Japanese Agriculture

Food prices in Japan are extremely high by international standards, and agricultural productivity is low. Why is Japan's performance in agriculture poor compared with its success in realizing high industrial output? This book analyses the recent stagnation of Japanese agriculture through international comparisons of growth and real productivity, and investigates the roles of Japan's rapid industrialization, agricultural protectionism, and in particular the high price support for agricultural commodities.

Japan's target is now to catch up with the EC in agricultural productivity, and since Dutch agriculture is a technological leader among EC countries, a comparison of Japanese and Dutch agriculture, is highly relevant. The authors also offer inter-country comparisons with Taiwan and the USA. They study the political and economic reasons for the eclipse of Japanese agriculture and assess the prospects for its future. The book concludes by discussing the relevance of Japan's experience for developing economies and suggests that there are several policy options which might mitigate the adverse effects of industrial pressure on agriculture.

Cornelis Van der Meer is at present Secretary for Social Sciences at the Netherlands Council for Agricultural Research. He was formerly Associate Professor of Development Economics and Agricultural Economics at the University of Groningen in the Netherlands.

Saburo Yamada is Professor of Agricultural Economics and Development Economics at the Institute of Oriental Culture and Graduate School of Agricultural Economics, University of Tokyo.

Japanese Agriculture

A comparative economic analysis

Cornelis L. J. Van der Meer
and
Saburo Yamada

Routledge
London and New York

First published 1990
by Routledge
11 New Fetter Lane, London EC4P 4EE

Simultaneously published in the USA and Canada
by Routledge
a division of Routledge, Chapman and Hall, Inc.
29 West 35th Street, New York, NY 10001

Printed and bound in Great Britain by
Biddles Ltd, Guildford and King's Lynn

British Library Cataloguing in Publication Data

Meer, Cornelis L. J. Van der, 1944–
Japanese Agriculture : a comparative analysis.
1. Japan. Agricultural industries
I. Title II. Yamada, Saburo, 1931–
338.1'0952

ISBN 0-415-02050-6

Library of Congress Cataloging in Publication Data

Meer, C.L.J. van der.
Japanese agriculture: a comparative economic analysis/Cornelis L.J. van der Meer and Saburo Yamada.
p. cm.
Includes bibliographical references.
ISBN 0-415-02050-6
1. Agricultural productivity—Japan. 2. Agriculture and state-Japan. I. Yamada, Saburō, 1931– . II. Title.
HD2092.M42 1990
338.1'0952—dc20 89-35968
CIP

Contents

Figures

Tables

Preface

The process of successful industrialization of Japan after the Second World War has significantly affected Japanese agriculture. Rapid industrial growth is one of the reasons for Japan's agricultural problems. A major problem is the very high prices of agricultural commodities in comparison with international prices. These high prices are caused by Japan's agricultural protective policies and associated stagnation of agricultural total factor productivity in recent decades. Through international comparative economic analyses, this study tries to reveal to what extent recent Japanese agriculture has stagnated and to analyse the reasons why.

Although this book focuses on Japan's agriculture, it is a part of a broader research project entitled 'Comparison of agricultural growth and productivity in Asian and European countries since the late 19th century' carried out by the authors since 1985. To pursue the joint study, Van der Meer visited the University of Tokyo in March 1985, and from April to November in 1986; Yamada visited the University of Groningen in September and October 1985, and from September to December in 1988. Parts of our joint studies have already been published as Research Memoranda from the Institute of Economic Research, University of Groningen. This book draws from those earlier publications.

Many institutions and persons co-operated for the study. Without their co-operation this book could not have been published.

The authors want to express their gratitude in particular to the following institutions for receiving financial and material support: the Netherlands Ministry of Education, the Fund for Promotion of Scientific Research of the University of Tokyo, the Japan Society for the Promotion of Science, the Mishima Kaiun Memorial Foundation, and the Institute of Economic Research of the University of Groningen. The Japan Economic Foundation provided financial support for the joint research with Professor Fumio Egaitsu, University of Tokyo, entitled 'Comparison of agricultural production efficiency between Japan and EC countries'.

In August 1988, Van der Meer moved his job from the Groningen University to the National Council for Agricultural Research. In spite of that the Council generously permitted him to finish the joint study and the University provided rooms and research facilities until the end of 1988.

The Agricultural Economics Research Institute (LEI), The Hague, provided data on the cost of production. The Instituut voor Mechanisatie, Arbeid en Gebouwen (IMAG) Institute for Mechanization, Labour and Building], Wageningen, provided information on prices for machinery and building. The Ministry of Agriculture, Forestry, and Fisheries, Tokyo, provided valuable support in finding and interpreting basic data. A.D. Kuipers of the Centraal Bureau voor de Statistiek (CBS), The Hague, provided basic information on prices. Yueh-eh Chen, Council of Agriculture, Executive Yuan, Taipei, provided basic data for Taiwanese agriculture.

The authors are indebted to Bart van Ark, J. C. Blom, Kees van Kooten, Angus Maddison, Dirk Pilat, H. Prins, J. M. H. Rutten, Ans Stanneveld and D. Strijker for advice and helpful comments on various parts of the study. The authors thank Fumio Egaitsu for co-operation in an earlier joint publication and for his permission to utilize the results in this book. The authors appreciate very much Yujiro Hayami's and Eddy Szirmai's detailed comments on the draft for the book. David Henebury helped to edit the English in the final draft; Natsuki Fujita checked the statistical validity; Dirk Strijker, Toshio Kuroyanagi, Yoshiharu Kubo, Ryohei Kada, Seiichi Fukui, and Kazutaka Nakano helped to organize field trips; Tineke Tadema typed drafts; and Jan Smit and Youngbong Yu helped process data for the book. All co-operation for this study is very much appreciated. Finally, the authors thank Andrew Lockett and Alan Jarvis for their editorial effort.

Abbreviations

Institutions

ADB	Asian Development Bank
APO	Asian Productivity Organization, Tokyo
CBS	Centraal Bureau voor de Statistiek [Central Bureau of Statistics], The Hague
FAO	Food and Agriculture Organization, Rome
ILO	International Labour Organization
IMF	International Monetary Fund
LEI	Landbouw-Economisch Instituut [Agricultural Economics Research Institure], The Hague
MAFF	Ministry of Agriculture, Forestry, and Fisheries, Tokyo
OECD	Organization for Economic Co-operation and Development, Paris
USDA	United States Department of Agriculture

Other abbreviations

AFF	Agriculture, Forestry, and Fisheries
CAP	Common Agricultural Policy (EEC)
c.i.f.	cargo, insurance, and freight
f.o.b.	free on board
GDP	Gross Domestic Product
Hp	Horse power
ISIC	International Standard Industrial Classification
NDP	Net Domestic Product
PPP	Purchasing Power Parity

Chapter one

Introduction

Japan's declining agricultural performance

In a few decades Japan has emerged as a major industrial country with a significant share in world trade. This is the result of a rapid economic spurt in which Japan caught up with productivity levels in industry in advanced industrial countries.

In the period 1870–1960 Japan's agricultural development was also rather successful. In particular, in the early phases of industrialization its contribution to economic development through foreign exchange earnings, capital formation, and food supply was significant. Despite a meagre resource base, agricultural output increased through technological progress of a mainly biological nature which raised land productivity. Japan's experience of agricultural growth and its relevance for late developing countries, in particular those in Asia, has been extensively studied and documented (see among others: Johnston 1951; Ishikawa 1967; Hayami *et al.* 1975; Ohkawa and Shinohara 1979; Yamada 1982a; and Hayami and Ruttan 1985 (1971)).

In recent decades, however, Japan's agricultural performance has been poor. Total factor productivity has stagnated since the late 1960s (Yamada 1987a) and growth of labour productivity lags far behind that in industry. In particular, after the recent appreciation of the yen against other major currencies Japan's agricultural prices have become among the highest in the world. These high price levels can only be maintained by increasingly expensive protective measures which not only form a burden to consumers and tax-payers, but are also a source of conflict with foreign trade partners. As a result, criticism has replaced praise. Recently Hayami has even characterized the situation as 'Japanese Agriculture under Siege' (Hayami 1988). Such a dramatic fall from 'AAA rating' to doubtful performance is most remarkable and deserves thorough analysis.

Japan's recent agricultural problems have received much attention

(Johnson, Hemmi, and Lardinois 1985; Anderson, Hayami, and Honma 1986; Hayami 1988; Hillman and Rothenberg 1988). These studies focus primarily on trade and agricultural policies and have provided important information on these topics. Our study mainly focuses on real productivity in Japanese agriculture from an international perspective, and on explanations for Japan's poor productivity performance. Productivity performance in modern Japanese agriculture has been a subject of earlier studies as well (Hayami and Ruttan 1985 (1971); Yamada 1975 and 1987a; Yamada and Hayami 1979; Yamada and Ruttan 1980). Some of these studies analyse growth of output and productivity by time-series analysis. Others compare productivity among countries on the basis of final output concepts. However the concepts of output and productivity used in these studies have shortcomings for inter-country comparison of real value added and economic efficiency.

Our study is the first to make a detailed real comparison of total production, current inputs, use of fixed capital and value added in Japan and other countries. It reveals that real net value added in Japan's agriculture at US and Dutch prices is negative. Our study also analyses the mechanisms by which this negative outcome has been attained: i.e. the dynamic interaction of over-protection of agriculture and excessive use of resources in this sector. This took place under conditions of rapid growth of output and productivity in industry, and a political system biased in favour of agriculture. On the basis of these findings the book discusses the prospects and the policy options for Japanese agriculture. Our study also assesses the extent to which Japan's experience is common to other rapidly industrializing economies, in particular South Korea (the Republic of Korea) and Taiwan. Finally, it raises the question of which policies might be adopted to avoid the development of such a serious imbalance between sectors as exists now in Japan.

Productivity growth in agriculture and other sectors in international perspective

Since the Second World War several important changes have taken place in world agriculture. Three notable phenomena have occurred in developing countries, each of which is discussed in turn below. The first is the so-called green revolution; the second is that in a considerable number of developing countries growth of agricultural productivity has lagged behind that of industry; and the last is the stagnation of African agriculture.

The term 'green revolution' is used for the significant expansion of cereal production, in particular rice and wheat, in developing countries, mainly in Asia, in the 1960s and 1970s through the generation and diffusion of new high-yielding varieties. This was the result of successful international transfer of technology in cereal production with technical and financial support from international research institutes and developed countries.

In many developing countries labour productivity in industry increased more rapidly than in agriculture, which means a relative increase in the gap in productivity between agriculture and industry. Such a growth pattern was most common in Asian countries, particularly the so-called Newly Industralizing Economies (NIEs). Quite a few of these countries felt compelled to start protecting their agriculture in order to maintain relative farm incomes and food self-sufficiency. But such a phenomenon is rather new and still limited to certain countries. In most developing countries priority has been given to industrialization, and low food price policies were often adopted to keep wages low.

In most African countries a significant stagnation of food production has occurred in recent decades. No significant breakthrough has been realized to supply more food for the rapidly increasing population. The environmental balance has been shaken by the population explosion after the Second World War, and forest resources are still being destroyed for fuel and feed. This was in many cases affected by political instability and unfavourable climatic conditions.

During the same period all industrial countries except Japan, have shown more rapid increases in labour productivity in agriculture than in industry. Food shortages occurred during and immediately after the war and Western developed countries stepped up their efforts in agricultural research and development. Consequently, the labour productivity gap between agriculture in developed and developing countries has increased, and comparative advantage in world agriculture generally moved away from developing countries to developed countries. Through their efforts the industrial countries succeeded in expanding production capacity to meet with increasing demand. The result was even a continuous over-supply of food in their own markets and in the international market.

Another important recent change among industrial countries is the relatively successful performance of European agriculture. From the later half of the nineteenth century until the Second World War the countries of Western Europe had experiences similar to Japan and some Asian countries in recent times. Their labour productivity in industry increased more rapidly than in agriculture, and the comparative advantage for agriculture moved partly to land-abundant countries like Argentina, Australia, Canada, New Zealand, Russia, and the USA (Van der Meer 1983a and 1983b). In recent decades, however, the gap in real labour productivity in agriculture between Western Europe on the one hand, and the USA and other countries of recent European settlement on the other, has narrowed significantly, and West European agriculture has increased its competitiveness. The catching-up of Western Europe in productivity may be partly attributed to the price support of the EC Common Agricultural Policy (CAP).

Over the past two decades Japan's agricultural performance contrasts poorly with that of the other developed countries. Despite much higher levels of price protection it has hardly been able to maintain output levels and, unlike Western Europe, high price support seems an obstacle rather than a stimulus to increased productivity. Recently South Korea and Taiwan have also rapidly increased their level of protection for agriculture, and their performance in agriculture has slowed down as well. At the same time several other developing countries show examples of very low price levels with negative effects on agricultural development. In this study we shall argue that both very low and very high prices may form an obstacle for productivity growth.

Japan's experience with growth of labour productivity in industry exceeding that of agriculture differs from the post-war experiences of West European countries. Some other Asian countries, on the other hand, follow Japan's experience. This suggests that the experience of a shift of comparative advantage from agriculture to industry is quite common in the process of rapid industrialization. Since Japan is the first developed Asian economy its performance and present problems deserve special attention.

Technological leadership and international transfer of technology

For a long time Japan has been the leader in agricultural technology in Asia, but its recent poor performance raises doubt whether it still remains as such. An important indicator of Japan's technological leadership in agriculture is its level of real productivity in this sector compared to its most successful followers, particularly the rapidly industrializing economies such as Taiwan and South Korea.

Japan's experience as a borrower of Western, and in particular European, technology is quite interesting. Striking is the fact that Japanese industry could rapidly bridge the gap in labour productivity with the West, while agriculture is still lagging behind. Was it really more difficult for Japan to borrow agricultural technology than industrial technology, was this an obstacle for more rapid growth of agricultural productivity, or can other factors explain the lag in agriculture? In Chapter Six we shall argue that Japan's relative stagnation in agriculture is not caused by lack of technology. There is in fact a backlog of technological knowledge which is not applied because of adverse institutions and policies. In order to substantiate this it is necessary to compare Japan's real productivity level and growth with that of the leading countries in Western Europe and the USA as well as that of other countries in Asia, and to explain differences.

European agriculture as a target for Japanese agriculture

Apart from theoretical considerations there is, for political reasons, at present much interest in comparing Japan with European countries. There is much pressure by Japan's trading partners, but also by domestic groups, to revise agricultural policies. As policy changes seem to be inevitable comparisons with other countries are conducted, mainly in search of productivity and protection standards. Comparisons with land-abundant countries like the USA, Canada, Australia, and New Zealand are deemed less relevant than with Europe, because the land-abundant countries have a different rural social structure. Moreover, one cannot realistically expect that Japan can in any way catch up with these countries in productivity for products that require relatively much land. Instead European productivity standards are increasingly marked as a target for Japanese agriculture. Hence, a major theme of the 1980 'Basic Guidelines of Government Agricultural Policy' was the adoption of the target of increasing Japanese agricultural productivity to the level of the EC countries (Johnson, Hemmi, and Lardinois 1985:19). For these reasons, this study provides a detailed comparison of growth performance and real productivity over the past decades between Japan and one of the technological leaders in Europe, the Netherlands.

Countries selected for in-depth comparisons with Japan: the Netherlands, Taiwan and the USA

Dutch agriculture as a technological leader in Europe

The Netherlands has been successful in its agricultural development since the last century, especially in the post-war period, and it has reached a labour productivity level in agriculture close to that of the USA. The Netherlands is situated at the centre of the EC's most important and most productive agricultural zone, which also comprises Belgium, northern Germany, Denmark, eastern England, and northern France. This zone forms one of the most relevant areas in the world for Japan for borrowing technology, and Dutch agriculture is fairly representative of this area. Agriculture in the larger European countries is rather heterogeneous, and therefore less suitable for comparison. The Netherlands is also one of the most land-scarce countries of Western Europe, but, just as in Japan, the quality of its scarce land area has been much improved over the past centuries in pursuance of increasing land productivity. Dutch agriculture is largely characterized by small family farms which have proved to form no obstacle for rapid agricultural growth. Since the Second World War large numbers of small inefficient farms have disappeared, and this has contributed to the enlargement of the remaining farms. Despite land scarcity in the Netherlands farms are big compared to those in Japan.

Agricultural policies form one of the most important differences between the two countries. Japan has long given priority to basic food self-sufficiency (either within the empire or within the country itself) and has been mainly inward looking in its agricultural policies. At present it does not have a single important agricultural export product. This is in great contrast to major parts of its manufacturing sector which have long followed an outward looking development strategy. Agricultural development in the Netherlands has been outward looking for centuries. The country has imported part of its grain requirement since the seventeenth century and exported other, mainly dairy agricultural products. When Europe was flooded with cheap grain from newly settled land-abundant countries during the late nineteenth century, little or no protection was given to grain producers, and agriculture adjusted itself by further specialization in products that required little land, such as intensive livestock production and horticulture. In the twentieth century the Netherlands became a major exporter of these products. These exports are based on the same principles as modern Japanese industrial exports: they use capital, little land, relatively advanced technology, efficient services, and imported raw materials.

Taiwan as a competitive leader in Asia

Another country chosen for a detailed comparison of productivity is Taiwan. Because of Japan's relative stagnation in agricultural productivity its leading role is challenged by Taiwan. Over the past decades Taiwan's agriculture has performed relatively better. Its agricultural productivity caught up despite the fact that its general economic development is still far behind Japan. This is an important fact that needs to be analysed because it may shed further light on Japan's agricultural performance. However, it is also significant to note that in recent years Taiwan has also experienced a slowdown of its agricultural growth when real wages increased rapidly as a result of successful industrialization. Taiwan is now rapidly losing its competitive edge in agriculture, and the successful exporter of agricultural products of the 1960s and 1970s has rapidly been building up protective measures for its depressed farming sector in the 1980s. The comparison with Taiwan therefore touches an important question: how relevant is Japan's recent experience for other rapidly industrializing economies?

The USA as a leader among land-abundant countries

For the past century the USA has been one of the most successful agricultural producers in the world. Its huge land areas allowed settlers to establish farms with sizes much larger than in Europe and Asia. With its good infrastructure, high level of economic development, and advanced level of agricultural technology it became one of the most productive agricultural producers in the world and the major exporter of agricultural produce. Since the 1870s it has dominated the world market for agricultural products. These characteristics have made US agriculture a kind of standard, or *numéraire*, for international comparative studies. This is already sufficient reason to select the USA for comparison, but there is one more reason. The USA represents a group of countries with abundant land resources and it is important to know how it compares with technological leaders of land-scarce regions - Japan in Asia and the Netherlands in Europe.

Concepts of output and productivity

There are several concepts of aggregate output which can all be relevant for a particular analysis, but which may have serious biases in other respects. Final output (total production minus intermediate input) is suitable to indicate the availability of produce for use outside agriculture, but it does not show the contribution of the agricultural sector to Gross Domestic Product (GDP). Neither is it a measure of sectoral income and efficiency. For this we have to use value added concepts. Gross value added, which is final output minus the use of current inputs from other sectors, is readily available in national accounts and probably therefore most commonly used. Since capital goods are also largely obtained from other sectors it is sometimes better to use net value added (gross value added minus depreciation), which corresponds to Net Domestic Product (NDP).

Corresponding to these output concepts are productivity concepts which indicate output per unit of input. A unit of input can be a unit of a single input, such as land or labour, or a unit of aggregate input, measured by relative prices as their weights. Kawagoe and Hayami (1985) measured aggregate input series for forty four countries in 1960 and 1980, assuming common weights for all countries and years, based on the estimates of production elasticities. In our study, however, we do not use such assumptions. Instead we essentially use single factor productivity ratios, which may of course give a biased comparison if the contribution of other factors differs strongly between the cases to be compared. However, since labour is by far the most important input factor, labour productivity is usually a fair indicator of net factor productivity.

Comparisons of aggregate output or productivity between countries or between years meet two basic problems. One is comparability of concepts chosen, which will be discussed first. The other is the elimination of price differences between countries or between periods, which will be treated subsequently. In the past, several comparative studies have been made of agricultural output and productivity. Early efforts, such as by Colin Clark (1957), and recently by Goossens (1986), focused on comparison of final output. This method was revised by deducting all seed and feed in several FAO publications, and publications by Hayami and Ruttan (1971 and 1985) and Yamada and Ruttan (1980). The results, however, raise a problem for economic comparison. They may give a biased picture of output and productivity of the agricultural sector in an economic sense, since the use of inputs from other sectors, apart from seed and feed, is neglected. Biases may be small for countries with low levels of purchased inputs and for countries with the same price and cost structure, but large in other cases. In the most developed countries inputs from other sectors typically constitute 40–60 per cent of the total value of production, whereas it is only 5–15 per cent in the least developed countries.

From the viewpoint of economic efficiency, problems of comparability are in principle much less for gross (or net) value added. Examples of such comparisons are studies by Paige and Bombach (1959) for the UK and the USA, by Mensink (1966) for the UK and the Netherlands, by Maddison (1970) for twenty two developing and seven developed countries, by Hayami and Ruttan (1971) for forty three countries, and by Van Ooststroom and Maddison (1985) for the agricultural sectors of fourteen countries. However, in this case the data problems are much more complicated as both outputs and inputs have to be included in the analysis.

National and international prices

Analyses of growth and productivity imply comparisons of quantities of inputs and outputs over time. In national accounts this is done at constant national prices and, consequently, results depend on the price base used. The use of another base year, or prices of another country, can give strongly different results. In Chapters Four and Five of this book such mechanisms are encountered in explaining differences in growth and productivity in agriculture between Japan and the Netherlands. In particular for Japan the choice of base year has a large effect on growth rates found. Although economists and statisticians are generally aware of such possibilities they usually ignore them because of lack of data. For international comparisons covering many countries, as presented in Chapter Two, there is no practical alternative to the use of national accounts data available in international statistics. In Chapter Three we use international prices for agricultural products, but not for inputs. In Chapter Four some comparisons of Japan and the Netherlands are made by use of other country's input and output prices. In Chapter Five, however, where detailed comparisons are made between Japan, the Netherlands, Taiwan, and the USA, we shall devote special attention to these problems, and to the interpretation of differences in growth rates for different base periods in Japan.

Explanations for the poor performance of Japan's agriculture

Japan's relatively poor recent performance in agricultural productivity growth can be analysed from two different perspectives. First, the performance of Japan's agriculture can be analysed in relation to Japan's overall economic and industrial growth. Such an analysis focuses on interactive relations between sectors. This is the main aim in Chapter Two where sectoral productivity performance is compared from an international perspective between groups of countries.

The post-war pattern of economic development in Japan had a strong impact on agricultural development. Because of rapid industrial growth, structural transformation of the economy and society lagged. Many small farmers remained part-time farmers and became an obstacle for farm-size enlargement. As a result, productivity in agriculture and services lagged and serious sectoral imbalances developed. In Western industrial nations industrialization started earlier than in Japan, it took a relatively long time, and society could transform its structure more gradually. Japan has more serious sectoral imbalances because of unequal growth rates of labour productivity by sector. To avoid social and political instability caused by such imbalances the Japanese government felt compelled to implement heavy support and protection measures for agriculture, but, as we shall argue, this aggravated external imbalances and added to trade conflicts with other countries.

Second, an analysis can be made on an intra-sectoral level with emphasis primarily on input–output relations, institutional factors, and policies that affect productivity changes. Agricultural economics literature contains a wealth of theories and opinions about factors affecting agricultural development and growth potential. Several of these are discussed since they give possible explanations for Japan's performance. Among these factors are land scarcity, unfavourable topography, investment in land, buildings and capital goods, expenditure on research and development, and government policies. Special attention will be given to technical progress in Japan and the effect of government policies in this field. Of particular interest is the effect of the high level of price protection in Japan on technical progress. Little is known about the long-term effect of input–output price relations on productivity in the long run. In Chapter Two of this book we shall develop an inverse U-shape hypothesis for the relation between productivity growth and price levels. The hypothesis assumes that there is an optimum price level where productivity growth is maximum, while at lower or higher price levels, lower growth rates are achieved. The hypothesis can be illustrated by micro-economic theory. Tests will be given in Chapters Two and Three while the subject is further analysed in Chapter Six. In Japan's case over-protection has contributed to excessive use of inputs and has reduced productivity growth. This is not primarily caused by lack of basic technology, but as we shall argue high support prices, related high land prices, and high input prices may significantly contribute to weak incentives for technical progress. As a result it seems that there is a considerable backlog of technical innovations awaiting necessary institutional reform and stronger incentives.

Outline of the book

Our study starts with a broad survey of trends in labour productivities by sector (agriculture, industry, and services) in eighty one countries over the period 1960–85 (Chapter Two). Data are obtained from national accounts statistics, published by international organizations. Chapter Three contains a more detailed analysis for twenty six countries based on estimates of real gross value added at 1975 international prices for 1963, 1975, and 1985. These data are in principle corrected for differences in price levels, although the corrections for inputs are based on assumptions. Analysis of these data shows that real productivity in Japan is low and falls short of levels predicted by regression analysis. It is interesting to note that the performance in Taiwan and Korea also shows a downward deviation from the predicted level. In Chapter Four long-term trends in agricultural development in Japan and the Netherlands are analysed and compared. A remarkable finding is that the gap in agricultural productivity in Japan and the Netherlands has increased gradually since 1880, while the gap for manufacturing closed rapidly. In particular, in the past twenty five years the difference is striking. In Chapter Five an in-depth comparison is made of real output and productivity in agriculture between Japan and the Netherlands. This comparison is in many respects more thorough than the comparison in Chapter Three. Price differences for products, current inputs, and capital goods are eliminated all the same way. For this purpose a new method was developed to eliminate differences in price levels between countries by making use of sector accounts for agriculture and basic material from agricultural price indexes. The results of the comparison between Japan and the Netherlands are put in international perspective by making similar comparisons with Taiwan and the USA (although in a somewhat short-cut way). This shows a dramatic real performance of Japan, not only compared to the Netherlands and the USA, but also compared to Taiwan. Chapter Six explains how various factors of an economic and a political nature have interacted, and caused the eclipse of Japan's agriculture. Chapter Seven tries to draw some conclusions about the prospects for Japan's agriculture. Reduction of price levels (in particular for rice), reduction of farm labour (in particular part-time farmers), and reduction of use of current inputs and capital goods are seen as prerequisites for rehabilitation of agriculture's economic performance. The last chapter discusses the relevance of Japan's recent experiences for developing economies. A rapid process of industrialization will cause severe pressure on agriculture which can have adverse effects on agricultural development. However, our analysis suggests that there are several policy options to mitigate adverse effects, policy options that have not yet been used in Japan.

Chapter two

Sectoral productivity performance in international perspective

Central issues for analysis in this chapter are trends in sectoral labour productivities in the past decades. By comparing trends some differences can be found in patterns of agricultural development in major regions of the world: Asia and the Pacific, Latin America, Africa south of the Sahara, the Middle East–Mediterranean, and the industrial economies (see Appendix Table A.1 p. 169 for definition of the regions). Main points of attention are differences in productivity growth in the major sectors of the economy (A, I and S sectors)[1], related changes in comparative advantage for agriculture and industry, changes in the factoral terms of trade between agriculture and other sectors[2], and resulting challenges for government policies. This comparison is put in the perspective of development experiences of the previous one hundred years. Therefore this chapter starts with a short review of these experiences, and related theoretical issues in literature which deserve further attention for the comparative analysis of Japan's case.

Experiences in agricultural development[3]

Productivity changes in agriculture directly affect the balance between agriculture and other sectors. In a closed economy, sectors with relatively slow productivity growth will experience improving terms of trade. The pessimistic view of the classical economists, Malthus and Ricardo, was based on the expectation that possibilities for increasing agricultural productivity were relatively limited, and that consequently prices for food would increase relative to other prices. This would put a downward pressure on real wages and profits in industry, and an upward pressure on land prices and rents. In the past century this pessimistic view has not been supported by facts. In retrospect Malthus and Ricardo appeared wrong because they overlooked the possibility of productivity increase generated by human capital and new technology.

Table 2.1 Long-term growth rate of gross value added per worker and terms of trade for agriculture and industry in selected developed countries

Countries	*Period*[g]	*Growth rate of gross value added per worker* *Agriculture* (1)	*Industry* (2)	*Difference* (1) – (2)	*Terms of trade*[a] *agriculture/ industry* (*% change*)
France	1840–1909	0.3	1.2	–0.9	1.3
	1909–54	1.8	1.5	0.3	–0.7
	1954–84	5.9	4.5	1.4	–1.1[d]
Germany	1850–1913	1.1	2.0	–0.9	1.3
	1950–84	5.6	4.3	2.3	–1.5[c]
UK	1852–1911	0.5	0.9	–0.4	—
	1911–50	1.9	1.7	0.2	0.8[e]
	1950–84	4.8	2.7	2.1	–3.3[c]
Denmark	1830–1913	0.9	1.4[b]	–0.5	1.3
	1913–50	2.2	0.8	1.4	–0.7
	1950–84	4.3	3.2[f]	1.1	–1.3
Netherlands	1950–84	5.8	4.3	1.5	–2.4
Sweden	1870–1913	1.6	1.9	–0.3	0.3
	1913–50	2.1	1.0	1.1	0.2
	1950–84	4.2	3.5	0.7	–0.2
Australia	1861–1913	1.9	1.8	1.0	–0.0
	1913–50	1.4	–0.3	1.7	–0.0
	1950–84	3.0	3.5	–0.5	–3.0
USA	1840–1913	0.7	1.4	–0.7	0.7
	1913–50	2.0	2.0	0.0	–0.1
	1950–84	3.9	1.9	2.0	–1.1
Japan	1885–1913	1.5	2.1[b]	–0.6	1.6
	1913–50	0.5	1.0	–0.5	–0.9
	1950–84	5.2	7.8	–2.6	3.0

Source Van der Meer (1983b: 46, 48). Data for 1984 updated from OECD, *National Accounts Statistics*, 1988a and OECD, *Labour Force Statistics*, 1988b.

Notes Data for the post-war period refer to three-year averages centred on the year shown. a. Growth rates for Denmark and Japan before 1913 are for industry and services together; b. See note 2 (p. 197) for definition of the (factoral) terms of trade; c. 1951 instead of 1950; d. Refers to the period 1951–84; e. Refers to the period 1920–50; f. Refers to the period 1956–84; g. See note 5 (p. 197) for another periodization.

The developed countries

In the nineteenth century, however, the incorrectness of the Malthusian view was not yet so clear. If we look at three periods of growth in the world economy, as distinguished by Lewis (1978) and Maddison (1982), i.e. the late nineteenth century–1913, 1913–1950, and the post-1950 period, we see important changes in agricultural growth performance. In the period before 1913 in most presently developed countries, including Japan, increases in real labour productivity (gross value added per worker) in agriculture lagged behind that in industry and the terms of trade moved in favour of agriculture[4] (see Table 2.1). The terms of trade for agriculture in several European countries increased, partly as a result of government protection. Despite the unfavourable trend in real food prices, real wages in the nineteenth century had started a slow but long-term upward trend contrary to the expectations of the classical economists.

The period 1913–1950 was very unstable, because of the two World Wars and economic crises in the inter-war years. Because of these experiences there were major differences between countries. Nevertheless, over this period as a whole, the relative performance of agriculture improved considerably in most developed countries, and the terms of trade moved against agriculture.[5] In many countries the turning point was after the First World War. Already in the early 1950s Schultz argued that the pessimistic view of the classical economists had proven wrong in all respects because of increased application of modern techniques and non conventional inputs (Schultz 1953). It appears indeed that over time labour productivity in agriculture has progressively increased, particularly in the post-Second World War period, and that the terms of trade have moved more and more against agriculture. As observed already by Cochrane (1958) gains of increases in productivity in agriculture go to an important degree to buyers of agricultural products by means of decreased real price levels.

Japan's experience of economic development is different from the other industrial countries after the Second World War. The difference lies in its very rapid industrialization. Its increases in labour productivity in agriculture during this period are close to those of the other developed countries, whereas its labour productivity in industry increased much more rapidly. However, this pattern of development is not unique to the Japanese economy if compared to the experiences of the Western countries in the period before 1913. In long-term perspective the recent experience of Japan and the pre-1913 experiences of the Western countries may be a basic feature for industrializing countries during a stage of sustained growth, and before a matured affluent stage of economy and society such as Western countries have realized now.

The developing countries

The growth experience of the developing countries has been different. In the century before 1950 labour productivity in agriculture in developing countries probably increased but little.[6] Some exceptions were export crops such as sugar, tea, and rubber, and food production in Taiwan and Korea, but in general productivity in food production probably changed little. In this period there was little transfer of agricultural technology from the developed countries. This changed around the time of the Second World War. Due to research efforts by developed countries better technologies were generated for developing countries, and they started to have an increasing impact on productivity of food grains in developing countries in the 1960s and 1970s. The effects are generally referred to as the 'green revolution'. Nowaways it is generally understood that it is technically possible to generate better technology for agriculture in developing countries. National and international research institutes have been established to develop such technologies, extension services have been created to disseminate them, and all kinds of other government efforts aim directly, or indirectly through improvement of infrastructure, at the adoption of better techniques (Ruttan 1982). However, the efforts and capabilities to generate technological innovation in developing countries are still far less than in developed countries. This is partly because most political leaders in developing countries tended to give priority to industrialization rather than to agricultural development. Also it appeared in the post-war period that industrial technology was easier to transfer than agricultural technology. It could be transferred in the form of joint-ventures and the results appeared rapidly. In many developing countries this resulted altogether in declining comparative advantage in agriculture.

The economic crisis of the 1980s has affected productivity growth in developing countries more than in industrial countries. In particular, industrial productivity declined much because of declining demand and disruption of input supply. However, this break in the trend is likely to be a temporary phenomenon only, since the underlying forces are still the same.

Agriculture and industry in international perspective

As mentioned before, if the productivity trend in agriculture differs from that in other sectors there will be an opposite pressure on relative prices. In a closed economy such a pressure will result in changes in the inter-sectoral terms of trade. In an open economy the price effect depends on foreign trade. For products that can easily be traded at low cost of transportation and small trade margins the price levels will closely depend on world price levels. For products that are perishable or have high handling margins, the prices between countries may fluctuate over a wide range before imports or exports become feasible.[7]

Discrepancies in productivity trends between agriculture and industry need not have much impact on comparative advantage between sectors – and thus on world trade – if ratios of sectoral productivity in major producing countries change in similar proportions. Only discrepancies in the relative performance of productivity in agriculture and industry between countries will affect comparative advantages and enhance trade.

Recent examples of such discrepancies can typically be found in the experiences of rapidly industrializing countries, such as Japan, Korea, and Taiwan, where relative income in agriculture came under serious pressure from domestic industry and international competition. The basic reason, at least initially, was not the poor performance of agriculture in these countries, but the fact that by international standards their industrial productivity grew so rapidly compared to agriculture. Income is the result of price and productivity, which means that at given international prices incomes of farmers in these small countries would seriously lag behind incomes in industry. However, the governments in these countries prevented this by providing increasing price protection for agriculture. This probably retarded structural change, since presumably, lower income would have induced more rapid reallocation of labour to other sectors.

Changes in the world production structure and transport can have similar effects on agriculture. In the mid-nineteenth century, for example, real productivity in agriculture in the USA, Australia, Argentina, Canada, and New Zealand was probably already much higher than in Europe,[8] but the costs of transportation were still too high and the populations in these countries too small to generate a large export. However, in the second half of the century major innovations and related investments took place in transportation systems. Transportation costs declined rapidly and massive immigration provided the work-force to generate large exports.[9] As a result, the world production structure changed and European markets were flooded with cheap agricultural products from these countries which put pressure on the incomes of European farmers. Therefore comparative advantage in European countries shifted from agriculture to industry.

The demand for protection

If farmers are facing declining relative prices because of cheaper imports (or declining export prices) they will usually turn to the government for protection. It depends on the political situation in a particular country as to what the government will do. Two factors play a major role. The first depends on the relative political power of farmers and other social groups such as traders, industrialists, and consumers. The second factor is whether a country, because of bad experiences in the past, precaution, or for mere nationalistic reasons, pursues a high self-sufficiency rate. The situation in importing and exporting countries is usually different. Exporting countries have in general fewer possibilities for providing price support than importing countries, because of higher government budget costs.

The case of Western Europe

When Europe was flooded with cheap imported grain in the last quarter of the nineteenth century there were distinct differences in reaction among European countries (Tracy 1982). Great Britain decided not to protect its farmers. As a result agricultural incomes were depressed and self-sufficiency for food declined. Low prices and lack of public support for research and investment in agriculture nearly resulted in stagnation of labour productivity in agriculture. The basic reasons for British agricultural policies were that Britain was the dominant world power that ruled the seas and could secure its supplies, and that it was the major industrial country in the world with powerful trade and industrial classes.

In France and Germany agriculture-based political groups were more powerful, and industrialists also wanted alliance with the landed interests (Tracy 1982; Hayami and Ruttan 1985:370). This combination of vested interests and nationalist feelings resulted in protectionist and autarchist policies.

Two smaller European countries Denmark and the Netherlands followed the British example of non-protection as they were both major exporters of livestock products to the British market. In both countries specialization in livestock products had started already before the fall in grain prices took place, and the crisis accellerated structural change (Tracy 1982:113–20; Knibbe (forthcoming); Pilat 1988:56). Protection of grain production could have increased the input prices for their livestock production, and this would have affected competitiveness for these export products. A difference with British policies was that both countries stimulated productivity and structural change in the farming sector by support for education, training, research, and institutional innovations.

These examples show that there can be different policy responses to competition challenges from outside. It is not easy to evaluate the long-term effect of these policies – not only because of different initial conditions in these countries, but in particular because of different experiences in both World Wars and the depression of the 1930s. In general the consumers in the protectionist countries were worse off than those in the other countries. Britain had bad experiences during the World Wars because its ignorance of agricultural productivity resulted in strong dependence on food imports during the World Wars, whereas the small exporting countries were hit hard by the protectionist wave during the slump of the 1930s. In any case the agricultural sector in the small countries was more compețititive and contributed more to overall economic growth than that of the other European countries.[10] After the Second World War labour productivity levels in agriculture in the small exporting countries were the highest in Europe, despite relatively low price levels in the preceding seventy-five years.

In the post-war period agricultural policies in several West European countries were gradually unified within the EC. EC policies resulted in a price protection which was about the average of that of the member countries. This implied a relative decline in protection for Belgium, Germany, and Italy and a relative increase for Denmark, France, the Netherlands, and the UK. Despite continuous protection, the terms of trade in EC agriculture declined rapidly (see Table 2.1 p. 14) which means that EC farmers experienced a considerable decline in real prices. For most countries this decline was stronger than for the USA. An important development is, however, that labour productivity in West European agriculture grew more rapidly than in the USA and other land-abundant countries. Consequently, the huge gap in labour productivity between the USA and EC countries narrowed significantly (see Van der Meer (1988) for a more detailed analysis). Analysis of total factor productivity in Kawagoe and Hayami (1985) supports this conclusion. The narrowing gap is one of the reasons for the increased competition in recent years between the US and the EC for foreign markets.

The case of post-war Japan

Adjustment of inter-sectoral resource allocation, particularly of labour, in response to the increasing comparative advantage in domestic industry within a very short time would have been very painful if it had only been left to the market mechanism. It could have caused a lot of unrest if farmers had been forced to bear the burden of the cost of adjustment without any social adjustment programme, and society might have become politically unstable. Japan felt obliged to adopt strong agricultural protection. In the post-war period, farmers' associations had increasingly strong political power because rural people were the most important supporters of the Liberal Democratic Party, the majority party, which was continuously in power. The farmers' organizations organized strong political lobbying for agricultural protection. If consumers or non-agriculturists had been strongly against such lobbying, the government could not have implemented agricultural protection so easily. However, the counter movement was very weak, and farmers' lobbying thus increased the cost of protection. The rest of the population could bear this because their income increased rapidly during the course of high economic growth. The Engel coefficient declined sharply and the increasing burden of protection did not hurt seriously. Besides Japan had a rather long period of food shortage in and after the war and the masses of population have tended to support policies aimed at improving self-sufficiency rates for food. In fact, however, as we shall see in Chapter Four, agricultural protection did not achieve a higher self-sufficiency rate. Since a rather wide range of groups in other sectors also benefited from agricultural protection political opposition against these government policies did not become so strong.

Agricultural protection in the early post-war period was not high in Japan. According to Hayami (1988), the average nominal rate of protection in 1955 in EC countries was 35 per cent and only 18 per cent in Japan. Later on, however, Japan's rate of protection exceeded the EC level very much. According to a recent FAO study (FAO 1986) the Japanese protection level in 1970 was about twice the EC level and the level increased even more later. The only country comparable to Japan is Switzerland. The increasing trend in agricultural protection is reflected in the terms of trade between agriculture and industry (see Table 2.1 p. 14). The government has supported agriculture not only by import quota and product price support, but also by heavy investment subsidies.

The role of prices

In the previous sections reasons have been given why governments embarked on price protection for agriculture. Here attention is given to the effects of price protection. An important question is why and how European countries could narrow the labour productivity gap with the USA. Did price protection in the EC countries induce technological innovation and accelerate growth of labour productivity, or did it form an obstacle to more rapid productivity growth? In what sense were experiences with protectionist agricultural policies different in Japan? There is little research that provides direct answers to these questions. In this section attention will be paid to the theoretical relationship between prices and the growth rate of productivity. At the end of this and in the following chapter some empirical tests will be made. In Chapter Six the relation will be further discussed for Japan.

Price level and technological change

In a dynamic perspective low product prices may retard innovation and, consequently, growth of productivity, because investment becomes less profitable. Designers and producers of new technology may face less demand and reduce their expenditure on research and development. On the other hand, high prices and high levels of profitability are likely to induce the development of better techniques. Farmers may experiment more and take more interest in learning new skills. New technologies are partly embodied in conventional inputs, and their introduction therefore partly depends on profit expectations. A positive response could be expected from profit maximizing behaviour. If this holds, as is assumed by neo-classical theory, one should expect a clearly positive relation between prices and the pace of technological change. However, it is doubtful whether this is fully realistic, mainly because supply and demand of resources on family farms may differ from standard neo-classical assumptions. For a discussion of various theories on farmers' economic behaviour see Ellis (1988), and also Mellor (1966). It is sometimes claimed that sustained high price levels make farmers less thrifty and less innovative or even lazy as they may enjoy a good life, whereas in times of depressed prices farmers make more efforts to reduce costs and to develop more efficient methods. Since they are self-employed they may respond to low prices by reducing consumption in order to generate sufficient investment to safeguard the continuity of their farm (Chayanov 1966). Of course there are limits to such behaviour. At very low prices farmers cannot generate investment, and at highly profitable prices everyone is willing to invest although the efficiency may be negatively affected by less intense efforts.

Growth rates of productivity are affected by many factors which are to a considerable extent independent of prices. For example, rapid technological change and related increases in productivity usually require structural change, such as farm-size increases. Moreover, productivity growth is bound by the so-called 'technological frontier' which reflects the level of basic knowledge in a society (Binswanger 1978). Given these opposite forces it is most likely that there is a degressively positive relation between output price levels and (long-term) trends in technological change. In principle at high price even a decline of the pace of technological change is imaginable, although not likely, but if it did occur it would strengthen the reasoning below.

Price level and input use

Price levels of final output also affect the use of inputs. In developed countries growth of demand for farm output is slow compared to changes in productivity, and the amount of factor input, and in particular labour required for production on farms declines rapidly. This means that reallocation of resources is required from agriculture to other sectors. Usually, however, reallocation is taking place slowly. Alternative prices for farm input factors, such as labour and fixed capital, and even land in most countries, may be persistently low. Although low remuneration of these input factors does not result in their immediate reallocation, it enhances a continuous decline of factors which are in surplus and have a low marginal productivity. However, if the government raises output prices, the due decline in stock of factor inputs will be retarded, and the use of variable inputs will be positively affected.

If the marginal productivity of inputs is equal to the average productivity a change in input results in an equal change in output, and does not affect productivity. However, marginal productivity of input in agriculture, in particular of labour input, is usually lower than average productivity, because of over-supply of labour and institutional obstacles for rapid input reallocation. Therefore, at given levels of technology, decreases of input levels will nearly always result in increases of net factor productivity (net value added per unit of factor input) and labour productivity.

Price level and labour productivity: the inverse U-shape hypothesis

The assumed opposite effects of output price levels on technological change on the one hand and input allocation on the other, give ground for the hypothesis that there is an inverse U-shaped relation between price levels and growth rate in total factor productivity (final output per unit of aggregate input) (see Figure 2.1). Before distinguishing different definitions of price level and productivity we want to show the working of the mechanism at national prices. We assume that the maximum pace of growth of total factor productivity is reached at price level P_m. At lower output prices, technological change is likely to be slower, and maximum growth cannot be achieved although marginal productivity of inputs is likely to be higher. At high price levels total productivity growth is negatively affected by too high input levels (in particular of labour). The inverse U-shape relation may also be observed for net factor productivity (net value added per unit of factor input) and the price level of final output relative to the given price level of non-factor input. The price P_m where total factor productivity is at its maximum, is not necessarily the same price where the growth rate of net factor productivity is at its maximum.

Up to now we have considered both relations at national prices regardless of the national price level relative to the international price level. However, in many cases the inverse U-shape relation

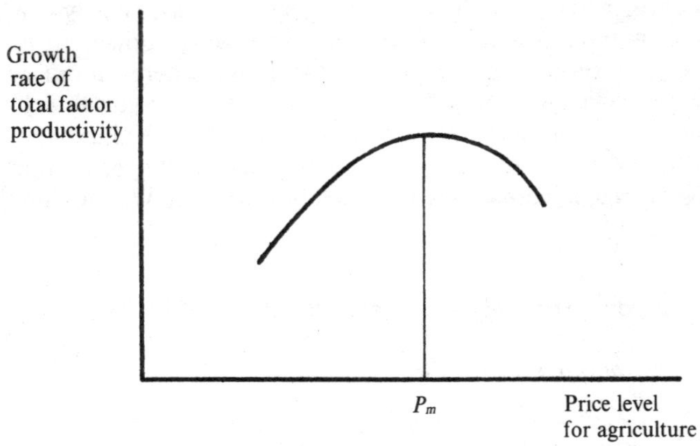

Figure 2.1 Assumed relationship between price level and growth rate of productivity

will be more pronounced from the perspective of international prices. In such cases prices can be expressed relative to the chosen international *numéraire*. In countries with high product price levels the output/input price ratio is artificially favourable and may induce excessive input use which from an international perspective, may reduce real productivity. We shall discuss the consequences of this mechanism in Chapter Six to explain Japan's poor productivity performance in agriculture over the past two decades. One the other hand, countries with output prices below the international level, such as Argentina, may use less than optimal amounts of inputs for achieving maximum real productivity and real productivity growth.

Empirical knowledge of long-term supply elasticities is crucial for the quantitative analysis of dynamic effects of government price policies, but difficult to obtain. First of all, the relations between price level and productivity growth are not easy to model. The suggested inverse U-shaped relation is likely to differ between countries depending on such basic supply factors as the quantity and quality of land and labour, the factor proportions, the level of technology, and past policies. In other words, the long-term price response curves are likely to be shaped differently among countries. Secondly, in order to make a comparative analysis of the hypothesis the productivity growth rates should preferably be measured at international prices, but in practice that is rather complicated as we shall show in the next chapters, and therefore it is rarely done. In that respect our study is exceptional. Moreover, growth of labour productivity may not always give a close approximation of increases in net (or total) factor productivity, particularly not in countries with considerable deviations from world prices.

Finally, it should be noted that the point where labour productivity reaches a maximum is not necessarily the social welfare optimum. If for example, marginal labour productivity in agriculture is lower than in other sectors, a transfer of labour to other sectors will increase the overall labour productivity within the economy.

Labour productivity trends in world agriculture, 1969–85

Growth of labour productivity by sector

In Table 2.2, part A, a comparison is given of growth rates of sectoral labour productivity (gross value added per worker) over the period 1960–85 for eighty-one countries grouped by major region and development status. Details for sub-periods are shown in Table 2.3. The sources and methods used for calculation are

Table 2.2 Growth of labour productivity by economic sector[a] 1960–85, countries grouped by major region and development status (average growth rates (%))

	Number of countries	Sectors[a] A	I	S	I&S	Total GDP
A. All countries by region						
All countries	81	2.5	1.9	0.9	1.3	2.2
Developing countries by area:						
Latin America	18	2.0	1.1	0.3	0.5	1.2
Africa south of Sahara	24	0.4	0.4	–0.7	–0.3	1.2
Asia and the Pacific	12	2.3	3.0	2.8	3.0	3.5
Middle East–Mediterranean	10	3.6	2.3	2.0	2.1	3.5
by income:						
Low Income Countries	14	0.2	–0.5	–0.7	–0.6	0.9
Middle Income Countries	50	2.2	2.0	1.1	1.3	2.3
Industrial economies	17	5.5	3.7	1.7	2.5	2.9
B. Countries with increases in labour productivity greater for agriculture than for industry						
All countries	56	3.2	0.9	0.7	0.8	1.9
Developing countries by area:						
Latin America	12	2.3	0.1	0.1	–0.1	0.7
Africa south of Sahara	15	0.8	–1.7	–1.0	–1.3	0.9
Asia and the Pacific	6	2.9	1.4	2.4	2.0	2.9
Middle East–Mediterranean	7	3.9	1.5	2.2	1.9	3.4
by income:						
Low Income Countries	8	0.5	–2.8	–1.4	–1.9	0.6
Middle Income Countries	32	2.6	0.5	0.8	0.6	1.8
Industrial economies	16	5.6	3.5	1.6	2.4	2.8
C. Countries with increases in labour productivity smaller for agriculture than for industry						
All countries	25	1.2	4.1	1.3	2.3	2.8
Developing countries by area:						
Latin America	6	1.5	3.2	0.8	1.6	2.1
Africa south of Sahara	9	–0.3	4.1	–0.2	1.3	1.8
Asia and the Pacific	6	1.7	4.6	3.3	3.9	4.1
Middle East–Mediterranean	3	2.9	4.3	1.7	2.8	3.9
by income:						
Low Income Countries	6	–0.1	2.5	0.3	1.0	1.1
Middle Income Countries	18	1.5	4.5	1.5	2.6	3.3
Industrial economies[b]	1	4.2	6.0	3.7	4.6	5.3

Sources See Appendix A.

Notes a. The text refers to the A, I, S and I&S sectors as 'agriculture', 'industry', 'services' and 'non-agriculture'; b. The industrial economy under C is Japan.

presented in Appendix A. The countries included are listed and classified in Appendix Table A.1 (see p. 169). This chapter is based on national constant prices as reported in national accounts statistics. In Chapter Three calculations are made in international prices.

It appears that of the twelve countries in Asia and the Pacific[11] for which data are available, average labour productivity in agriculture increased at a slightly higher growth rate than in Latin America, but at a much higher rate than in Africa (2.3, 2.0 and 0.4 per cent respectively). Performance in the more developed countries in the Middle East–Mediterranean region was better (3.6 per cent), and in the industrial economies the average growth rates of labour productivity in agriculture were even more than twice as high as in Asia. Labour productivities in industry give a different picture. The highest rates were still found in the industrial economies, but the differences with the Asian and Middle East–Mediterranean countries are only 0.7 and 1.4 per cent. The average growth for Latin America is much lower than for Asia.

The growth rates for agriculture on the one hand and the other sectors (I&S) on the other show strongly different patterns between the regions. It appears that in all regions except Asia agriculture performs better: by 1.5 per cent in Latin America; 0.7 per cent in Africa; 1.5 per cent in the Middle East–Mediterranean; and by even 3.0 per cent in the industrial economies. In Asia agriculture lags by 0.7 per cent. Gaps in productivity growth rates for agriculture and industry are smaller for all regions, except Asia.

In so far as comparative advantage is indicated by changes in labour productivity ratios, the overall average picture shows that the comparative advantage for industry has relatively moved from industrial countries and Latin America to the Asian countries. The Middle East–Mediterranean countries take a position in between. Since the industrial countries dominate world exports because they have the largest share the impact of the shift in comparative advantage in agriculture to these countries is significant for the world market, and is likely to be felt in the long-term trends in terms of trade between both.

Successful agricultural and industrial performers

In Table 2.2 a break-down in two groups (B and C) is given of countries with increases in labour productivity greater (B) and smaller (C) respectively for agriculture than for industry. It appears that sixteen of the industrial countries belong to the first group (B); Japan is the only industrial country in the second group (C). Of the twelve Asian countries six belong to this second group (C). Their growth of agricultural labour productivity is better than that of the other developing countries in this group, except for the three countries in the Middle East–Mediterranean group. The reason for being situated in this group is their high industrial performance. Most countries of Latin America, Middle East–Mediterranean, and Africa perform better in agricultural than in industrial labour productivity. It is important to notice that labour productivity for the whole economy increased at an average rate of 1.9 per cent for the first group (B) and 2.8 per cent for the second (C). Apparently the better overall performers are the countries with rapid industrial growth.

Table 2.3 Growth of labour productivity by economic sector and sub-period, countries grouped by major region and development status (average growth rates (%))

	Number of countries	*Sectors*				
		A	*I*	*S*	*I&S*	*Total GDP*
A. 1960–75						
All countries	81	3.0	3.0	1.5	2.0	3.1
Developing countries						
by area:						
Latin America	18	2.8	2.9	1.5	1.8	2.7
Africa south of Sahara	24	1.2	1.8	–0.4	0.3	2.1
Asia and the Pacific	12	2.3	3.6	3.3	3.4	3.7
Middle East–Mediterranean	10	3.8	3.6	2.6	3.0	4.4
by income:						
Low Income Countries	14	0.3	0.7	–0.3	–0.1	1.4
Middle Income Countries	50	2.8	3.3	1.7	2.2	3.3
Industrial economies	17	5.7	4.2	2.3	3.1	3.7
B. 1975–85						
All countries	81	1.8	0.3	0.1	0.2	0.9
Developing countries						
by area:						
Latin America	18	1.0	–1.3	–1.3	–1.4	–1.0
Africa south of Sahara	24	–0.9	–1.5	–1.0	–1.1	–0.1
Asia and the Pacific	12	2.3	2.3	2.4	2.4	3.3
Middle East–Mediterranean	10	3.4	0.9	1.5	1.2	2.4
by income:						
Low Income Countries	14	–0.1	–2.3	–1.3	–1.5	–0.1
Middle Income Countries	50	1.2	0.2	0.3	0.2	0.9
Industrial economies	17	5.3	2.8	0.8	1.7	1.8

Notes and Sources As for Table 2.2

In the first group (Table 2.2 part B) agriculture out-performs industry on average by about 2 per cent per year in Latin America, the Middle East–Mediterranean, and in the industrial economies. The other regions show a more pronounced difference between both sectors. For the African countries this coincides with a poor overall economic performance.

The period 1960–85 falls into two sub-periods of rather different performances in the world economy. The trends for the sub-periods are shown in Table 2.3. In the sub-period 1960–75 all regions had high rates of growth of productivity. In all regions the developing countries showed on average more rapid growth of labour productivity in industry than in agriculture. Only the industrial economies and the Middle East–Mediterranean region showed the opposite. In this sub-period the shift of comparative advantage in agricultural production to the industrial economies was more pronounced than in the period 1960–85 as a whole.

The oil crises, the monetary instability, the financial crisis and the slow-down of growth in the industrial economies had a strong impact on labour productivity performance in most developing countries in the period 1975–85. Most affected by the crises were developing countries, in particular in Africa and Latin America. The effect of the crises was much stronger on labour productivities in industry than in agriculture. This is not surprising, because agricultural production is less sensitive to prices, income, and business cycles. Consequently, the past decade partly forms a break with the long-term trend in which comparative advantage for agriculture shifted to the industrial economies and that for industry in the opposite direction. But the trend is not reversed completely, and probably only temporarily. The divergence in labour productivity growth between agriculture and industry is still about 2.5 per cent per year in the industrial economies and the Middle East–Mediterranean region, whereas in Africa and Latin America the gap is less and in the Asian countries there is no divergence at all. However, when an economic recovery occurs in countries which are performing poorly at present the divergence in labour productivity in many of these countries is likely to move in favour of industry. It can be expected that the shift in comparative advantage to industry in developing countries is a longer term phenomenon.

Trends in terms of trade

Table 2.4 presents average compound growth rates of the factoral terms of trade between agriculture and other sectors. There is an inverse relation between the relative productivity performance of agriculture and changes in the factoral terms of trade between agriculture and the other sectors. In the industrial economies and in Latin America the terms of trade moved against agriculture, whereas in Asia the opposite occurred. In Africa on average there was not much change. The countries of the Middle East–Mediterranean form an exception. They show improved terms of trade for agriculture despite relatively favourable trends of labour productivity. The reason for this is probably that some of these countries have significant oil production and used income from this sector to boost agricultural output and productivity by high prices.

The relation between agricultural labour productivity and agriculture's terms of trade is even more pronounced if the countries are again divided in groups with labour productivity performance of agriculture better and worse respectively than of industry (parts B and C of Table 2.4). Over the twenty-five-year period average relative price levels for agriculture versus industry in the first group went down by -0.7 per cent per year and up by 0.3 per cent in the second group. For services the difference is small.[12] It is interesting to contrast the industrial and the Asian countries. The divergence of their relative price levels for agriculture and industry is about 1.6 per cent per year, but over 2.7 per cent per year if related to services. The contrast between Japan and the other industrial economies is even bigger for industry (Japan and other industrial economies are given in Table 2.4, parts C and B) with a divergence of 3.5 per cent, but it is only 1.3 per cent for services.

The terms of trade for agriculture were much less favourable over the second period than for 1960–75 (Table 2.5). This may to some extent be affected by the still high prices for 1975 in the aftermath of the price boom of the previous years, while the international agricultural crisis of the 1980s with depressed price levels forms another explanation. In some of the countries, government policies may have played a dominant role. The stronger decline of the terms of trade for agriculture in the industrial economies in the second period largely reflects the relatively rapid increase of labour productivity in agriculture. This change in terms of trade affects other countries through changes in price ratios in the world market and affects the country's barter terms of trade.

Share of employment in agriculture

Table 2.4 also shows the share and trend in agricultural employment. Agricultural employment in industrial economies is low and decreasing faster than in other regions. In the Middle East–Mediterranean region it is also declining. If the regions are

Table 2.4 Changes in inter-sectoral factoral terms of trade and agricultural employment 1960–85, countries grouped by major region and development status

	Number of countries	Factoral terms of trade[a] (average annual change (%)) A/I	A/S	A/(I&S)	Agricultural employment: Share of total employment 1975 (%)	Average growth rate (%)
A. All countries by region						
All countries	81	–0.4	–0.5	–0.4	44.6	–0.2
Developing countries						
by area:						
Latin America	18	–0.9	–0.2	–0.5	38.1	0.6
Africa south of Sahara	24	–0.5	–0.2	–0.3	73.0	1.5
Asia and the Pacific	12	0.5	0.3	0.4	47.9	0.3
Middle East–Mediterranean	10	0.5	0.8	0.7	43.4	–0.9
by income:						
Low Income Countries	14	–0.8	–0.7	–0.7	75.9	1.6
Middle Income Countries	50	–0.1	0.2	0.1	47.7	0.4
Industrial economies	17	–1.1	–2.4	–1.8	9.8	–3.5
B. Countries with increases in labour productivity greater for agriculture than for industry						
All countries	56	–0.7	–0.5	–0.6	40.4	–0.6
Developing countries by area:						

Latin America	12	–0.4	0.8	0.3	32.8	0.2
Africa south of Sahara	15	–1.1	–0.2	–0.4	73.4	1.7
Asia and the Pacific	6	–0.6	–0.1	–0.3	52.6	0.2
Middle East–Mediterranean	7	0.4	0.7	0.6	43.1	–0.8
by income:						
Low Income Countries	8	–1.7	–0.9	–1.1	78.4	1.4
Middle Income Countries	32	–0.2	0.6	0.3	46.4	0.4
Industrial economies	16	–1.3	–2.5	–2.0	9.4	–3.5
C. Countries with increases in labour productivity smaller for agriculture than for industry						
All countries	25	0.3	–0.4	–0.2	54.0	0.6
Developing countries by area:						
Latin America	6	–1.9	–2.3	–2.2	48.7	1.4
Africa south of Sahara	9	0.6	–0.2	0.0	72.3	1.3
Asia and the Pacific	6	1.5	0.7	1.1	43.3	0.3
Middle East–Mediterranean	3	0.6	0.9	0.8	44.3	–1.1
by income:						
Low Income Countries	6	0.5	–0.4	–0.1	72.7	1.8
Middle Income Countries	18	0.1	–0.4	–0.2	50.0	0.4
Industrial economies[b]	1	2.2	–1.2	0.3	15.6	–3.2

Sources See Appendix A.

Notes a. See note 2 (p. 197) for a definition of factoral terms of trade. The text refers to the A, I, S, and I&S sectors as 'agriculture', 'industry', 'services', and 'non-agriculture'. b. The industrial economy under C is Japan.

Table 2.5 Changes in inter-sectoral factoral terms of trade and agricultural employment by sub-period, countries grouped by major region and development status

	Number of countries	Factoral terms of trade (average annual change (%)) *A/I*	*A/S*	*A/(I&S)*	Agricultural employment Share of total employment* (%)	Average growth rate period (%)
A. 1960–75						
All countries	81	0.4	0.3	0.3	51.5	–0.3
Developing countries by area:						
Latin America	18	–0.3	0.8	0.3	45.2	0.5
Africa south of Sahara	24	0.5	0.5	0.4	78.8	1.4
Asia and the Pacific	12	1.5	1.7	1.7	54.5	0.4
Middle East–Mediterranean	10	0.7	0.6	0.7	54.1	–0.7
by income:						
Low Income Countries	14	1.0	0.9	0.9	80.4	1.6
Middle Income Countries	50	0.4	0.8	0.6	55.5	0.4
Industrial economies	17	0.0	–1.7	–0.9	16.0	–3.8
B. 1975–85						
All countries	81	–1.3	–1.3	–1.2	41.3	0.0
Developing countries by area:						
Latin America	18	–0.9	–0.9	–0.9	34.6	0.8
Africa south of Sahara	24	–1.3	–0.8	–0.9	70.5	1.7
Asia and the Pacific	12	–0.8	–1.6	–1.2	44.1	0.2
Middle East–Mediterranean	10	0.2	1.0	0.7	37.2	–1.1
by income:						
Low Income Countries	14	–2.8	–2.3	–2.3	72.7	1.6
Middle Income Countries	50	–0.3	–0.2	–0.3	44.0	0.5
Industrial economies	17	–2.7	–3.5	–3.2	7.7	–2.9

Sources As for Table 2.4

Notes *Percentages under A are for 1965 and under B for 1980

subdivided again in groups with labour productivity growth in agriculture bigger and smaller than in industry (Table 2.4 parts B and C, pp. 30–1), there appear to be some differences. For Latin America the countries in the second group are still more agricultural, for the Asian countries the opposite holds.

As shown in Table 2.2 (p. 25) the Low Income and Middle Income Countries in the second group have a better overall economic performance (total growth of productivity) than those in the first group. However, contrary to expectation for the Middle Income Countries, agricultural employment in both groups grows at 0.4 per cent. The Low Income Countries in the second group, which have better general economic performance, have even more rapid growth of agricultural employment (compare parts B and C in Table 2.4). Apparently a rapid decline in agricultural employment is no prerequisite for a rapid growth of overall labour productivity.

Trends in agricultural employment also differ between the subperiods 1960 and 1975 and between 1975 and 1985 (Table 2.5). In the industrial countries there is a slow-down in the rate of decrease, probably caused by higher unemployment levels and less opportunity for off-farm employment. Nevertheless, labour productivity growth in agriculture is not severely affected. Only in the Middle East–Mediterranean region has the decline in agricultural employment accelerated. In Latin America and Africa the growth rate of agricultural employment increased, but in Asia the opposite took place.

Causes of differences in agricultural labour productivity growth

The findings in the previous section show big differences in overall and agricultural labour productivity performance. An in-depth analysis of the causes of this would require sophisticated models and large amounts of data other than that presently available. Within the scope of this study only a few factors can be discussed and conclusions are necessarily tentative. We restrict our analysis to some comparisons of growth rates between groups of countries with distinctive characteristics and to some correlations between labour productivity in agriculture and other variables. First of all, the effects of productivity growth in non-agricultural sectors and the general level of economic development on growth of labour productivity in agriculture will be tested. Although the main focus of this chapter is on interactions between agriculture and other sectors, we shall also give some attention to the role of resource endowments, in the form of availability of land and irrigation, as possible dominant factors for labour productivity growth in developing countries. Next, some effects of government price policies will be tested, and we shall give a test for the inverse U-shape hypothesis.

Non-agricultural growth and structural transformation

The level and pace of development of the economy as a whole forms a major explanation for agricultural labour productivity performance. We selected the share of agriculture in employment as an indicator of a high level of development, and the rate of growth of labour productivity in non-agricultural sectors as an indicator for the pace of development. If the share of agriculture in employment is still high then the development of other sectors may still form a limitation to the pace of productivity growth in agriculture. This is partly because the other sectors cannot yet provide a large variety of material inputs and services of good quality and at low prices. It is also because a relatively small size of non-agricultural sectors poses limitations on the pace at which the agricultural labour force can be absorbed. The shift of labour to other sectors also depends on the pace of development in these sectors, whereas development of other sectors implies increasing demand for agricultural products. Growth of labour productivity in the non-agricultural sectors is an indicator of the development in these sectors. In any case, lack of sectoral transformation may form a constraint on increases in labour productivity in agriculture, and when the results of Table 2.2 and 2.4 are taken together it is clear that this is the case. The countries with the lowest share of employment in agriculture have high rates of decline in agricultural employment and high growth of labour productivity. Furthermore, productivity growth in agriculture is clearly related with that in other sectors.

By means of regression analysis this is further analysed for the countries covered in Table 2.9 (p. 39).[13] The two variables appear to have a fair explanatory value (Table 2.6). The correlation coefficients indicate that 51–69 per cent of variance can be explained. This finding suggests that in particular, growth of labour productivity in non-agricultural sectors contributes strongly to agricultural performance, especially after 1975. This means that, compared to other industrial countries, Japan's higher growth rates in non-agricultural sectors forms a relatively favourable factor for achieving labour productivity growth in agriculture.

Table 2.6 Regression of growth of labour productivity in agriculture on the share of agriculture in total employment and growth of labour productivity in non-agricultural sectors for sixty four countries

	Constant	*Percentage growth rate of labour productivity non-agriculture*	*Percentage share of agriculture in total employment*	R^2
1960–75[a]	5.43	0.214	–0.054	0.51
	(1.64)	(0.104)	(0.009)	
1975–85[b]	5.03	0.436	–0.075	0.68
	(1.76)	(0.085)	(0.009)	
1960–85[b]	5.10	0.280	–0.063	0.69
	(1.33)	(0.089)	(0.007)	

Sources See Appendix A for growth rates of labour productivity and share of agriculture in employment.
Notes Countries covered are the same as for Table 2.9. See note 13 (p. 199) for explanation. Standard error of coefficients in parentheses. a. employment share 1965; b. employment share 1975.

Resource endowment in developing countries

In early stages of development, land is a dominant factor of production. Scarcity of land is often seen as a negative factor for achieving growth of labour productivity in agriculture, in particular in Asia. In modern agriculture the effects of land scarcity are presumably less, but for Japan land scarcity is often still seen as a drawback for achieving productivity growth. The general argument, which follows the classical economists and Boserup (1965: 28–42), is that raising production per worker is less costly by expansion of the land area per worker than by increasing production per hectare. This would imply that availability of abundant land resources makes increases of labour productivity easier. A counter argument is that the establishment and maintenance of the infrastructure, which is often a prerequisite for expanding the cultivated areas, is relatively more expensive in land-abundant countries, and also that government systems in these countries tend to be more loosely structured and less effective (Boserup 1981, Chapter 7 and pp. 210–11).

A good indicator of land scarcity is difficult to obtain. Land input per capita is not very suitable because of major differences in climatic conditions and quality of land. What is needed is some kind of weighting of land based on quality. In a recent study the

FAO made detailed estimates of the productive capacities of land resources in 1975 in fifty-seven developing countries (FAO 1983). The FAO made estimations in terms of the potential food production in each country under three levels of input use. By dividing potential food production by the per capita food requirement the FAO derived the 'potential population' at each of these input levels. We used these data for thirty-two countries which are part of our data set as well, and took the ratio between the actual population in 1975 and the thus calculated 'potential population' at low levels of input as an indicator of the pressure on land. This pressure index is a reliable indicator of land scarcity in which land is weighted for its productive capacity. For two groups, one with an index < 0.75 (low pressure on land), and the other with an index ⩾ 0.75 (high pressure on land), growth rates of labour productivity in agriculture are compared in Table 2.7.

Among seven Asian countries two have low population pressure. Their growth rates of labour productivity in agriculture are almost twice as high as those of the other countries. The findings for Latin

Table 2.7 Pressure on land and average growth rate of labour productivity in thirty-two developing countries 1960–85

	Index pressure on land <0.75		⩾0.75	
	Number of countries	*Growth of labour productivity in agriculture (%)*	*Number of countries*	*Growth of labour productivity in agriculture (%)*
All developing countries	32	1.5	23	1.3
by area:				
Latin America	14	2.1	4	1.7
Africa south of Sahara	15	0.8	9	–0.2
Asia and the Pacific	2	2.5	5	1.3
Middle East–Mediterranean	1	1.4	5	3.5
by income:				
Low Income Countries	6	0.3	8	0.1
Middle Income Countries	26	1.8	15	1.9

Sources See Appendix A. Potential population from FAO (1983: Table 2.4).
Note Pressure on land is the ratio of actual population in 1975 and the potential population that can be supported with food at low levels of input.

America and Africa also indicate that the countries with low pressure on land perform relatively better. Thus, on a regional base land scarcity seems to play a negative role for raising agricultural productivity, but differences between regions are much more important. In the Middle East–Mediterranean region, irrigation is quite important and there is only one country with low pressure on land, but the region as a whole has a high growth rate compared to other regions. Correlation for all countries (without distinction between regions) between growth of labour productivity and pressure on land gave a correlation coefficient of 0.08, which means that the relationship is statistically meaningless.

Irrigation is originally related to pressure on land. Literature on agricultural development suggests that traditional irrigated agriculture requires more labour per unit of product than rain-fed agriculture, and that historically irrigation was an innovation to cope with scarcity of land (e.g. Boserup 1965). Present day irrigated agriculture does not necessarily reflect this any more because of the use of modern technology and application of irrigation in areas too dry for other forms of cropping. But to some extent irrigated agriculture may still be a relatively costly form of agriculture. Therefore a test was carried out about the role of irrigation. For the same group of developing countries the FAO study also indicates the percentage share of irrigation in food production (FAO 1983). The correlation coefficient between the growth rate of labour productivity over 1960–85 and the share of irrigation in food production in 1975 was only 0.1 and therefore also insignificant.

The conclusion is that the available data do not confirm a significant negative overall effect of scarcity of resource endowment on growth of labour productivity growth. Only on a regional scale do such differences seem to be meaningful. In so far as Japan still shares characteristics with Asian developing countries the experiences point at some comparative disadvantage.

Price policies

Prices are of dominant importance for agricultural development. A distinction can be made between the effects of price distortions and the effects of price levels. Schultz (1979) and the World Bank, *World Development Report* (1983) have stressed the effect of price distortion by governments. In the latter source a distortion index is calculated for twenty-nine developing countries for the 1970s from price distortions related to exchange rates, trade restrictions, interest rates, labour cost, and prices of infrastructural services. In Table 2.8 these countries are split into two almost equal groups with low and high distortion indexes on which growth rates of labour productivity are compared. The results show clearly that countries with little distortion perform much better in growth of agricultural labour productivity. The Latin American countries appear to have on average more price distortion than the Asian countries.

The price level in countries may not have been optimal for growth of labour productivity. As suggested in a previous section, pursuance of higher farm incomes and higher self-sufficiency rates by increased prices may be inefficient and ineffective in the long run. A strategy of high price levels may, despite increasing costs, result in relatively lower income levels and self-sufficiency rates in the long run, given mechanisms described. Pursuance of low food prices may also have adverse effects. Here we provide the correlation between the growth of labour productivity (gross value added per worker) and the price level for final output. Price levels by

Table 2.8 Price distortion and average growth rate of labour productivity in agriculture for twenty-nine developing countries 1960–85

	Distortion index <2.00		≥ 2.00	
	Number of countries	*Growth of labour productivity in agriculture (%)*	*Number of countries*	*Growth of labour productivity in agriculture (%)*
All developing countries	14	2.8	15	1.4
by area:				
Latin America	2	3.9	6	2.2
Africa south of Sahara	4	1.8	5	0.2
Asia and the Pacific	6	2.5	2	0.9
Middle East–Mediterranean	2	5.1	2	2.3
by income:				
Low Income Countries	3	0.5	2	0.9
Middle Income Countries	11	3.5	13	1.4

Sources See Appendix A for growth rates of labour productivity. Distortion index from the World Bank, *World Development Report* (1983: 60).

Note The distortion index is a composite index of price distortions in the 1970s related to the exchange rate, trade restrictions, interest rates, labour cost and prices for infrastructural services country relative to international prices can be obtained from an FAO study for the years 1970, 1975, and 1980 (FAO 1986:26). Data are available in the FAO and in our data set for sixty-four countries.[14] The relative price levels in the FAO study are calculated as the ratio of the Purchasing Power Parity for agriculture and the exchange rate both in terms of units of local currency per US $. Tests are made of an inverse U-shape relation between labour productivity growth and these price indexes at one of these benchmark years (Table 2.9).

Although the relative price level shows some relation with productivity increases as assumed, the correlation coefficient shows that the relation is weak and not more than 20 per cent of the variance is explained. For the period 1960–75 and the 1970 price level the coefficients are not significant statistically, but for the period 1975–85 as well as for the whole period 1960–85 statistically significant coefficients were found for the 1980 price level. The weak statistical relation is not surprising. Many factors affect productivity growth rates and, as indicated in an earlier section, the relation might be country-specific. Moreover, growth of labour productivity is measured at national prices, and as argued before growth of value added may be considerably unwardly biased for high-price countries, and underestimated for countries with low price levels. It is also important to note that differences in prices of

Table 2.9 Test of inverse U-shape relationship between growth rate of labour productivity and price level for sixty-four countries

	Intercept	*Price index*	*Squared price index*	R^2
1960–75[a]	–0.58	4.58	–0.78	0.15
	(2.16)	(3.79)	(1.60)	
1975–85[b]	–2.94	5.32	–0.92	0.17
	(2.84)	(1.50)	(0.27)	
1960–85[c]	–3.00	8.04	–2.32	0.15
	(2.19)	(3.26)	(1.21)	

Sources See Appendix A for growth rates of labour productivity. Price index from the FAO (1986: 26)

Notes The sixty-four countries for which the data are available are those listed in Appendix Table A.1 minus the countries mentioned in note 14 (p. 199). Price levels are measured in international prices and expressed as indexes with USA = 1.00. The index is the ratio of the Purchasing Power Parity for agriculture and the exchange rate both expressed in terms of units of local currency per US $. The standard error of coefficients are in parentheses. a. the price index for 1970 is applied; b. the price index for 1980 is applied; c. the price index for 1975 is applied current inputs can play an important role as well, but are ignored here because of lack of data.

Conclusion

This chapter provides a broad comparative overview of labour productivity growth by sector and inter-sectoral factoral terms of trade for different groups of countries and regions in the world. It shows that Japan's post-war pattern of growth differs considerably from that of the other industrial countries. In Japan labour productivity in industry has been increasing more rapidly than labour productivity in agriculture. This is not a unique feature of Japan's economic development, but rather common for industrializing countries. It was shown that the same happened in the West European countries in the period before 1913, and during 1960–85 a substantial number of developing countries with rapid economic growth had the same experience. In the period since the Second World War the other industrial countries performed quite differently from Japan. These countries achieved much more rapid growth of labour productivity in agriculture than in industry. Since they dominate in the world market comparative advantage in agriculture has shifted away from Japan to the other industrial countries. A loss of comparative advantage results in declining relative incomes, and, consequently, farmers urge for protection. The Japanese government has responded with rapidly increased protection for agriculture. However, despite high levels of protection, growth of labour productivity was relatively slow in Japan. This is in contrast to the EC where rapid growth of productivity was achieved at much lower levels of protection and in this way, the productivity gap between the EC and US agriculture has narrowed. At the other extreme, there are countries where very low price levels seem to be harmful for technological progress and growth of labour productivity in agriculture. In order to explain this an inverse U-shape relationship is assumed between the pace of productivity growth and price levels. In this chapter the inverse U-shape hypothesis was developed and a first test was made. In the next chapter a more detailed test will be made and the hypothesis will be further developed in Chapter Six to explain Japan's poor productivity performance in recent decades.

Chapter three

International comparison of agricultural productivity

The analysis in this chapter focuses on agricultural productivity and mainly on intra-sectoral factors for its explanation. It applies an international comparative analysis for which differences in product price levels between countries are eliminated.

In 1987 world population reached five billion – double the 1950 figure. The rapid growth of population since 1950 was accompanied by a significant increase in food production which reflects the successful agricultural development in the post war-period. However, agricultural development did not follow the same pattern in different countries and periods. Some countries achieved rapid growth while others lagged behind. Even if a country performed successfully in one period, it did not necessarily repeat this in the next one. Besides, different patterns exist in agricultural development among different regions of the world. To identify and assess such differences is important for understanding what has happened in world agriculture in the past and what could happen in the future. Through such a study we can identify which positions Japan and the Netherlands took, how these positions changed in the past and what the relevance of their performance is in international perspective.

To make such an assessment, this chapter makes an international comparison of agricultural productivity. We take gross value added per worker as an indicator of economic efficiency in agriculture. Furthermore, land productivity, i.e. gross value added per hectare of agricultural land, is also taken into account to understand past agricultural performance. Our sample covers twenty-six countries in Asia, Europe, the Americas, and Oceania.[1]

The comparison is carried out for three benchmark years: 1963 (or the 1961–5 average), 1975, and 1985 (or the 1984–6 average). The year 1963 was selected as the earliest year because the 1961–5 average was once a base period for the FAO's production data and 1961–5 averages are readily available in the *FAO Production Yearbook*.[2] The year 1985 (or the 1984–6 average) is selected as the latest year for which relevant data are available in international sources.[3] There are two reasons for selecting 1975 as an intermediate benchmark year. After the first oil shock and the so-called world food crisis in 1973–4 world economic growth as well as Japanese economic growth slowed down and Japanese agricultural policy shifted to more protection. The second reason is that several related studies and international statistics use 1975 as a benchmark year.[4]

The method and the data

In this study gross value added per agricultural worker and per hectare of agricultural land are used as indicators of labour and land productivities. As discussed in Chapter One, gross value added is a good economic indicator of production since it is free from double counting and gross value added per unit of labour is a good indicator of economic efficiency.[5] Gross value added per worker is a fairly consistent labour productivity measure which was also used for comparison with the other sectors in the previous chapter. By comparing the levels of labour productivity in agriculture among countries and their changes over different periods, we can identify patterns of agricultural development among countries in the past.

Gross value added in agriculture

For international comparison of 'real' productivity gross value added data should preferably be measured in common international prices, which means measured as the difference between output and current input at international prices. In this manner gross value added would be free from bias in price levels and price structures among countries. However, in practice it is very difficult to find sufficient data for a large group of countries. Even for comparison between a few countries, as carried out in Chapter Five, a complete set of data is difficult ot obtain. Under the limited availability of international data sources, in particular for inputs, we measure real gross value added series internationally and over time according to the following formula:

$$V_j^t = v_j^t \Sigma P_i Q_{ij}^t \qquad (1)$$

where V is gross value added, v the gross value added ratio to total production value at national 1975 prices, P the international price in 1975 'International dollar', and Q the quanity of each product.

The superscript *t* indicates year *t*, and the subscripts *i* and *j* indicate commodity *i* and country *j*, respectively.

Prices in International dollars, P_i, are a kind of international weighted averages of the prices of the *i*th commodity in all producing countries.[6] In past studies by Hayami and Ruttan (1971 and 1985) and Yamada and Ruttan (1980), American, Japanese, and Indian prices, in terms of wheat units, were used to get three aggregate series first, then their geometric averages were aplied in analysis. Yamada (1975 and 1987b) applied the wheat units which were used as the weights for FAO Production Indexes, whereas Van Ooststroom and Maddison (1985) used USA prices. Here we take prices in International dollars measured by Prasada Rao in FAO (1986) as the best set of prices presently available for comparative purposes.

The quantity of each product in each country for year *t*, Q_{ij}^t, is taken from the *FAO Production Yearbook*. One deficiency of these data is their incomplete coverage of agricultural products by country. Many commodities are not included in the FAO statistics such as flowers, mushrooms, radish, and many various local fruits and vegetables. Thus inevitably estimates of total production based on FAO data are underestimates. The extent of such underestimation differs by country. However, when we need data for many countries the *FAO Production Yearbook* is the only practical international data source available.[7]

To estimate real gross value added, we use the share of gross value added in total production in national prices because of the limitation of data availability for inputs. In earlier studies various methods were applied to estimate gross value added. Some of them are compared with this study in Appendix B.[8]

In this study the share of gross value added in total production in national prices has been used for estimating real gross value added from the real value of total production. This method was previously applied in Stanneveld, Van Ooststroom, and Van der Meer (1984), and assumes theoretically that Purchasing Power Parities of agricultural outputs and those of inputs are the same, but in general this is not likely to be the case. However, we prefer this to other methods which intend theoretical consistency, but need many bold assumptions. Our method resembles a single deflation method used to obtain constant price time-series of GDP data by deflating current GDP series by the production price index. This method is usually accepted in cases of limited data availability.[9] The estimates of total production, the gross value added ratio, and gross value added are presented in Appendix Table B.1 (see p. 172).

Labour and land

The number of people employed in agriculture, or economically active in agriculture, is taken as an indicator of labour input.[10] A major problem is that agricultural labour data often comprise not only agriculture in a narrow sense (crop growing and livestock raising), but also forestry and fisheries. Sometimes the term 'agriculture' refers to the three together, but here our focus is on the narrow concept of agriculture only, not on the other two. Since gross value added estimates refer to the narrow concept of agriculture, we need corresponding labour data for measuring labour productivity. For most countries such data are not available in international statistics. We solved this by assuming that gross value added per worker is the same for both the sub-sector agriculture and for forestry and fisheries, and employment in agriculture was therefore split off from the total on the basis of agriculture's share in total production for the three sub-sectors.

Another input for which data are required for productivity comparison is agricultural land. The concept of agricultural land is the total area of arable land and permanent pasture. Data are taken from the *FAO Production Yearbook*, Eurostat, *Agricultural Statistics*, or national data sources. The land and labour data used are presented in Appendix Table B.2 (see p. 175).

Productivity comparisons

Labour productivity

Table 3.1 shows estimates of gross value added per worker for 1963, 1975, and 1985 in 1975 international prices and growth rates for the two intervening periods. Inter-country differences in labour productivity are quite large. Labour productivity was highest in Australia in 1963 and 1975, and in the USA in 1985, while it was always the lowest in India. The ratio between the highest and the lowest increased from 43 to 68 during the period. Agricultural productivity in the other countries ranges between these two extremes, but there are clear regional differences in the level of labour productivity. The Asian countries are at the lowest level, the developed countries in the Americas–Oceania at the highest level, the European countries in between, and the other American countries are mixed. Certain differences also exist within each region. In Asia the level of East Asian countries is highest, particularly in Taiwan and Japan. The Netherlands, Belgium, and Denmark show the highest levels in Europe, the South European

Table 3.1 Estimates of labour productivity in agriculture, 1963, 1975, and and 1985, in 1975 prices (1975 International dollars)[a]

Country	*Gross value added per worker* *1963*[b]	*1975*	*1985*[b]	*Annual growth rate %* *1963–75*	*1975–85*	*1963–85*
Asia						
East Asia						
Japan	549	1,299	1,590	7.4	2.0	5.0
Korean Rep.	368	548	915	3.4	5.3	4.2
Taiwan	662	991	1,430	3.4	3.7	3.6
Other Asian countries						
Indonesia	245	300	425	1.7	3.6	2.5
Philippines	461	585	579	2.0	–0.1	1.0
Thailand	263	356	461	2.6	2.6	2.6
India	239	293	277	1.7	–0.6	0.7
Pakistan	402	607	708	3.5	1.5	2.6
Europe						
North West Europe						
Sweden	2,391	5,028	8,047	6.4	4.8	5.7
Belgium–Lux.	5,311	9,565	15,143	5.0	4.7	4.9
Denmark	5,681	8,396	14,265	3.3	5.4	4.3
Netherlands	4,149	9,749	15,193	7.4	4.5	6.1
France	3,340	6,422	10,074	5.6	4.6	5.1
Germany FR	2,554	4,989	7,251	5.7	3.8	4.9
Ireland	2,674	5.756	8,326	6.6	3.8	5.3
UK	3,548	6,575	10,558	5.3	4.8	5.1
South Europe						
Greece	1,068	2,404	3,063	7.0	2.5	4.9
Italy	1,706	3,520	4,805	6.2	3.2	4.8
Portugal	504	778	869	3.7	1.1	2.5
Spain	1,152	2,470	3,802	6.6	4.4	5.6
EC total	2,143	4,083	6,128	5.5	4.1	4.9
Americas–Oceania						
Australia	10,390	15,634	18,403	3.5	1.6	2.6
USA	6,935	14,098	18,773	6.1	2.9	4.6
Canada	7,313	12,093	13,132	4.3	0.8	2.7
Argentina	3,917	5,571	7,653	3 0	3.2	3.1
Brazil	1,000	1,487	2,102	3.4	3.5	3.4
Mexico	560	786	1,109	2.9	3.5	3.2

Source Appendix Tables B.1 and B.2.
Notes a. See note 6 (p. 199) for the definition of International dollar. b. The 1963 and 1985 data are averages of the years 1961–5 and 1984–6 respectively.

countries the lowest. In the Americas the USA and Canada are at the top, Argentina is comparable to the average European level, Brazil is at the South European level, and Mexico at the East Asian level.

Except for the Philippines and India in 1975–85, all labour productivities increased for both sub-periods. However, there are notable inter-regional differences in growth rates. European countries realized sizeable high growth ranging from 4 to 6 per cent per annum for the entire period. The growth rate was especially high in 1963–75, and ranged between 5 and 7 per cent, except for Denmark and Portugal. This high growth was generally associated with a significant decline in agricultural labour and moderate increases in gross value added during the period. From 1963–75 to 1975–85 the growth rate of labour productivity declined for all the European countries except for Denmark. The growth rate for the EC total declined from 5.5 to 4.1 per cent during the period. It was mostly related to a slower decline in the agricultural work-force for the latter period, which can be attributed to a significant increase in unemployment for unskilled workers by which opportunities for farm workers for shifting to other sectors were significantly affected. Table 3.2 shows growth rates of gross value added, and labour and land input for 1963–85. The Netherlands realized the highest growth rate for gross value added with 3.7 per cent while the decline of agricultural employment was among the lowest during the entire period. This is in fact a significant characteristic of Dutch agriculture. However, the Dutch productivity growth rate also declined in the latter period because of a slower decline in agricultural labour similar to the other European countries.

The East Asian countries followed after Europe in growth rates of labour productivity. They ranged from 3.6 to 5.0 per cent per annum for the whole period. The highest growth rate was for Japan, but it declined significantly from 7.4 per cent in 1963–75 to 2.0 per cent in 1975–85 while the growth rate in the other two countries increased. The high growth rate of 7.4 per cent in Japan for 1963–75 was largely the result of a rapidly declining rate of labour input by 5.0 per cent, among the largest of the selected countries.[11] A notable fact in Japan's case is that in 1975–85 labour input and gross value added both declined. However, the declining rate of labour input was larger, so the growth rate of labour productivity was still positive.

The growth rate of labour productivity in the Americas–Oceania ranged from 4.6 per cent in the USA to 2.6 per cent in Australia. Because of an exceptionally high growth rate the USA was able to catch up with Australia in 1985. This was associated by a much

Table 3.2 Annual growth rates of gross value added, and input of labour and land in agriculture, 1963, 1975, and 1985 (%)

Country	*Gross value added*			*Labour*			*Land*		
	1963 –75	*1975 –85*	*1963 –85*	*1963 –75*	*1975 –85*	*1963 –85*	*1963 –75*	*1975 –85*	*1963 –85*
Asia									
East Asia									
Japan	2.1	–0.7	0.8	–5.0	–2.6	–3.9	–0.7	–0.4	–0.5
Korean Rep.	5.0	1.3	3.3	1.6	–3.8	–0.9	0.7	–0.2	0.3
Taiwan	2.6	1.2	2.0	–0.8	–2.4	–1.5	0.4	–0.3	0.1
Other Asian countries									
Indonesia	3.2	4.0	3.6	1.5	0.4	1.0	0.7	0.6	0.7
Philippines	4.1	1.6	2.9	2.0	1.7	1.9	1.2	1.1	1.2
Thailand	4.0	4.0	4.0	1.4	1.4	1.4	4.4	1.8	3.2
India	3.3	1.0	2.3	1.6	1.6	1.6	0.3	0.1	0.2
Pakistan	5.5	3.7	4.7	2.0	2.1	2.0	1.0	0.5	0.8
Europe									
North West Europe									
Sweden	1.3	1.9	1.6	–4.8	–2.8	–3.9	–0.7	–0.3	–0.5
Belgium–Lux.	–0.3	1.9	0.7	–5.1	–2.7	–4.0	–0.6	–1.1	–0.8
Denmark	0.2	3.9	1.9	–3.0	–1.4	–2.3	–0.4	–0.3	–0.3
Netherlands	3.6	3.7	3.7	–3.5	–0.8	–2.3	–0.5	–0.4	–0.5
France	0.6	1.3	0.9	–4.7	–3.1	–4.0	–0.5	0.0	–0.3
Germany FR	1.4	1.2	1.3	–4.1	–2.5	–3.4	–0.5	–0.4	–0.5
Ireland	2.9	0.3	1.7	–3.5	–3.4	–3.4	1.8	0.0	1.0
UK	1.2	4.2	2.6	–3.8	–0.6	–2.4	–0.3	–0.1	–0.2
South Europe									
Greece	5.0	0.0	2.7	–1.9	–2.4	–2.1	0.2	0.1	0.2
Italy	1.8	–0.4	0.8	–4.2	–3.5	–3.9	–0.9	–0.2	–0.6
Portugal	1.5	0.0	0.8	–2.1	–1.1	–1.6	–2.9	–0.4	–1.8
Spain	3.5	0.6	2.2	–2.9	–3.6	–3.2	–0.3	–0.5	–0.4
EC total	1.7	1.3	1.5	–3.6	–2.9	–3.3	–0.4	–0.2	–0.3
Americas–Oceania									
Australia	2.5	1.9	2.2	–1.0	0.3	–0.4	0.4	–0.3	0.1
US	2.1	2.7	2.4	–3.7	–0.2	–2.1	–0.8	–0.4	–0.6
Canada	1.1	1.0	1.1	–3.0	0.2	–1.6	0.7	0.2	0.5
Argentina	2.2	2.2	2.2	–0.8	–0.9	–0.8	0.2	0.0	0.1
Brazil	3.5	3.3	3.4	0.1	–0.2	–0.1	2.4	1.1	1.8
Mexico	3.8	4.3	4.0	0.9	0.8	0.8	0.0	0.1	0.0

Source Appendix Tables B.1 and B.2.

larger decline in labour input for the USA.

The growth rates of labour productivity in other Asian countries were the lowest at 0.7 to 2.6 per cent. This was not due to a slower

Table 3.3 Estimates of land productivity in agriculture, 1963, 1975, and 1985, in 1975 prices (International dollars[a])

Country	*Gross value added per ha* 1963[b]	1975	1985[b]	*Annual growth rate (%)* 1963–75	1975–85	1963–85
Asia						
East Asia						
Japan	980	1,369	1,327	2.8	–0.3	1.4
Korean Rep.	704	1,165	1,354	4.3	1.5	3.0
Taiwan	1,240	1,608	1,871	2.2	1.5	1.9
Other Asian countries						
Indonesia	199	267	372	2.5	3.4	2.9
Philippines	370	517	544	2.8	0.5	1.8
Thailand	291	277	344	–0.4	2.2	0.8
India	197	280	308	3.0	1.0	2.1
Pakistan	146	247	338	4.5	3.2	3.9
Europe						
North West Europe						
Sweden	276	349	433	2.0	2.2	2.1
Belgium–Lux.	756	788	1,062	0.3	3.0	1.6
Denmark	472	510	770	0.6	4.2	2.2
Netherlands	760	1,239	1,858	4.2	4.1	4.1
France	360	413	473	1.1	1.4	1.2
Germany FR	484	609	709	1.9	1.5	1.7
Ireland	210	240	247	1.1	0.3	0.7
UK	300	358	543	1.5	4.2	2.7
South Europe						
Greece	182	320	317	4.8	–0.1	2.5
Italy	453	625	608	2.7	–0.3	1.3
Portugal	143	244	253	4.6	0.3	2.6
Spain	126	196	219	3.8	1.1	2.6
EC total	316	406	470	2.1	1.5	1.8
Americas–Oceania						
Australia	9	12	15	2.1	2.2	2.1
USA	76	108	146	3.0	3.1	3.0
Canada	77	80	86	0.4	0.8	0.6
Argentina	36	46	57	2.0	2.2	2.1
Brazil	78	88	109	1.0	2.1	1.5
Mexico	36	56	84	3.8	4.2	4.0

Source As for Appendix Tables B.1 and B.2.
Note a. and b. As for Table 3.1.

growth of gross value added, which was among the highest of the selected countries, but mainly the result of the absolute increase in agricultural labour at annual growth rates ranging from 1 to 2 per cent. The same characteristic, which is typical for developing countries, can be observed in Mexico.

Land productivity

There are also significant differences in land productivities. Table 3.3 indicates land productivity in terms of gross value added per hectare for 1963, 1975, and 1985 in 1975 international prices and annual growth rates. During the entire period, Taiwan ranked at the top and Australia at the bottom. The ratio between the two was as big or bigger than 1:120. Again there are clear inter-regional differences in land productivities.

Contrary to the case of labour productivity, land productivity in Americas-Oceania countries ranked lowest. At highest it was only 146 International dollars per hectare for the USA in 1985. East Asian countries were at the highest level of land productivity, ranging 1,327 to 1,871 International dollars per hectare in 1985. Land productivity in European countries ranged widely between the Netherlands, which is at the East Asian level, to Spain or Ireland which are at the level of the lowest in Asia. The EC total average is close to the level of the Philippines.

Growth patterns of land productivity are different from labour productivity. Labour productivity has clear regional patterns, but in the case of land productivity no particular pattern is observed. In Asia Pakistan achieved the highest growth rate with 3.9 per cent and Thailand the lowest at 0.8 per cent. In Europe the highest was 4.1 per cent for the Netherlands, while the lowest was 0.7 per cent for Ireland. And in the Americas the highest was 4.0 per cent for Mexico and 0.6 per cent the lowest for Canada. Since all regions had the same wide ranges of growth of land productivity, it is difficult to identify particular trends by region. However, there are regional differences in growth of land input. For the entire period, agricultural land increased in Asia, except for Japan, and in the Americas, except for the USA, while it decreased in Europe, except for Ireland and Greece. In Asia and the Americas, however, growth of land input slowed down in 1975–85 compared with 1963–75, and, furthermore, it decreased absolutely in Korea, Taiwan, and Australia.

Some national experiences deserve special notice. In Japan land productivity decreased absolutely in 1975–85 and its level was surpassed by Korea in 1985. The Netherlands achieved the highest growth among the countries and overtook Taiwan in 1985. And the USA, whose land productivity was half of Pakistan in 1963, could reach the 1963 Pakistan level in 1985.

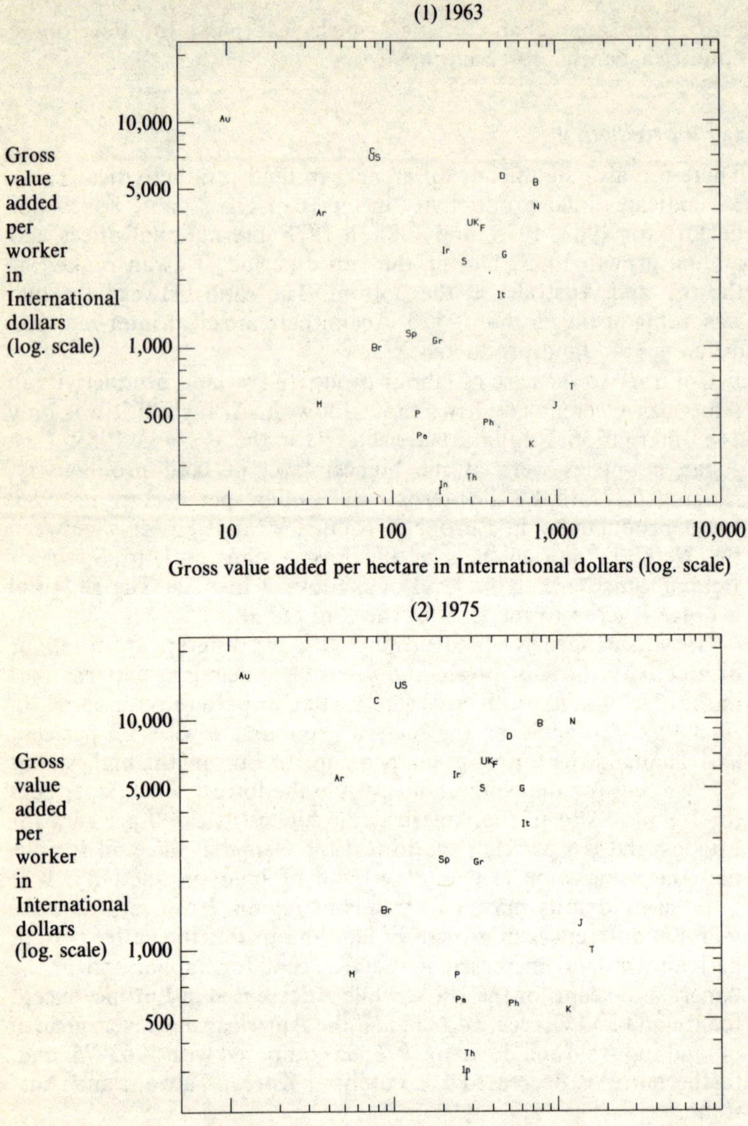

Figure 3.1 International comparison of labour and land productivities in agriculture, 1963, 1975, and 1985 (International dollars)

(3) 1985

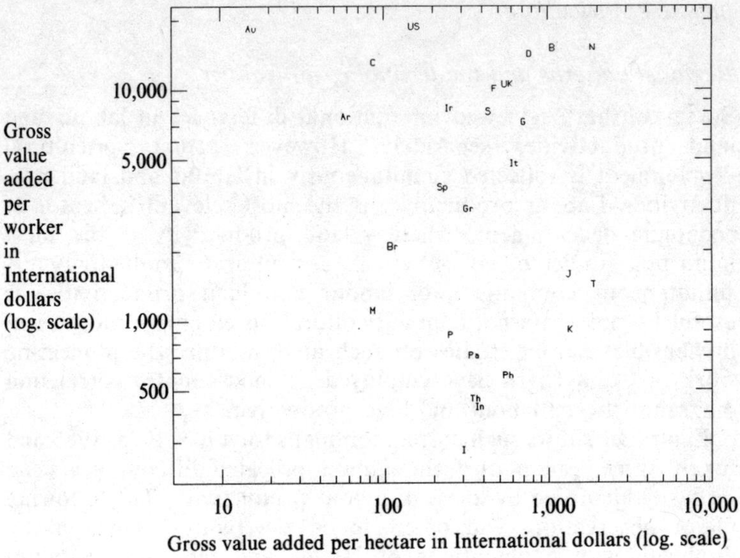

(4) 1963, 1975 and 1985, pooled

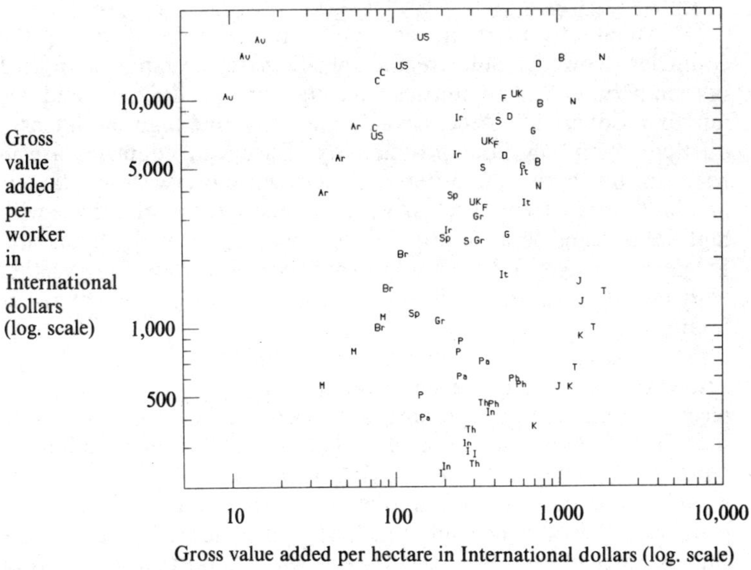

Notes Keys are as follows:

Argentina	Ar	France	F	Japan	J	Spain	Sp
Australia	Au	Germany FR	G	Korea	K	Sweden	S
Belgium (-Luxembourg)	B	Greece	Gr	Mexico	M	Taiwan	T
		India	I	Netherlands	N	Thailand	Th
Brazil	Br	Indonesia	In	Pakistan	Pa	United Kingdom	UK
Canada	C	Ireland	Ir	Phillipines	Ph	United States	US
Denmark	D	Italy	It	Portugal	P		

Source Tables 3.1 and 3.3.

Regional patterns and the technological frontier

So far we have reviewed international differences in labour and land productivities separately. However, actual agricultural development is reflected simultaneously in labour and land productivities. Labour productivity is the most relevant indicator of economic development, whereas land productivity is the most important indicator of physical agricultural productivity. A simultaneous comparison of labour and land productivities is useful to make international agricultural development more comprehensible. Earlier studies on such analysis since the pioneering work of Colin Clark have employed an inter-country correlation diagram between labour and land productivities.

Figure 3.1 shows such correlation maps for 1963, 1975, 1985 and for the three years pooled, though not indicated different years can be easily identified by levels of labour productivity. The following major observations can be made on the figures, which partly duplicate with explanations of labour and land productivities above.

(1) Apparently there are no significant correlations among the countries. However, some region specific patterns can be identified in each period. Asian countries have high land productivity and low labour productivity. Americas–Oceania combine high labour productivity with low land productivity. European countries are in between, but with wide differences between those with low labour and land productivity, such as Portugal and Greece, and those with high labour and land productivities, such as the Netherlands and Belgium. Mexico and Brazil, however, could be classified together with the low productive European countries such as Portugal or Spain.

(2) The observed inter-regional differences are strongly associated with resource endowment conditions of countries in terms of land area per agricultural worker (Table 3.4). It is natural that the technological choice where land is scarce relative to labour, tends to bias towards land-saving technological progress. This means that where the amount of land per worker is small, land productivity would be high and labour productivity not so high. This is particularly observed in Asia, where land per worker is at most two hectares. On the contrary, if land is abundant compared to labour, labour productivity is the major concern in agricultural development and land productivity growth is often disregarded. This was the case in Americas–Oceania where land per worker was more than 100 hectares or even more than 1,000 hectares, except for Brazil and Mexico where land labour ratios were at the same level

Table 3.4 Agricultural land area per worker, 1963, 1975, and 1985 (hectares)

Country	*Hectares per worker*			*Annual growth rate (%)*		
	1963	*1975*	*1985*	*1963–75*	*1975–85*	*1963–85*
Asia						
East Asia						
Japan	0.6	0.9	1.2	4.5	2.4	3.5
Korean Rep.	0.5	0.5	0.7	–0.9	3.7	1.2
Taiwan	0.5	0.6	0.8	1.2	2.2	1.6
Other Asian countries						
Indonesia	1.2	1.1	1.1	–0.8	0.2	–0.3
Philippines	1.2	1.1	1.1	–0.8	–0.6	–0.7
Thailand	0.9	1.3	1.3	3.0	0.4	1.8
India	1.2	1.0	0.9	–1.2	–1.5	–1.3
Pakistan	2.8	2.5	2.1	–0.9	–1.6	–1.2
Europe						
North West Europe						
Sweden	8.7	14.4	18.6	4.3	2.6	3.5
Belgium–Lux.	7.0	12.1	14.3	4.7	1.6	3.3
Denmark	12.0	16.5	18.5	2.6	1.2	2.0
Netherlands	5.5	7.9	8.2	3.1	0.4	1.9
France	9.3	15.6	21.3	4.4	3.2	3.9
Germany FR	5.3	8.2	10.2	3.7	2.2	3.1
Ireland	12.8	24.0	33.8	5.4	3.5	4.5
UK	11.8	18.4	19.5	3.7	0.6	2.3
South Europe						
Greece	5.9	7.5	9.7	2.1	2.5	2.3
Italy	3.8	5.6	7.9	3.4	3.4	3.4
Portugal	3.5	3.2	3.4	–0.9	0.8	–0.1
Spain	9.2	12.6	17.4	2.7	3.3	2.9
EC total	6.8	10.1	13.2	3.3	2.7	3.1
Americas–Oceania						
Australia	1,112.0	1,311.0	1,239.0	1.4	–0.6	0.5
USA	91.0	131.0	128.0	3.0	–0.2	1.5
Canada	96.0	151.0	152.0	3.9	0.1	2.1
Argentina	109.0	122.0	135.0	0.9	1.0	1.0
Brazil	13.0	17.0	19.0	2.3	1.3	1.9
Mexico	16.0	14.0	13.0	–0.9	–0.7	–0.8

Source Appendix Table B.2.

as Europe. The land area per worker in Europe ranged from 3 to 26 hectares.

(3) Relative positions of individual countries within each region with respect to labour and land productivities are, by and large, unchanged through the entire period. Leading countries are always Taiwan and Japan in Asia, the Netherlands, Belgium, and Denmark in Europe and the USA and Canada in the Americas.

(4) Except for Japan from 1975–85, leading countries relatively improved their labour and land productivities, and the differences within each region have widened. The productivity ratio between countries with highest and lowest labour productivity changed over time from 2.8, 4.4, to 5.7 in Asia, from 11.3, 12.5 to 17.5 in Europe, and from 18.6, 19.9 to 16.9 in Americas–Oceania for 1963, 1975, and 1985, respectively. Only in the case of the Americas–Oceania in 1985 has the gap declined.

(5) Changing patterns of differences in land productivity within the same region were different from that of labour productivity. In Asia the ratio in land productivity between the highest and the lowest countries has declined from 8.5, 6.5 to 6.1 in the period 1963–85, respectively. Thus a relative catching-up has taken place. However, in Europe and Americas-Oceania the productivity ratios within regions widened, from 6.0 in 1963 to 8.5 in 1985 in Europe and from 8.7 to 9.7 in Americas–Oceania.

(6) The phenomena observed above can be interpreted consistently in the context of the concept of a technological frontier. The leading countries in each region may form a technological frontier of international agricultural development possibilities. The technological frontier can be considered as the meta-production function (Hayami and Ruttan, 1985). This means that Taiwan and Japan (and recently also Korea) in Asia, the Netherlands, Belgium, and Denmark in Europe, and the USA, Canada and the extreme case of Australia in Americas–Oceania occupy the highest possible productivity positions on the world-wide technological frontier line. In the course of economic development and structural transformation of the respective countries, the direction of technological change in agriculture was geared to meet the respective current conditions. For leading Asian countries, Japan and Taiwan, where a high level of economic development has now also been achieved, particularly in Japan, labour productivity only recently became a major concern in agricultural development. In the past an increase of land productivity was the most important objective since land was scarce. Leading countries in Europe and Americas–Oceania could increase agricultural land area per worker considerably in 1963–75, and labour productivity could also

increase, regardless of changes in land productivity. In 1975–85, however, the land area per worker could not increase as much as in the previous period, but labour productivity could increase by improving land productivity.

(7) The relative position of Japan to Taiwan, the leading countries in Asia, has changed during the period: in 1963 Japan was behind Taiwan in both labour and land productivity, but exceeded Taiwan in labour productivity and narrowed the land productivity gap in 1975. But after 1975 the growth rate of labour productivity in Japan slowed down and that of land productivity even became negative. As a result Taiwan exceeded Japan considerably in land productivity and almost caught up with Japan in labour productivity. In 1985 Japan's land productivity was even behind that of Korea.

Sources of international productivity differences

As we have seen, sizeable productivity differences exist among countries. Many partly interdependent factors contribute to such differences. Below some major factors for labour productivity differences are analysed.

General level of economic development

Many economic activities can be expected to be more efficient in advanced systems of an economy and society. We may expect that developed countries have better infrastructures, more advanced scientific know-how, better educated people, cheaper manufactured farm inputs, and more job opportunities to absorb excess labour from rural areas than developing countries. Thus it is natural to expect a high correlation between the agricultural productivity level and the general economic development level, indicated by GNP per capita. To test this for the benchmark years GNP per capita was correlated with agricultural labour productivity (Figure 3.2).

There is a high correlation coefficient between the two variables of 0.89. But the positions of Japan and Argentina are not on the trend line. One of the major factors for the two outliers could be the contrasting resource endowment, which is relatively small for Japan and big for Argentina. However, for Japan there may be some other reasons as well, which we will try to identify later on. The Netherlands was exactly on the trend, but tended to increase labour productivity rapidly during the entire period. Japan, on the contrary, increased productivity only little in spite of the fact that GDP per capita increased considerably in 1975–85. Japan remains relatively backward in agricultural development while the

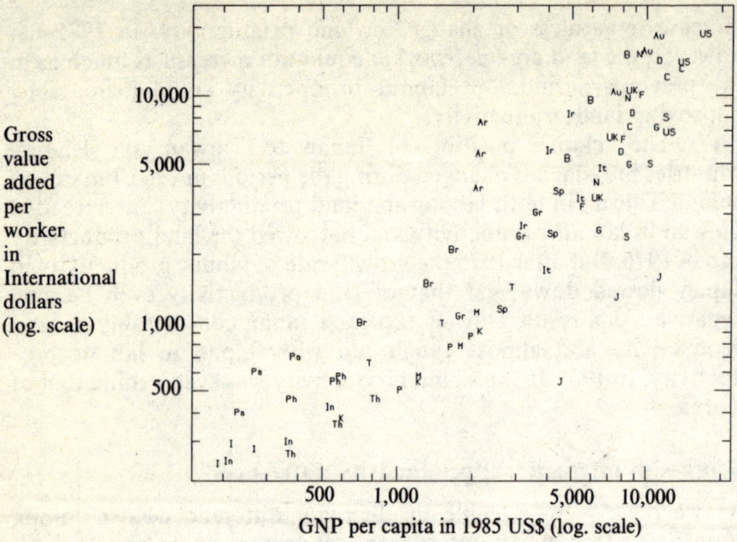

Figure 3.2 International comparison of labour productivity in 1975 International dollars and GNP per capita in 1985 US$, 1963, 1975, and 1985

Source Table 3.1 and GNP per capita calculated from World Bank, *World Development Report*, various issues.

Note See Figure 3.1 for keys.

Netherlands enjoyed a sizeable productivity improvement. The USA has kept its leading position in the Americas, but labour productivity growth stagnated a little in the period 1975–85 compared to 1963–75.

Diversified economy and society

In a traditional society where agriculture is the dominant sector, agriculture cannot utilize services from other sectors to improve agricultural productivity. Where, on the contrary, other sectors are developed and provide goods and services sufficiently, agriculture can fully utilize such goods and services. As an indicator we may apply shares of agriculture in employment, or GDP in the total economy. Figure 3.3 shows the correlation between the agricultural share in total employment and labour productivity for 1963, 1975, and 1985. We can observe a clear negative correlation between agricultural labour productivity and agricultural employment share with a correlation coefficient of -0.90.

Again Japan's position was lower than the trend and its 1985 position moved further away from the trend while the Netherlands

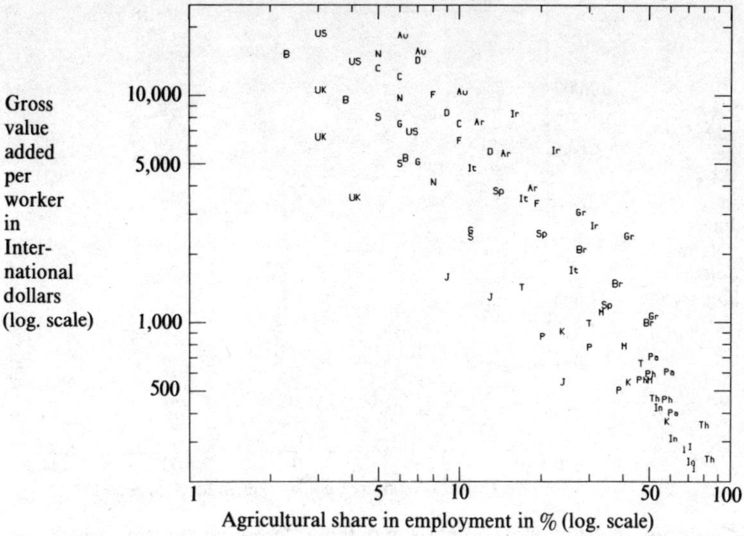

Figure 3.3 International comparison of labour productivity and agricultural share in employment, 1963, 1975, and 1985

Sources Table 3.1., OECD *Labour Force Statistics*, various issues, Asian Development Bank, *Key indicators*, various issues, and *FAO Production Yearbook*, various issues.

Note See Figure 3.1 for keys.

showed a higher increase in productivity than average. There are two additional notable matters in Figure 3.3. One is the fact that in 1985 Taiwan and Korea seemed to follow Japan's downward deviation from the trend, which may imply that in the near future these two countries may face problems similar to Japan. Another is the fact that the UK came back on the trend line from an outlier position, such as Japan is occupying now.

Resource endowment

Land is a very important resource for agricultural activity. Where land is relatively abundant to labour, farmers can achieve rather easily high labour productivity by use of labour-saving inputs such as tractors. Figure 3.4 shows that in Australia, where land area per worker is over 1,000 hectares, labour productivity is among the highest in the world, and in the USA and Argentina where land area per worker is over 100 hectares, labour productivity follows Australia. Under the land scarcity conditions such as in Japan, Taiwan, and Korea, where the land area per worker is about only

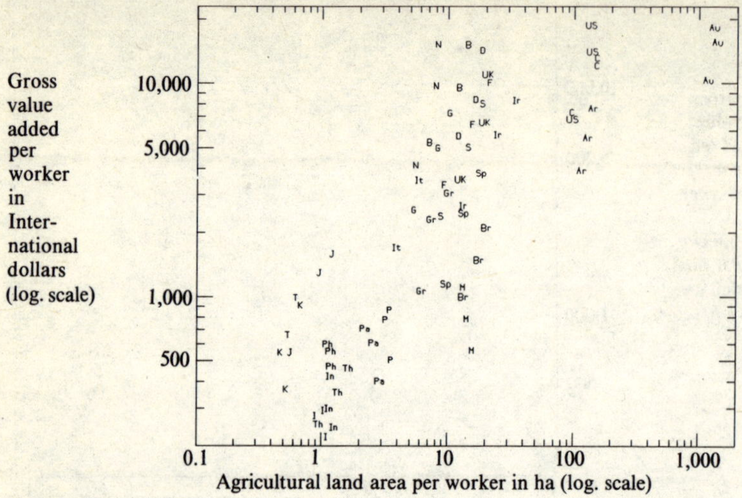

Figure 3.4 International comparison of labour productivity and agricultural land area per worker, 1963, 1975, and 1985

Sources Tables 3.1 and 3.4.
Note See Figure 3.1 for keys.

one hectare, it is hard to realize a high labour productivity, since labour productivity is equal to land productivity multiplied by land area per worker, and land productivity in these countries is already at the top level in the world. Remarkably, there is no convergence between regions, but parallel paths with steeper slopes than for the overall trend. This implies that there is a possibility of increasing labour productivity under less favourable resource conditions. However, Asian countries' resource endowment conditions are too low to expect that the other regions' level can be approached without considerable further expansion of land availability per worker. There is apparently no possibility for Japan and other East Asian countries to catch up with EC countries in the near future.

Input substitution

We can expect that labour productivity can improve if inputs of better quality or technically more advanced inputs become available for substitution of labour at reasonable prices. This is of course true for agricultural activities as well. It is difficult to estimate the optimum use of such inputs, but in an international comparison which includes several developing and developed countries, we may assume that higher application of such input can generate higher

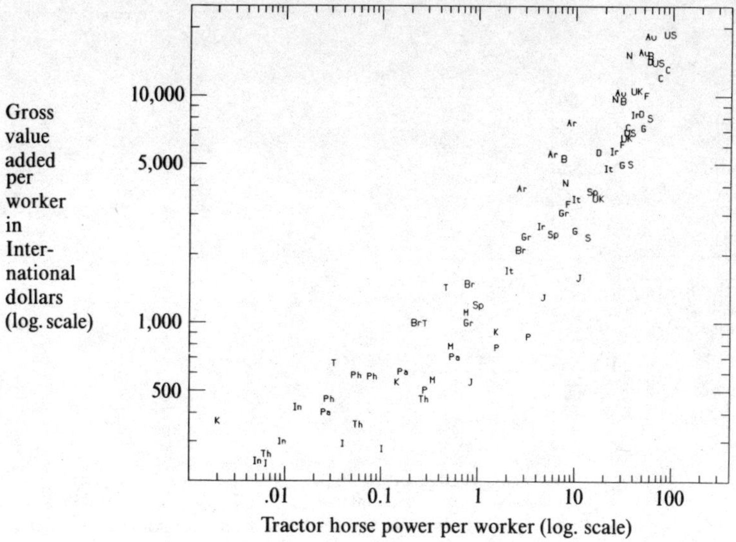

Figure 3.5 International comparison of labour productivity and tractor horse power per worker, 1963, 1975, and 1985

Sources Table 3.1 and Appendix Table B.3.
Note See Table 3.1 for keys.

productivity. As an indicator representing input that can be substituted for labour, we used tractor horse power per worker for 1963, 1975, and 1985. The relation with labour productivity is shown in Figure 3.5. There is a clear high correlation between labour productivity and the tractor horse power per worker. The correlation coefficient is as high as 0.93. The position of Japan is clearly below the trend line which suggests a significant over-investment of machinery in Japan.

Current inputs are used in agricultural production with the aim of obtaining more production. Actually some current inputs can be considered as substitutes for labour. For instance herbicides can save the work of weeding, and feed can save the work of cutting grass or taking animals to the fields for feeding. Of course these inputs will only be applied if there is a positive margin left after these costs are deducted. Thus they most likely raise labour productivity. Even on a gross value added concept basis, i.e. after deduction of the value of current inputs from total production value, this relation can be observed. Figure 3.6 shows the relationship between gross value added per worker and current inputs per worker with a correlation coefficient as high as 0.95.

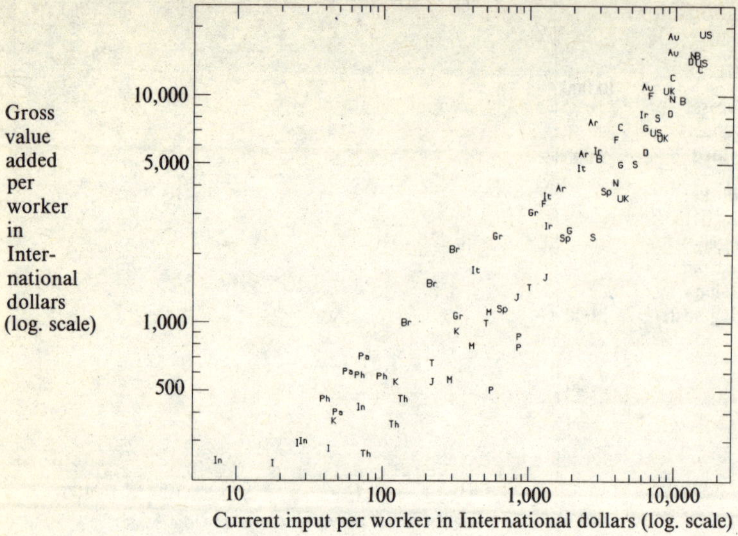

Figure 3.6 International comparison of labour productivity and intermediate input per worker, 1963, 1975, and 1985

Sources Table 3.1 and Appendix Table B.1.

Notes Intermediate input can be obtained by deducting gross value added from total production.

Statistical test of the divergence of Japanese agriculture from the international productivity level

So far we have observed inter-country productivity differences and some relevant determining factors. One significant finding is that the Japanese position is several times below the productivity level that it is expected to achieve given the overall trend. In actual production all the variables affect labour productivity simultaneously. To test whether Japanese agricultural productivity really lags behind the international trend, given its use of input factors, aggregate productivity functions of the Cobb–Douglas type are estimated first, then the possible divergence of Japanese agriculture from the international productivity trend is measured by comparing the level predicted by the functions with the actual productivity level.

The regression results are presented in Table 3.5. The regression coefficients are statistically significant and the equations acceptable.[12] Table 3.6 shows the gaps between the actual labour productivity level and the predicted level derived from the regression results for the technologically leading countries in different regions. There is a significant difference in the gap for

Japan and for the other countries. Japan's actual gross value added per worker was much below the predicted level. The gap decreased in 1975 because of large decline of labour and partly due to an exceptionally good crop in that year, but widened significantly again in 1985. For Taiwan, the competitive technological leader in Asia, actual performance was always above the predicted level, but its relative performance shows a declining trend. For Korea, another competitor in Asia, actual performance was better than the trend in 1963 and 1975, but its performance deteriorated and dropped to below the trend in 1985. This implies that it is following Japan's example.

Contrary to Asia, for the other regions the actual productivity level of the technical leaders deviates in an upward direction from the predicted level, in particular in 1985. Leaders in Europe recently realized levels much higher than the trend prediction level. For the Americas–Oceania the actual levels were significantly lower than the trend in 1963, approached the trend level in 1975, and exceeded the trend level in 1985.

The observations above may imply that Japanese agriculture recently became relatively more inefficient in contrast to the continuous improvement of Western countries, and even to its neighbours in East Asia, though they also show signs of relative deterioration.

Why did such a significant deterioration occur in Japan? A possible explanation for that deterioration can be found in the

Table 3.5 Regression results of labour productivity functions*

Equation number	*(1)*	*(2)*	*(3)*	*(4)*
Explanatory variables:				
land area per worker	0.197	0.202	0.201	0.183
	(0.029)	(0.035)	(0.030)	(0.036)
Tractor horse power per worker	0.178	0.228	0.161	0.340
	(0.033)	(0.051)	(0.046)	(0.028)
GNP per capita		0.251	0.052	
		(0.103)	(0.096)	
Agricultural employment share	–0.512		–0.492	
	(0.085)		(0.093)	
Intercept	6.022	2.136	5.653	3.422
	(0.336)	(0.395)	(0.338)	(0.408)
R^2	0.937	0.913	0.937	0.906

Note *Equations are estimated by ordinary least squares, and the standard errors of coefficients are in parentheses.

Table 3.6 Gaps between actual performance in gross value added per worker and the predicted values in per cent of the predicted value, for the technically leading countries 1963, 1975, and 1985 (%)

Equation number		*Japan*	*Taiwan*	*Korea*	*Netherlands*	*Belgium*	*Denmark*	*USA*	*Australia*
(1)	1963	–71	44	46	7	15	29	–45	–17
	1975	–49	30	9	40	12	4	–6	–6
	1985	–79	25	–19	55	17	33	4	1
(2)	1963	–113	47	53	19	39	13	–39	–29
	1975	–69	30	1	48	45	19	11	–8
	1985	–94	32	–26	63	55	45	26	3

Note The equation number corresponds to the number in Table 3.5.

inverse U-shape hypothesis of the relationship between the agricultural price level and changes in growth rate of labour productivity which was presented in Chapter Two.

Statistical test of the inverse U-shape hypothesis

There must be some reasons for the relatively low productivity performance other than the factors included in the equations. We assume that the increase in the unexplained productivity, in particular for 1975–85, was caused by the price distortion which emerged in that period in Japan in the context of the inverse U-shape hypothesis. In Chapter Two (Table 2.9 p. 39) we tested the validity of the hypothesis by use of quadratic equations which used the growth rates of productivity derived from national accounts at 1975 national prices. Table 3.7 shows the same test for the twenty-six observations at 1975 international prices. The results indicate similar findings as in the case of national prices. Accordingly we may tentatively confirm the validity of the inverse U-shape hypothesis by use of international price data as well as national data. However, the optimum price level at which maximum labour productivity growth occurs, may differ by country. Considering this possibility, an alternative statistical test is carried out.

In this section the validity of the inverse U-shape hypothesis as a key factor for explaining recent changes in Japanese agricultural productivity is tested with the following model:

Table 3.7 Test of inverse U-shaped relationship between growth rate of labour productivity and price level of twenty-six countries

	Intercept	*Price index*	*Squared price index*	R^2
1963–75[a]	–1.32 (1.66)	7.49 (4.18)	–1.74 (1.63)	0.34
1975–85[b]	–4.20 (1.57)	8.74 (3.00)	–2.22 (0.84)	0.29
1963–85[c]	–3.20 (1.11)	8.85 (2.65)	–2.24 (0.86)	0.47

Source Growth rates of labour productivity from Table 3.1. Price indexes from the FAO (1986: 26)

Notes The difference of this regression with that of Table 2.9 is that here growth rates of gross value added are measured at international prices as explained at the beginning of this chapter. Price levels are measured at international prices and expressed as indexes with USA = 1.00. The index is the ratio of the Purchasing Power Parity for agriculture and the exchange rate, both expressed in terms of units of local currency per US \$. The standard errors of coefficients are in parentheses. a. The price index for 1970 is applied; b. The price index for 1980 is applied; c. The price index for 1975 is applied.

$$g(P)_j = M - a\,[(R+\Sigma d_k D_k) - r_j]^2 \qquad a > 0 \qquad (2)$$

where $g(P)$ is the actual growth of labour productivity in agriculture and M the maximum growth rate, R the optimum price index at which maximum labour productivity growth occurs, $d_k D_k$ dummy variables of the optimum price index for different regions (country groups) k, r each country's actual price index, and j indicates country j. The actual agricultural product price level in a country is defined as the ratio of agricultural Purchasing Power Parities (PPPs) (estimated by the FAO 1986) to the exchange rate both expressed in local currency units per US dollar, and referred to here as the price index. This model implies that $R + d_k D_k$ is assumed to be different by region, but the same within the regions. If country j's ratio r_j was at the level R_k of region k to which country j belongs, the actual growth rate of labour productivity $g(P)$ would be the maximum, and $g(P)$ smaller if r is smaller or larger than R. The calculation is simplified as follows. Instead of direct estimation of the quadratic form with dummy variables, equation (2) was transformed into a linear form:

$$a^{1/2}(R + \Sigma\, d_k D_k - r) = \pm\,[M - g(P)]^{1/2} \qquad (3)$$

For countries for which the left side of the equation was negative (when r_j is bigger than R_k), the sign on the right side was also set negative. M could be different by country or region, but it was assumed to be equal for all countries. Many factors affect the optimum price level for countries or regions. In countries like Japan and Korea, where industrial growth is rapid and comparative advantage in agriculture is low, the optimum price level is likely to be considerably higher. On the contrary, in countries with a comparative advantage in agriculture, the level could be relatively low. For countries where the absolute income or productivity level in agriculture lags far behind that in industrial sectors the optimum price level may be relatively high compared to the opposite case. There is also probably a dynamic interaction between policies and changes in the optimum price level. In countries where farmers' organizations are politically powerful, structural transformation may be delayed and by this the optimum price level could become higher than in countries where farmers' organizations lack power. For countries with free import and low prices, structural adjustment may be rapid and the optimum level is likely to be relatively low, while the opposite is the case under agricultural protection. Other factors, such as institutions and various economic and social policies, will also have a dynamic effect on the optimum price level.

Considering the differences among countries, the optimum price level is likely to be different by country. However, for practical purposes, we had to assume that it is different by region but the same for countries within the same region. For *M* in equation (3) we took the highest actually achieved growth rate. *G*(*P*) was taken from Table 3.1 and *r* from the FAO (1986). *R* and d_k were estimated by regressions, and thus the optimum price levels by region can be measured (in the form of indexes). By using these results the gap between the optimum price level and the actual index of each country is compared with the growth rate of labour productivity of the country. An arbitrary element of this model is that the estimated level by region is in particular affected by the necessary subjective grouping of countries, and also by the selected value for *M*. To test the effect of the choice of groupings, the calculation was carried out for several alternative groupings and the results compared.

The test was made separately for the periods 1963–75 and 1975–85. The 1970 price index was used as an indicator of the price level for the first period (1963–75) and that of 1980 for the latter period (1975–85). Some of the results are shown in Table 3.8. For the first

Table 3.8 Regression results of the equation (3) with different regional groupings, 1963–75 and 1975–85[a]

Period *Regression number*	*1963–75*[b] *(1)*	*1963–75*[b] *(2)*	*1975–85*[c] *(3)*	*1975–85*[c] *(4)*
Price index (*r*)	2.528 (1.193)	1.949 (1.156)	4.081 (0.528)	3.947 (0.601)
Regional dummy: D1 (East Asia)[d]	-1.551 (1.330)	-1.185 (1.261)	-4.819 (0.923)	-4.631 (1.012)
D2 (Western developed countries)[e]	-0.043 (0.723)		-0.858 (0.306)	
D3 (North West Europe)		0.633 (0.759)		-0.763 (0.365)
D4 (North American-Oceania)[f]		-1.592 (1.031)		-1.039 (0.479)
Intercept	-2.346 (1.699)	-1.799 (1.594)	-4.854 (0.722)	-4.698 (0.734)
R^2	0.174	0.306	0.745	0.748

Notes a. The standard errors of coefficients are in parentheses; b. The 1970 price indexes (r_{1970}) are used and the maximum growth rate (*M*) is assumed to be 7.5 per cent; c. The 1980 price indexes (r_{1980}) are used and the maximum growth rate (*M*) is assumed to be 4.8 per cent; d. Japan and Korea; e. D3 + D4; f. The USA, Canada, and Australia.

period the results are not statistically significant. During that period international price distortion was not so important yet, and the relation found was statistically not significant. This means that the inverse U-shape was not observed. However, in the latter period, 1975–85, protectionism increased, and we find a distinct inverse U-shape. The regression results for 1975–85 are all statistically significant.

By combining the estimates from the regression (3) in Table 3.8 with the equation (3), we obtained the regional optimum levels of the price index as 2.37 for Japan and Korea, 1.40 for the countries included in the D2 dummy, and 1.19 for the rest of the countries. The gap between the price level of each country and the regional optimum price level (both presented in Appendix Table B.4, p. 178) are shown in Figure 3.7 in relation with the growth rates of gross value added per worker (Table 3.1, p. 45). When the regression (4) is applied, we obtain as regional optimum levels of price indexes 2.36 for Japan and Korea, 1.38 for the North West-European countries, 1.45 for the USA, Canada and Australia, and 1.19 for the

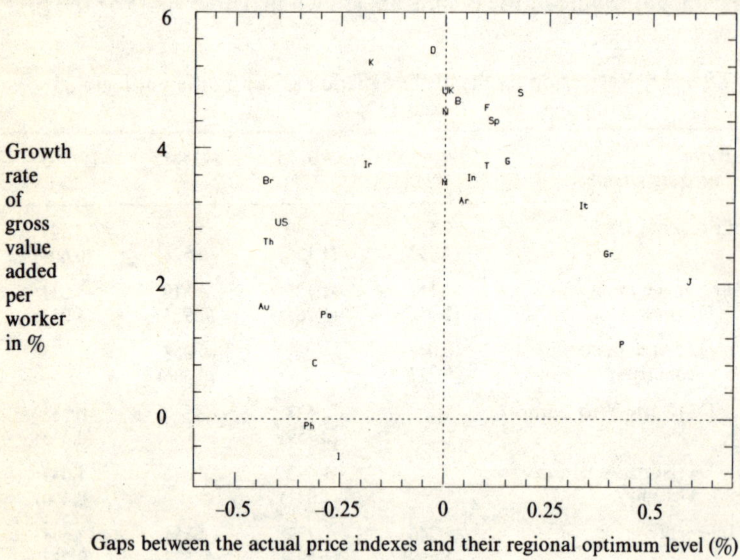

Figure 3.7 International comparison of the growth rate of labour productivity and gaps between the price level and the regional optimum level, 1975–85

Source Table 3.1 and Appendix Table B.4.
Note See Figure 3.1 for keys.

rest of the countries. Figure 3.7 shows a rough but clear inverse U-shape relationship between the two variables. The alternative figure based on regression (4) shows almost the same. Thus, the present test roughly supports the hypothesis, though it is statistically still weak.

Conclusion

Through the international comparison we have identified stagnation of gross value added per worker in Japanese agriculture in the 1975–85 period, poor performance relative to the predicted level on the basis of international comparison, and a negative effect of the high price level on productivity performance based on the confirmed inverse U-shape hypothesis.

Japan has been one of the technological leaders in agricultural development in Asia. However, Japan is now losing or has already lost that position to Taiwan, and next perhaps even to Korea. Without drastic changes in price policy, structural transformation and adjustment policy, international trade policy and land policy, it is impossible for Japanese agriculture to catch up with the EC level or even that of Taiwan.

In various aspects, Japanese agricultural performance contrasts with Dutch agriculture, one of the leaders of European agriculture. Through an in-depth analysis of differences in agricultural performances in the past between the two countries in the next chapter, we shall try to find more detailed reasons for the poor performance of Japanese agriculture, and perhaps indications for measures required to maintain leadership in Asian agricultural development.

Chapter four

Agricultural development in Japan and the Netherlands

In this chapter agricultural development in Japan and the Netherlands since 1880 will be compared. Both countries are densely populated and have relatively small areas of agricultural land. Nevertheless, both countries have achieved rapid agricultural growth and are technological leaders in Asian and European agriculture. However, there still exists a considerable productivity gap between the two, a gap which has not significantly narrowed over the past one hundred years. This chapter aims at in-depth comparison of growth in Dutch and Japanese agriculture and extends a preliminary effort by Van der Meer and Yamada (1986).

Japan is one of the countries with the best documented growth experience in the world. Basic information on the whole economy and agricultural sector over the period since 1880 is found in Ohkawa and Shinohara (1979), Hayami *et al.* (1975) and Yamada (1982a and 1987a). For the Netherlands, however, the data base for the period before 1948 is much poorer. Official national income data by sector are available from 1900–48, but in current prices only. In this chapter use is made of tentative current and constant price estimates for the period 1880–1948 from research by Knibbe (forthcoming) and Van der Meer and Van Ark (1987).[1]

A detailed analysis of sources of agricultural growth, as carried out for Japan by Hayami *et al.* (1975) and Yamada (1987a) is not possible within the limited scope of this chapter. A problem for comparison of growth is that phases of acceleration and retardation of growth differ over time between both countries. As we are not primarily concerned with cycles but rather with long-term trends in growth, we selected 1880, 1913, 1938, 1950, 1975, and 1985 as benchmark years. We distinguished four sub-periods:

(1) the period before the First World War, 1880–1913, which was a period of continuous growth in both countries;
(2) the First World War and inter-war period 1913–38, during

which there were major disruptions in the European economies;[2]

(3) the period of recovery and rapid growth after the Second World War, 1950–75[3], and
(4) the recent decade of international economic instability and slow growth, 1975–85.

The period 1938–50 is disregarded because Japan and the Netherlands were seriously affected by the Second World War. Years of decline and recovery were not the same in both countries, and data are not very reliable. The data used are not corrected for annual fluctuations. For long periods annual fluctuations have a minor influence on compound growth rates.[4]

General conditions, 1880–1985

Land and population

The land area of Japan is 377,000 sq km, ten times larger than that of the Netherlands. Its population in 1985 was 121 million or eight times larger than that of the Netherlands (Table 4.1). With a population density of 320/sq km and 388/sq km Japan and the Netherlands are among the most densely populated countries in the world. Since 1880, Japan's population has increased by a factor of 3.3 and in the Netherlands by 3.6 or 1.1 and 1.2 per cent at compound growth rates. Compared to other Asian countries Japan's population grew slowly, whereas compared to other European countries the Dutch population grew rapidly.

Despite its greater overall population density the Netherlands has three times more agricultural land per capita. Until the Second World War, both countries had been able to slowly expand their

Table 4.1 Population and land use in Japan and the Netherlands, 1880–1985

	Population (1,000)		*Agricultural land (ha)*			
			Per capita		*Per agricultural worker*	
	Japan	*Netherlands*	*Japan*	*Netherlands*	*Japan*	*Netherlands*
1880	36,857	4,027	0.129	0.489	0.30	3.93
1913	51,742	6,161	0.110	0.337	0.36	3.64
1938	71,976	8,655	0.085	0.258	0.46	3.65
1950	83,662	10,114	0.070	0.231	0.40	3.94
1960	94,118	11,486	0.065	0.203	0.50	4.97
1975	111,520	13,656	0.050	0.159	0.94	7.87
1985	120,750	14,497	0.045	0.144	1.20	8.22

Source Appendix Tables C.1 and C.2, and OECD *Labour Force Statistics.*

agricultural land area, but afterwards the area declined because of rapid urbanization, and demand for infrastructure and recreation. There is a great difference in the area of agricultural land per worker. Because of a higher overall employment participation of nearly 50 per cent in Japan (compared to one third in the Netherlands), and because of a much higher share of agriculture in employment (see Table 6.2 p. 134), the amount of agricultural employment is much larger than in the Netherlands (Appendix Table C.1, p. 184). The land area per worker in the Netherlands was some ten times that of Japan in the pre-war period. In the post-war period, the difference decreased, yet in 1985 it is still nearly seven times larger in the Netherlands.

General economic performance

There is a big difference between the economic performance of Japan and the Netherlands. The Netherlands was a rich country at an early stage. If we take the real GDP in international prices as calculated by Kravis, Heston, and Summer (1982) then we find that in 1980 GDP per capita of Japan had slightly surpassed the level of the Netherlands. A hundred years ago, however, the Dutch level was still about four times higher. Since then, Dutch GDP per capita increased five times and that of Japan more than twenty times. Japan's increase in GDP per capita was rapid, in particular in the post-war period. Its average growth rate in the total post-war period is more than 7 per cent while it was merely 3 per cent in the Netherlands. As shown in Chapter Two and further to be discussed in Chapter Six, industrial growth in Japan was very rapid and agricultural productivity growth always lagged behind that of industry. Industrial growth was the engine of Japan's general economic growth, and it strongly affected agricultural performance.

Foreign trade in agricultural produce

Japan is a major exporter of manufactured goods. Exports formed the basis for rapid industrialization and economic development in Japan. Foreign trade is a really important element of general economic development in Japan. However, in comparing both countries it should first be noted that total foreign trade is of much more importance to the Netherlands than to Japan. Compared to GDP it has been three to five times higher in the Netherlands, except in the inter-war period when the Netherlands suffered from import restrictions imposed by its trading partners (Table 4.2). The relative importance of trade in the Netherlands can be explained by

Table 4.2 Ratios of trade to GDP and agricultural shares in total trade in Japan and the Netherlands in current prices, 1880–1985 (%)

	Exports[a] in % of GDP		*Imports[b] in % of GDP*		*Agricultural exports in % of total export*		*Agricultural imports in % of total import*	
	Japan	*Netherlands*	*Japan*	*Netherlands*	*Japan*	*Netherlands*	*Japan*	*Netherlands*
1880	5[c]	32	8[c]	43	42	34	12	30
1913	15	42	17	64	13	30	56	22
1938	16	19	15	26	12	47	42	43
1950	9	29	13	43	7	46	70	30
1960	9	37	10	41	9	31	44	21
1975	11	42	12	42	2	24	24	16
1985	13	57	10	54	1	22	20	16

Source Van der Meer and Yamada (1986), Kayo (1977), MAFF (1988), Pilat (1988) and LEI/CBS, *Agricultural Statistics*, 1983 and 1988.
Notes a. f.o.b.; b. c.i.f.; c. 1890.

the fact that the Netherlands is well integrated in the European economy, whereas Japan is more isolated, and also because the size of the domestic market in the Netherlands is much smaller than in Japan which has a more than eight times larger population. Besides, the Netherlands' traditional favourable attitude towards trade plays an important role.

A striking feature is the great importance of agricultural trade to the Netherlands. Until the Second World War, about 50 per cent of its exports and 40 per cent of its imports were of 'agricultural origin'. Only in recent years has the share of agriculture declined significantly. In Japan, contrary to the Netherlands, the share of agricultural exports in total exports was important in the late nineteenth century when silk was the most important exporting commodity, but in the twentieth century the share has declined sharply, to only 1 per cent in 1985. However, in the 1950s the share of agricultural imports in total imports in Japan was more than twice that in the Netherlands. During that period there was a serious shortage of food in Japan, and large amounts of food imports were inevitable. But even in 1985 the share was 20 per cent, significantly more than the Dutch level. Since Japan's total imports amount is large, the magnitude of Japan's agricultural imports in the international market is quite significant as well and Japan has now become the largest food importer in the world.

Per capita agricultural production and self-sufficiency in food

For Japan self-sufficiency in food and food security were important political issues after the Second World War and protection was

Table 4.3 Agricultural total production per capita, in 1975 prices, and self-sufficiency in food in Japan and the Netherlands, 1880–1985 (1975 International dollar, %)

	Agricultural total production per capita[a]		Self-sufficiency in food: Grains[b]		Meat		Total	
	Japan	*Netherlands*	*Japan*	*Netherlands*	*Japan*	*Netherlands*	*Japan*	*Netherlands*
1880	46	86						
1913	54	112						
1938	51	117	85		97			
1950	41	107	77		93			
1960	56	139	83	40	93	157[c]	90	116
1975	61	198	40	42	76	178	74	123
1985	60	266	31	23	81	241	71	127

Source Kayo (1977), MAFF (1988), LEI/CBS, *Agricultural Statistics*, various issues, Knibbe (forthcoming), Van der Meer and Van Ark (1987), and FAO (1986).

Notes Self sufficiency rates are defined as final output divided by domestic consumption and use in industry. a. Total production series in 1975 prices are linked at 1975 prices with the 1975 value in 1975 International dollar (FAO, 1986), which was utilized in Chapter 3, then divided by population; b. For the Netherlands production and use of straw included; c. All livestock products for 1960.

applied for this purpose (Yamada 1982b). This particularly applied to food grains. Gradually, however, income support claims became a more important force to maintain protection than the aim of a high self-sufficiency rate. Table 4.3 shows that in 1985 self-sufficiency rates in total food, grain, and meat were much lower for Japan than for the Netherlands. However, for grains it is lower in the Netherlands. The main reason is the huge demand from the livestock sector. Unlike Japan this is not a reason for major political concern in the Netherlands. During the two World Wars the Netherlands had to rely on domestic food production which was achieved by reducing the livestock sector and by increasing the production of wheat and potatoes. Dependency on imports of feed grains in order to obtain self-sufficiency in livestock production has a low food security risk. These sectors, just like major parts of the manufacturing industries, exist by the virtue of adding value to imported raw materials.

There is a big difference in per capita domestic agricultural production between the two countries. The real amount of total agricultural production per capita, measured at international prices, in the Netherlands was about double of that in Japan for the pre-war period, and afterwards the gap enlarged to more than four times in 1985. This means that the per capita food production in Japan is much smaller than in the Netherlands. This may partly explain why food security is more a concern in Japan than in the Netherlands.

Long-term trends in agricultural performance, 1880–1985

Trends in output and input

Our main aim is a comparison of agricultural productivity between Japan and the Netherlands. Long-term trends in agricultural output and input are reviewed first. The input and output data in 1975 national prices for the benchmark years are shown in Appendix Table C.1 (p. 184). The growth rates between the benchmark years are shown in Table 4.4.

Except for the period 1950–60, Dutch agriculture had a better growth performance than Japan. In 1950 Japanese agriculture had not yet recovered from war damage and the production level was still very low compared to its historical trend. Thus the growth rate of Japanese agriculture for that period includes the rehabilitation effect from the war. The trend for Japanese agriculture in the pre-war period was slightly different from the Netherlands and the Western countries. Japanese agriculture could realize a relatively

Table 4.4 Growth rates of final output, value added, and inputs of agriculture in Japan and the Netherlands in 1975 national prices, 1880–1985 (%)

	1880–1913	*1913–1938*	*1938–1950*	*1950–1960*	*1960–1975*	*1975–1985*	*1880–1938*	*1950–1985*	*1880–1985*
Japan									
Final output	1.6	1.2	–0.6	4.4	1.8	0.6	1.5	2.2	1.5
Gross value added	1.5	1.0	–0.7	4.2	0.2	–0.6	1.3	1.1	1.0
Net value added	–	–	–	4.0	–0.5	–1.2	–	0.6	–
No. of workers	0.1	–0.7	0.8	–1.9	–4.7	–2.7	–0.3	–3.3	–1.2
Hours worked	0.9	–0.5	0.8	–3.3	–4.4	–3.9	0.3	–3.9	–1.1
Land area	0.6	0.3	–0.4	0.4	–0.6	–0.4	0.4	–0.2	0.1
Capital	–	–	–	2.2	3.3	1.5	–	2.5	–
Non-farm current input	3.3	3.4	0.0	5.4	6.6	2.4	3.4	5.0	3.5
Depreciation	–	–	–	10.2	6.7	2.7	–	6.5	–
The Netherlands									
Final output	2.1	1.5	2.6	4.6	3.8	3.6	1.9	4.0	2.9
Gross value added	1.5	1.9	0.9	3.4	3.0	4.1	1.7	3.4	2.2
Net value added	–	–	–	3.5	2.9	4.2	–	3.4	–
No. of workers	0.4	0.3	–0.3	–2.3	–3.5	–0.8	0.4	–2.4	–0.6
Hours worked	0.4	0.2	–0.2	–2.5	–4.3	–2.0	0.3	–3.2	–0.9
Land area	0.2	0.3	0.4	–0.1	–0.5	–0.4	0.2	–0.3	0.1
Capital	–	–	–	0.3	2.4	2.4	–	1.8	–
Non-farm current input	4.4	0.5	6.9	6.5	4.7	3.0	2.7	4.7	3.8
Depreciation	–	–	–	2.1	4.3	3.6	–	3.5	–

Source Appendix Table C.1.

high growth rate until around 1920, but stagnated afterwards.[5]

Even though the growth rate of Japanese agriculture lagged behind Dutch agriculture, its performance up to the 1960s was rather successful compared to other Asian developing countries, since its population grew only at an average rate of 1.2 per cent. In both the pre-war and in the earlier post-war period Japanese agriculture contributed to general economic growth. However, in the 1960–75 period net value added started to decline and in the 1975–85 period both gross and net value added declined.[6] Recently Japanese agriculture has definitely stagnated.

In contrast the growth of Dutch agriculture is remarkable. As indicated in Table 4.4, the annual growth rates of final output and gross value added for the whole period of 1880–1985 are 2.9 and 2.2 per cent compared to 1.5 and 1.0 per cent respectively for Japan.

The number of workers in Japanese agriculture was stable until 1913, but declined after the boom of the First World War. Immediately after the Second World War, former armed forces personnel and emigrants repatriated to Japan where industrial employment opportunities were still bleak. Many of them returned to their native villages and engaged in farming so that the number of agricultural workers increased suddenly. However, since then it has decreased sharply, in particular for 1960–75 when it decreased at nearly 5 per cent per annum. The trend in hours worked (flow concept of labour input) shows the same direction as that of the number of workers, except for the period 1880–1913 when hours worked increased a lot, due to progress in double cropping and expansion in sericultural production (Hayami *et al.* 1975: 24–5). In 1975–85 hours worked continued to decline at 4 per cent, but the number of workers declined much slower. For Dutch agriculture both the number of workers and hours worked increased until 1938, and declined continuously afterwards. Hours worked declined faster, particularly in 1975–85.

In both countries the land area increased up until the Second World War. In the Netherlands it increased until 1950. In Japan it decreased once in the war period 1938–50, then increased again in the 1950–60 period. During that period the government promoted land reclamation, because of the severe food shortage after the war. After the land reform farmers also had positive incentives to expand their own farm land. However, in the Netherlands after 1950 and in Japan after 1960, the area of farm land was reduced because of use for infrastructural purposes and urbanization.

The use of non-farm current input increased continuously in both countries, particularly after the Second World War. Its growth was very rapid in both countries with rates of about 5 per cent after the war and over 3.5 per cent for the entire period. Since the analysis in this book focuses mainly on gross value added, the role of non-farm current input as a source of expansion of farm production or final output is not analysed. It should be remembered, however, that both countries could not have realized agricultural development without intensive use of non-farm current input. Fertilizer was the most important input in pre-war Japan. Feed was always the most dominant input in the Netherlands and became important in post-war Japan as well.

For the Netherlands data on capital and depreciation are only available for the post-war period which limits our comparison to this period. These variables are not strictly comparable between the two countries because of their different definitions.[7] However, growth rates of recorded depreciation (capital consumption) are much higher in Japan while in contrast growth rates of output are lower. As we shall argue, there is obviously over-investment in Japan. Although growth rates of depreciation in 1975–85 declined to less than half of the 1960–75 level, net value added declined absolutely in that period. In contrast, in the Netherlands, the growth rate of depreciation is almost constant after 1960, but the growth rate of value added increased from 1975–85. This may imply that capital efficiency recently improved in the Netherlands.

Trends in productivity

To assess differences in economic efficiency, or the level of agricultural development, between Japan and the Netherlands, a comparison of real productivity, measured at a common set of price data, is necessary. For this purpose three alternative value added series in common 1975 prices are calculated (Appendix Table C.2). The first series is at 1975 Japanese prices. Data for the Netherlands is obtained as follows. For the period 1950–85 each of the Dutch series at 1975 prices of agricultural products by sub-sector and by groups of current input items is converted into Japanese prices, but use of the respective price ratio for that group between the two countries.[8] The price ratios are calculated at Dutch 1975 weights (see Chapter 5). The converted series are aggregated to get total production, total current inputs, depreciation, and gross and net value added at 1975 Japanese prices. For 1880–1938, a break-down of data per group is not available, and for that period gross value added series at 1975 Dutch prices are linked in 1950 to the series at 1975 Japanese prices.

The second set of value added series is at 1975 Dutch prices, and the same method is appied to convert Japan's value added data for

Table 4.5 Value added per hour and productivity ratios in Japanese and Dutch agriculture in alternative common 1975 prices, 1880–1985[a]

	1880	*1913*	*1938*	*1950*	*1960*	*1975*	*1985*
Gross value added per hour							
In 1975 Japanese prices (yen/hour)							
Japan (J1)	89	108	157	132	277	555	780
Netherlands (N1)	196	287	436	502	944	2,694	4,489
Ratio (N1)/(J1)	2.2	2.7	2.8	3.8	3.4	4.9	5.8
In 1975 Dutch prices (yen/hour)[b]							
Japan (J2)	39	53	75	61	131	240	372
Netherlands (N2)	120	175	266	306	551	1,659	3,035
Ratio (N2)/(J2)	3.1	3.3	3.6	5.0	4.2	6.9	8.2
In the 1975 International dollar[c] (per 1,000 hours)							
Japan (J3)	177	143	207	174	365	731	1,028
Netherlands (N3)	289	422	641	738	1,325	3,993	7,300
Ratio (N3)/(J3)	2.5	3.0	3.1	4.3	3.6	5.5	7.1
Net value added per hour							
In 1975 Japanese prices (yen/hour)							
Japan (J1)				128	262	475	626
Netherlands (N1)				460	878	2,454	4,067
Ratio (N1)/(J1)				3.6	3.4	5.2	6.5
In 1975 Dutch prices (yen/hour)[b]							
Japan (J2)				58	117	170	237
Netherlands (N2)				270	492	1,448	2,665
Ratio (N2)/(J2)				4.7	4.2	8.5	11.2
In the 1975 International dollar[c] (per 1,000 hours)							
Japan (J3)				168	345	626	825
Netherlands (N3)				650	1,185	3,485	6,411
Ratio (N3)/(J3)				3.9	3.5	5.6	7.8

Source Appendix Tables C.1 and C.2.

Notes a. J1, J2 and J3 and N1, N2 and N3 correspond to the same codes in Appendix Table C.2; b. Dutch prices are converted into yen at 1975 exchange rates (1 Dfl. = 117.36 yen) to make comparison easier; c. See Chapter 3 for the definition of 'International dollar'.

Table 4.6 Growth rates of value added per hour and per hectare in Japanese and Dutch agriculture in 1975 Japanese and Dutch prices, 1880–1985 (%)[a]

	1880–1913	*1913–1938*	*1938–1950*	*1950–1960*	*1960–1975*	*1975–1985*	*1880–1938*	*1950–1985*	*1880–1985*
Gross value added per hour									
In 1975 Japanese prices									
Japan (J1)	0.6	1.5	-1.5	7.7	4.7	3.5	1.0	5.2	2.1
Netherlands (N1)	1.2	1.7	1.2	6.5	7.2	5.2	1.4	6.5	3.0
In 1975 Dutch prices									
Japan (J2)	0.9	1.4	-1.6	7.9	4.1	4.5	1.1	5.3	2.2
Netherlands (N2)	1.2	1.7	1.2	6.1	7.6	6.2	1.4	6.8	3.1
Net value added per hour									
In 1975 Japanese prices									
Japan (J1)				7.5	4.1	2.8		4.7	
Netherlands (N1)				6.7	7.1	5.2		6.4	
In 1975 Dutch prices									
Japan (J2)				7.4	2.5	3.3		4.1	
Netherlands (N2)				6.2	7.5	6.3		6.8	
Gross value added per ha									
In 1975 Japanese prices									
Japan (J1)	1.0	0.7	-0.4	3.9	0.7	-0.2	0.8	1.3	0.9
Netherlands (N1)	1.4	1.6	0.6	3.9	3.1	3.6	1.5	3.5	2.0
In 1975 Dutch prices									
Japan (J2)	1.3	0.6	-0.5	4.0	0.2	0.7	0.9	1.4	0.9
Netherlands (N2)	1.4	1.6	0.6	3.4	3.5	4.5	1.5	3.8	2.1
Net value added per ha									
In 1975 Japanese prices									
Japan (J1)				3.6	0.1	-0.9		0.8	
Netherlands (N1)				4.1	3.0	3.5		3.4	
In 1975 Dutch prices									
Japan (J2)				3.5	-1.4	-0.4		0.3	
Netherlands (N2)				3.6	3.4	4.6		3.8	

Sources Tables 4.5 and 4.7.
Note a. As for Table 4.5. The growth rates for the J3 and N3 series are the same as for the J1 and N2 series since their time-series are the same; only the level differs.

1880–1985 at 1975 prices into 1975 Dutch prices. But the grouping for Japan is slightly different from the Dutch case because of the data availability.[9] Moreover, to make a comparison with the Japanese price series easier, the Dutch price series for both countries are converted into yen terms by exchange rate.

The third set of comparable series is expressed in terms of the International dollar, estimated by the FAO (1986), for both countries. Gross value added in 1975 in international prices (expressed in the International dollar) was estimated in the previous chapter (see also Appendix Table B.1, p. 172). By use of those estimates time-series of value added in 1975 national prices were converted into the series in 1975 International dollars.

Table 4.5 shows value added per hour for both countries and their productivity ratios in alternative common 1975 prices, which are derived from the above estimated series (see Appendix Table C.2, p. 185) and the hours worked data (see Appendix Table C.1, p. 184). Table 4.6 shows growth rates by different periods. As stated earlier, in 1950 Japanese agriculture had still not fully recovered from war damage, and productivity in that year was far below the trend. Thus 1950 was an extra-ordinary year for Japan. If we exclude 1950 from the comparison, we can draw three conclusions about the trends in labour productivity shown in Table 4.5: (a) growth rates in Dutch agriculture were higher than in Japan in all sub-periods, so that the productivity ratios of the Netherlands to Japan increased continuously; (b) the ratios in Dutch prices are always highest, those in Japanese prices lowest, and those in the International dollar just in between. This implies that both countries' agriculture performed better under their own price structure than under the counter-factual price structure of the other country; and (c) the ratios for net value added per hour were smaller than those for gross value added until 1960, but became larger after 1975. This is related to increasingly inefficient use of capital in Japan. The ratios for gross value added per hour increased from ranges of 2.2–3.1 in 1880 to 5.8–8.2 in 1985 and those for net value added per hour increased from 3.6–4.7 in 1950 to 6.5–11.2 in 1985. The ranges indicate the different results of the price bases.[10]

The productivity ratios in our comparisons are not influenced by the exchange rate. Often, however, inter-country productivity comparisons use exchange rates to convert productivity data into another country's currency. In our case this would mean that Japan's labour productivity in Japanese prices (J1) is compared with Dutch data in Dutch prices, converted to yen by exchange rate (N2) in Table 4.5. In that case the ratios for gross value added per hour would be 1.3 in 1880, 1.7 in 1938, 2.0 in 1960 and 3.9 in 1985, which gives a much better performance for Japan than our real comparison results.

Table 4.7 indicates land productivity in terms of value added per hectare of agricultural land for both countries in 1880–1985.[11]

Table 4.7 Value added per hectare and productivity ratios in Japanese and Dutch agriculture in alternative common 1975 prices, 1880–1985[a]

	1880	*1913*	*1938*	*1950*	*1960*	*1975*	*1985*
Gross value added per hectare							
In 1975 Japanese prices (1,000 yen/ha)							
Japan (J1)	411	563	665	637	930	1,039	1,015
Netherlands (N1)	144	226	335	359	526	836	1,182
Ratio (J1)/(N1)	2.9	2.5	2.0	1.8	1.8	1.2	0.9
In 1975 Dutch prices (1,000 yen/ha)[b]							
Japan (J2)	181	275	316	296	438	450	484
Netherlands (N2)	88	136	205	219	307	515	799
Ratio (J2)/(N2)	2.1	2.0	1.5	1.4	1.4	0.9	0.6
In the 1975 International dollar[c] (dollar per ha)							
Japan (J3)	542	741	876	839	1,225	1,369	1,337
Netherlands (N3)	211	332	493	528	738	1,239	1,922
Ratio (J3)/(N3)	2.6	2.2	1.8	1.6	1.7	1.1	0.7
Net value added per hectare							
In 1975 Japanese prices (1,000 yen/ha)							
Japan (J1)				617	878	890	815
Netherlands (N1)				329	489	762	1,071
Ratio (J1)/(N1)				1.9	1.8	1.2	0.8
In 1975 Dutch prices (1,000 yen/ha)[b]							
Japan (J2)				279	393	319	308
Netherlands (N2)				193	274	449	702
Ratio (J2)/(N2)				1.5	1.4	0.7	0.4
In the 1975 International dollar[c] (dollar per ha)							
Japan (J3)				812	1,157	1,173	1,073
Netherlands (N3)				456	660	1,081	1,688
Ratio (J3)/(N3)				1.8	1.8	1.1	0.6

Sources and Notes As for Table 4.5.

We can also draw three conclusions about trends during the entire period: (a) until 1960 all the indicators show higher land productivity for Japan, but the ratios decline from 2.1–2.9 in 1880 to 1.4–1.8 in 1960. After 1975 land productivity in the Netherlands at Dutch prices became higher, and in 1985 the other two ratios indicate the same; (b) the ratios in Japanese prices are always the highest, those in Dutch prices the lowest, and those in the International dollar in between, which is of course similar to the findings for labour productivity; and (c) similarly ratios for net value added per hectare were larger or at least the same as those of gross value added per hectare up to 1960, but after 1975 net productivity ratios became smaller.

Again, if Japanese data at current prices (J1) are compared with Dutch data at current prices, converted into yen by the exchange rate (N2), the result is not reliable. For example in that case, even in 1985, land productivity in Japan is still higher than in the Netherlands.

Effect of price changes on productivity measurement

So far a long-term series of output and productivity measured in 1975 prices has been analysed. As stated earlier, there are several reasons to use 1975 as the basis year for our comparative analysis. However, the measured productivity indicators in 1975 prices are in no way unique. They are affected by price structures of agricultural products and inputs in 1975. For instance, the first oil crisis and the drastic increases in food prices on the international market in 1973 and 1974 may have affected the 1975 price structure and cause a specific bias in the measurements.

As indicated in Table 4.8, changes in prices of various items differ significantly during the past thirty five years. This means that the price structure changed significantly during this period, more clearly in Japan than in the Netherlands. Choice of base year affects productivity measurement. To assess the magnitude of this, sets of output and input indexes are first calculated for 1960, 1975, and 1985 at national prices and weights, then productivity indexes are measured for the three base years.

Table 4.9 indicates indexes of final output and non-farm current input for each of the three base years.The original base years are 1960, 1975, and 1985, respectively, but all indexes are expressed as 1950=100 for easier comparison. The Japanese indexes show rather big effects of choice of different base years while differences for Dutch indexes are minor. The earlier the base year the larger the final output index in Japan. This is caused by the fact that production in the livestock sector, for which prices were relatively high until 1960, expanded very rapidly after that year. From 1975 to 1985 the index at 1960-prices did not decline whereas indexes at 1975 and 1985 prices did. A major factor for this is a sizeable decline in the share of rice production. All final output indexes for

Table 4.8 Price indexes of outputs and inputs in Japanese and Dutch agriculture, 1950–85 (1975 = 100)

	Japan			*Netherlands*		
	1950	*1960*	*1985*	*1950*	*1960*	*1985*
Arable crops }	16.3	26.3	136.4	49.7	52.7	109.2
Horticulture }						160.0
Livestock	32.9	38.8	96.0	56.6	57.1	128.7
Current inputs						
Feed	32.2	48.7	99.4	55.3	59.8	127.1
Fertilizer[a]	38.8	44.6	132.0	29.6	43.7	176.8
Agricultural chemicals	94.2	70.0	117.6			
Fuel	24.8	40.7	169.1	34.6	44.4	351.9
Labour[b]	6.4	11.4	164.0	8.2	16.2	197.8
Land[c]	3.4	29.8	185.5	NA	49.1	180.2
Capital						
Buildings	16.0	36.6	146.5	18.3	31.2	168.9
Machinery	32.4	58.3	125.8	38.3	49.6	148.2
Livestock	18.2	25.5	110.9	39.6	53.4	126.9
Plants	13.6	24.6	142.2	NA	NA	NA

Sources Yamada (1987a), MAFF, *Agricultural Statistical Yearbook* (1987), MAFF (1988), and Kayo (1977) for Japan; and Van der Meer (1987a), LEI/CBS, *Agricultural Statistics*, various issues, and Van der Meer and Yamada (1989) for the Netherlands.

Notes NA = not available; a. For the Netherlands including agricultural chemicals. b. For Japan male worker's wage per day, but for the Netherlands average wage cost per hour; c. For Japan paddy field price, and for the Netherlands the weighted average land rent.

the Netherlands increase more rapidly than for Japan during the entire period, and the differences among them are very small. Highest is the 1985-prices index because the price level of horticulture was high in that particular year.

The non-farm current input indexes show similar patterns of continuous increase in both countries for the entire period. The index at 1985 prices shows the slower growth. This is because of increased use of non-farm current inputs whereas modern inputs are more expensive in the earlier base year while their share in total inputs increased relatively. However, there are differences of growth rates in current input use in different periods between the countries. In the Netherlands growth is faster than in Japan in 1950–60, but slower in 1960–75, and again faster in 1975–85. As a whole, use of non-farm current input has increased faster in Japan than in the Netherlands. The faster increase in non-farm current input in Japanese agriculture contrasts with the decline in final output, and this together results in a much faster increase of gross value added in the Netherlands.

In Japan the gross value added index at 1960 prices shows a pattern very different from the indexes at other prices bases. The

Table 4.9 Indexes of final output and non-farm current input in Japanese and Dutch agriculture in 1960, 1975, and 1985 prices[a]

	Japan			*Netherlands*		
	1960 prices	*1975 prices*	*1985 prices*[b]	*1960 prices*	*1975 prices*	*1985 prices*[b]
Final output						
1950	100	100	100	100	100	100
1960	161	154	149	162	161	163
1975	223	201	187	263	258	267
1985	224	195	176	372	365	380
Non-farm current input						
1950	100	100	100	100	100	100
1960	182	168	165	191	176	172
1975	508	437	393	358	305	300
1985	653	552	495	510	435	417
Gross value added						
1950	100	100	100	100	100	100
1960	154	151	146	147	152	156
1975	138	155	147	212	226	237
1985	96	125	115	298	317	346

Sources For Japan: Yamada (1978a) and MAFF, *Agricultural Statistical Yearbook* (1987); and for the Netherlands: LEI/CBS, *Agricultural Statistics*, various issues, and Van der Meer and Yamada (1989).

Notes a. Original base years of indexes in 1960, 1975, and 1985 prices are 1960, 1975, and 1985, respectively, but all indexes are converted into 1950 = 100 to facilitate comparison; b. 1984 weights are taken due to data availability.

index at 1960 prices started to decline after 1960 due to the very high use of non-farm current input in 1960 prices, and it indicates a level even lower in 1985 than in 1950. The indexes in 1975 and 1985 prices both show the same pattern: a rapid increase in the period 1950–60, stagnation in 1960–75 and a sharp decline in 1975–85. This can be explained by the different trends in final output and non-farm current inputs. On the contrary all the Dutch gross value added indexes show the same patterns of continuous increase during the entire period. The index at 1985 prices shows the most rapid increase because the corresponding non-farm current input index inidcated slower growth.

Table 4.10 shows indexes of labour, land, and capital inputs for both countries in the different base year prices. The first two indexes are single indexes and are therefore the same for different base years. Labour input declined fast, but land did not decline so much in both countries.

The capital indexes indicate similar patterns to the non-farm current input indexes, except for the indexes at 1960 prices which show a higher increase in Japan than in the Netherlands. As a

Table 4.10 Indexes of labour, land, and capital used in Japanese and Dutch agriculture, 1950–85

	Japan					*Netherlands*				
			Capital[a]					*Capital*		
	Hours worked	*Land area*	*1960 prices*	*1975 prices*	*1985*[b] prices	*Hours worked*	*Land area*	*1960 prices*	*1975 prices*	*1985*[b] *prices*
1950	100	100	100	100	100	100	100	100	100	100
1960	72	104	126	124	124	78	99	103	103	103
1975	37	95	229	202	199	40	93	149	147	146
1985	25	92	274	235	230	33	89	188	186	186

Sources For Japan: Yamada (1987a), MAFF, *Agricultural Statistical Yearbook* (1987) and Appendix Table C.1; and for the Netherlands: Van der Meer and Yamada (1989), LEI/CBS, *Agricultural Statistics*, various issues, and Oskam/CBS (unpublished).

Notes a and b as for Table 4.9.

whole, the Japanese indexes increased faster than the Dutch indexes.

The total input index is defined as the aggregate index of labour, land, capital, and non-farm current input (aggregated by respective weights of input share) (see Table 4.13, p. 87). The input index corresponding to final output includes all inputs, while the index corresponding to gross value added excludes non-farm current inputs (Table 4.11).

There are significant differences between the total input indexes for final output. The Japanese index in 1960 prices declined slightly in 1960, but increased afterwards, while the other Japanese indexes declined continuously. In the Netherlands the index in 1960 prices increased continuously, but the other indexes declined until 1975, and increased subsequently until 1985. Contrary to such diverging patterns in the above indexes, the indexes of total factor input for gross value added, in which non-farm current inputs are not included, declined continuously. The indexes of later base years show a faster decline. This may imply that the resource factors such as labour, land, and capital in agriculture tend to decline as a whole and are partly substituted by non-farm current inputs. An obvious reason for the faster decline of the indexes based on prices of later

Table 4.11 Indexes of total input in Japanese and Dutch agriculture, 1950–85, in 1960, 1975, and 1985 prices

	Japan In prices of			*Netherlands In prices of*		
	1960	*1975*	*1985*	*1960*	*1975*	*1985*
Total input for final output[a] (including non-farm current inputs)						
1950	100	100	100	100	100	100
1960	98	81	82	107	90	88
1975	122	72	66	125	78	70
1985	135	70	62	158	89	76
Total input for gross value added[b] (excluding non-farm current inputs)						
1950	100	100	100	100	100	100
1960	87	81	78	83	81	80
1975	74	56	51	58	52	49
1985	70	48	42	56	50	46

Sources Tables 4.9, 4.10 and 4.13.

Notes [a]Indexes of labour, land, capital and non-farm current inputs are aggregated by respective factor shares.

[b]Indexes of labour, land and capital are aggregated by respective factor shares.

Table 4.12 Indexes of gross value added per hour, per ha, and per unit of capital in Japanese and Dutch agriculture, 1950–85, in 1960, 1975, and 1985 prices

	Japan			*Netherlands*		
	1960 prices	*1975 prices*	*1985 prices*	*1960 prices*	*1975 prices*	*1985 prices*
Gross value added per hour						
1950	100	100	100	100	100	100
1960	214	210	203	188	195	200
1975	373	419	397	530	565	593
1985	384	500	460	903	960	1,048
Gross value added per ha						
1950	100	100	100	100	100	100
1960	148	145	140	148	153	158
1975	145	163	154	228	243	255
1985	104	158	125	335	357	388
Gross value added per unit of capital						
1950	100	100	100	100	100	100
1960	122	122	117	143	148	151
1975	60	77	74	142	153	162
1985	35	53	50	159	170	186

Sources Tables 4.9 and 4.10.

base years is the decline of labour input, of which the price (wage rate) increased rapidly. The working hours index for Japan declined in 1985 to 25 and for the Netherlands to 33 while the land index declined to about 90 in 1985 (see Table 4.10, p. 84).

Indexes of labour, land, and capital productivities in terms of gross value added per hour and per hectare in the different base year prices based on Tables 4.9 and 4.10 are compared in Table 4.12. All indexes of gross value added per hour show an increasing trend in both countries. Over the period 1950–60 growth in both countries is similar, but later on the Dutch indexes increased much faster. For the Dutch indexes, the 1985-base index grew most rapidly because of the faster increase in the gross value added in agriculture with the slower increase in total factor input in the later base year index. For Japan, the highest growth was indicated by the 1975-base index. This was caused by the relative increase of the gross value added index compared to the total factor input index which was at its best in the 1975 base year.

The indexes of gross value added per hectare reflect the patterns of gross value added indexes because land area did not change so

Table 4.13 Factor shares in final output and in gross value added in Japanese and Dutch agriculture, 1960, 1975, and 1984 (%)

	Japan[a]				Netherlands[b]			
	Labour	*Land*	*Capital*	*Current input*	*Labour*	*Land*	*Capital*	*Current input*
Final output								
1960	38.8	28.8	11.6	20.8	45.5	5.0	9.2	40.3
1975	35.1	22.4	13.4	29.1	40.5	3.2	16.5	39.8
1984	31.3	20.0	13.5	35.2	35.7	3.0	16.4	44.9
Gross value added								
1960	49.0	36.4	14.6		76.2	8.4	15.4	
1975	49.5	31.6	18.9		67.3	5.3	27.4	
1984	48.3	30.9	20.8		64.8	5.5	29.7	

Sources For Japan: Yamada (1987a), MAFF (1988), Statistics Bureau (1986) and Appendix Table C.1; and for the Netherlands: LEI/CBS, *Agricultural Statistics*, various issues, and CBS (1982).

Notes: a. Shares of each input in the total input costs. Individual input costs are estimated as follows: labour, the total working hours are multiplied by the wage rate; land, agricultural land area is multiplied by the land price to get the land value, which is multiplied by the interest rate; capital, interest on gross capital; and current inputs, the value of non-farm current input. b. The concept is the same as for Japan. However, estimating methods for land and capital are different. For land, agricultural land area for horticulture, arable crops and grass are multiplied by their respective rent; and for capital, interest on net capital plus depreciation.

much for both countries. For the Netherlands the indexes indicate the same pattern as those per hour. However, those of Japanese agriculture indicate different patterns from the indexes per hour: the index at 1960 prices increased up to 1960, but decreased afterwards; both other indexes increased up to 1975, but declined afterwards.

The indexes of gross value added per unit of capital, the inverse indexes of the capital-output ratio, indicate sharp contrasts between the two countries: Japanese indexes increased once in 1950–60, but declined sharply afterwards, while Dutch indexes indicate an increasing trend all the time. This indicates a considerable decline in efficiency of use of capital, which is consistent with the findings of poorer Japanese agricultural performance in net valued added terms compared to gross value added terms. In Chapter Six we shall argue that there is considerable over-investment in Japanese agriculture.

The index of total factor productivity is defined as the index of the ratio of the output index to the total input index. The estimated total factor productivity indexes are shown in Table 4.14. According to Table 4.13, the share of labour was the largest in 1960 and 1975,

Table 4.14 Indexes of total factor productivity in Japanese and Dutch agriculture, 1950–85, in 1960, 1975, and 1985 prices

	Japan			*Netherlands*		
	1960 prices	*1975 prices*	*1985 prices*	*1960 prices*	*1975 prices*	*1985 prices*
Final output basis[a]						
1950	100	100	100	100	100	100
1960	164	190	181	152	178	187
1975	182	279	282	212	331	382
1985	166	302	284	235	411	500
Gross value added basis[b]						
1950	100	100	100	100	100	100
1960	177	188	186	178	188	203
1975	187	275	287	369	433	500
1985	137	302	272	532	639	971

Sources Tables 4.9 and 4.11.
Notes a. The index of final output is divided by the index of total input including non-farm current inputs. b. The index of gross value added is divided by the index of total input excluding non-farm current inputs.

but the share of current inputs became largest in 1984 in both countries.[12] The share of capital increased for 1960–75, but later on it was stable in both countries. The share of land has decreased in both countries. There are big differences in the magnitude of land share between the two countries, which is partly caused by different estimation methods. Land rent is regulated by the government in both countries so that the real economic rent should be higher than the reported rent. There is no way to find real land rent. For Japan, an imputed rent was calculated by use of land price and interest rate, but such a method was not suitable for the Netherlands because available land prices and interest rates are deemed inappropriate for such a method of valuation. Thus different methods were applied for both countries as indicated in the note for Table 4.13.[13]

Table 4.14 shows significant contrasts between the two countries, except for the period 1950–60 during which roughly similar trends are observed. For the Netherlands, the indexes always increased, with faster increases for later base year indexes, and with faster increases in the productivity indexes for gross value added than for final output. In contrast, the trend for Japan is different among the three base year indexes. The 1960-base-year indexes increased until 1975, and declined sharply in 1985 due to the sizeable decline in gross value added. Growth indicated by the 1960-base index was the lowest. The 1975 base-year index always increased and indicated the highest growth except for 1960–75. In this case growth of the productivity indexes of final output and gross value added were almost the same. The 1985 base-year index for final output increased to 1975, and did not change much afterwards while the corresponding index for gross value added increased to 1975, and declined again in 1985. Compared to the corresponding Dutch total factor productivity performance, Japanese agriculture lagged much behind the Netherlands, in particular for the period 1975–85, and for the index on gross value added basis (see Table 4.14).

According to the above analysis, productivity measurement for Japanese agriculture in 1975 prices shows slightly higher growth performance than for the 1960 and 1985-base year productivity indicators, while Dutch agriculture productivity growth at 1975 prices is just in between the 1960 and 1985 base year indicators. Our study mainly focuses on comparisons of gross value added per hour in 1975 prices while disregarding changes in the other input factors, land and capital, which may of course result in a bias. The difference in productivity levels between the two countries indicated by gross value added terms is smaller than differences found on the base of final output or net value added. Thus our observations, which are mainly based upon gross value added per hour, do not over-estimate the 'real' productivity gaps between the two countries.

Chapter five

How productive is present Japanese agriculture? In-depth comparisons of productivity in Japan, the Netherlands, Taiwan, and the USA

Method of comparison

In the previous chapter a detailed comparison was made of growth and productivity performance between Japan and the Netherlands over the period 1880–1985. In this chapter the main emphasis is on comparison of levels of output and productivity. First an in-depth comparison is made of real productivity in Japanese and Dutch agriculture for three benchmark years: 1975, 1980, and 1984. Not only is attention given to agriculture as a whole but also to the sub-sectors' arable products, livestock, and horticulture, and to some livestock products. Subsequently, a comparison of real productivities for the agricultural sector as a whole is made with Taiwan and the USA.

The international comparison in Chapter Three was based on the FAO production statistics valued at international prices. Since international statistics on input use are scanty, an assumption had to be made about the price level of current input for the estimation of gross value added. Inputs at international prices were assumed to be in the same proportion of real total production as at national prices. This implicitly means that a single deflation method is used. For some countries this may result in considerable errors. In Japan, for example, protection for most agricultural inputs is low or zero, whereas output prices are very high as a result of protection. In such cases single deflation under-estimates the volume of inputs. In countries with depressed agricultural prices and high input prices the opposite will occur.

The use of agricultural statistics from the FAO has several limitations as explained in detail in Appendix B and can give biased results. In spite of such deficiencies, a study covering many countries has to use the FAO's international statistics since it would take too much time to use national statistics. For the few countries selected for this chapter, however, national statistics could be used, and this permits a more in-depth comparison of outputs and inputs than Chapters Two and Three of this book and other studies did. These studies only focused on final output or at most on gross value added (Paige and Bombach, 1959; Mensink, 1966; Maddison, 1970; Van Ooststroom and Maddison, 1985; and Hayami and Ruttan, 1985), but there are good reasons to give attention to net value added as well. For example, capital consumption should be taken into account to evaluate economic results. Furthermore, when comparing real productivity between sectors in different countries there may be great differences between both concepts. One reason for this is that national accounting practices differ among countries with regard to the distinction between investment and current inputs. Another is that the ratio between gross value added and depreciation in international prices may differ strongly from that in national prices.

Real comparison of output implies the elimination of differences in price levels. Instead of making a direct estimation of real values by multiplying quantities and prices as done in Chapter Three and in other studies, this chapter first estimates deflators for groups of outputs and inputs. Relevant data on prices and weights could be derived from material used for the estimation of price index series for agriculture. The deflators were applied to corresponding groups of outputs and inputs in the sector accounts for agriculture at current prices. A schematic presentation of this method is given in Appendix D. The reason for adopting this practice is that it is very difficult to collect all prices and quantities of farm commodities and inputs even for a limited number of countries. It is assumed that prices for different products are fairly well related within groups and that the products and inputs included in the price index are representative for the respective groups. In the case of Japan and the Netherlands the number of these items that could be matched ranged from about 50 to 70 per cent and their weight ranged between 60 and 90 per cent.

The (inter-country) deflators give interesting information as well. The deflators for total production are equal to one plus the nominal rate of protection, whereas the implicit deflator for (net) value added equals one plus the effective rate of protection. The rates of protection estimated in this way refer to differences in price level at the farm gate between both countries. They can originate in differences in natural protection, such as cost of transportation and margins of the agribusiness, as well as all kinds of trade barriers. The information from these estimated rates of protection is very useful for an analysis of the effects of trade liberalization. Inefficiency of enterprises processing and trading agricultural inputs is reflected in high deflators for inputs.

A multi-country comparison as conducted by the FAO (1986) has the advantage that real output and 'average' international price levels can be calculated simultaneously. However, international prices are difficult to obtain. For a binary country comparison, therefore, direct use of prices of the two countries may be required for an in-depth study. Use of the average prices of Japan and the Netherlands as a proxy for international prices is not so suitable. Therefore, in this chapter sets of Dutch and Japanese prices are used. This leads to two different estimates of rates of protection and productivity: one from the Japanese and one from the Dutch point of view (i.e. production and price structure). The different results show the effects of differences in structure, which is also important information in binary comparisons.

There is always some fiction involved in real comparison because of structural differences and differences in the product mix and inputs used. For instance, rice forms a particular problem in this comparison. It is the major product in Japan, but it is not grown in the Netherlands. Since this study aims at a comparison of Japan with the Netherlands and more in general with Europe, the price ratio of rice and wheat in Italy was taken to calculate a shadow rice price for the Netherlands. More than for products and current inputs fiction is involved in comparing capital goods. There are huge differences in sizes and qualities of machines and tractors used. Despite its good engineering qualities very little of the kind of machinery used in Japanese agriculture is also used in Dutch (and American) agriculture, because it is basically inefficient in labour use under Dutch (or American) conditions. Nevertheless, despite such fictional assumptions, we believe that the binary comparisons bring about various interesting findings which could not be derived from other comparisons.

Real productivity in agriculture in Japan and the Netherlands in 1975, 1980, and 1984

Table 5.1 contains the shares[1] of groups of products and inputs for both countries obtained from the sector accounts for 1975 and 1980.[2] In the Netherlands livestock raising accounts for two thirds of production, in Japan for only one quarter. Arable crops still form 40 per cent of the value of production in Japan, mainly because of high support prices for rice. It is not surprising that feed accounts for not less than 60 per cent of the inputs in the Netherlands, but at first sight a share of over 40 per cent for Japan seems very high, given its small livestock sector. The reason for this is that Japan has relatively little domestic fodder production.

Table 5.1 Structure of output and input in Japanese and Dutch agriculture in national prices, 1975 and 1980

	Share in sector accounts			
	Netherlands		*Japan*	
	1975	*1980*	*1975*	*1980*
Total Production	1,000	1,000	1,000	1,000
of which:				
Arable crops	131	110	462	416
Horticulture	199	232	301	322
Livestock products	670	658	237	262
Total Current Inputs	1,000	1,000	1,000	1,000
of which:				
Agro-chemicals	15	13	70	58
Fertilizer	62	66	140	139
Feed	635	608	428	423
Seed & seedlings	43	42	46	46
Animals for use	3	2	0	0
Maintenance mach. & buildings	76	58	65	70
Energy & lubricants	53	100	52	67
Agricultural services	21	13	52	57
Auto costs	18	16	34	50
Other costs/miscellaneous	73	81	113	90

Source Van der Meer and Yamada (1988: annex A, Tables A.1 – A.8).
Note Value added tax included in the Dutch data.

Fodder crops, especially grassland products, are very important in the Netherlands but many of them are not recorded in the sector accounts. Energy consumption seems to be more important in the Netherlands, which reflects the extensive use for heating greenhouses, and perhaps also a higher degree of mechanization.

The relative price indexes between the two countries shown in Table 5.2 reveal that output and input price levels are in general higher in Japan, and that the difference has increased in particular since 1980. This increase is related to changes in the exchange rate. The appreciation of the yen in this period was not significantly reflected in a downward adjustment of the price levels for output and input (see Table 5.3). The price indexes, expressed in national currencies, show that in Japan non-factor prices and output prices increased at similar rates, whereas in the Netherlands prices for non-factor costs increased about twice as fast as output prices. Apparently Dutch farmers had to operate under much less favourable price conditions than their Japanese colleagues. If the Dutch price indexes are expressed in yen, the output and input prices show a significant decline after 1980.

Table 5.2 Relative price indexes for groups of inputs and products in Japanese and Dutch agriculture, 1975, 1980, and 1984

	Price index Japan (Netherlands = 100)					
	Dutch weights			*Japanese weights*		
	1975	*1980*	*1984*	*1975*	*1980*	*1984*
Total Production[a]	141	150	191	201	215	264
of which:						
Arable crops	136	237	287	268	312	381
Horticulature	121	139	175	139	147	180
Livestock products	148	139	180	148	144	183
Total Current Inputs[a]	131	128	167	121	118	164
of which:						
Agro-chemicals	131	118	154	110	113	165
Fertilizer	99	124	182	132	152	230
Feed	127	120	159	130	120	159
Seed & seedlings	390	283	339	187	177	295
Animals for use	100	180	208	150	166	241
Maintenance mach. & buildings	86	88	125	79	76	101
Energy & lubricants	135	160	183	130	140	152
Agricultural services	55	61	100	55	61	100
Auto costs	63	54	68	57	59	90
Gross Value Added	152	180	218	352	905	659
Depreciation	114	113	162	114	107	138
Net Value Added	157	195	228	602	b	b

Source Van der Meer and Yamada (1988: 23).

Notes Value added tax included in the Dutch data. Price indexes are by definition equal to the Purchasing Power Parity divided by the exchange rate. Price indexes for gross and net value added are implicit. See Appendix D for the method of calculation. a. the shares in production and inputs in Table 5.1 are used to calculate aggregated indexes. b. is negative and cannot be interpreted.

Table 5.3 Price indexes and exchange rates in Japanese and Dutch agriculture, 1975, 1980, and 1984

		Netherlands			*Japan*		
		1975	*1980*	*1984*	*1975*	*1980*	*1984*
Price indexes (1975 = 100)							
Total Production	in Yen	100	110	84	100	122	126
	in Dfl.	100	113	133			
Non factor input (excl. depreciation)	in Yen	100	132	103	100	124	127
	in Dfl.	100	136	163			
Exchange rate (Yen/Dfl)		117	114	74			
(Yen/US $)		297	227	238			

Source Price indexes: Japan from MAFF, Yearbook; Netherlands from LEI/CBS, *Agricultural Statistics*. Exchange rates from World Bank (1987).

The price levels and trends in Table 5.2 for horticultural products, livestock products, and the most important input groups show strong similarities, regardless of the use of Dutch or Japanese weights. The major difference between both countries is formed by the gap in output prices for arable crops (rice and field crops). The weight of arable crops is about three-and-a-half times higher in Japan, and moreover, this group is dominated by rice which is not grown in the Netherlands and more heavily protected in Japan than most other crops. Consequently, the price index for total production in Japan is much higher at Japanese than at Dutch weights as in the latter, rice has zero weight.

On the input side indexes for seed and seedlings and maintenance of machines and buildings appear to be sensitive to the weights used. The first group contains a limited number of products and is dominated by seed potatoes in the Netherlands, but has a small share in total inputs. The difference in the index for maintenance is highly affected by the wage cost. An explanation for the low price levels of agricultural services may be found in the relatively low level of wages in Japan, but the figure is not very reliable either as it is only based on some rough comparisons of fees for veterinary services and artificial insemination.

In each case the effective rate of protection is higher than the nominal rate. Of main interest are the implicit price indexes for gross and net value added as they indicate the price level of factor input and price support for factor income. At Dutch weights (i.e. excluding rice) there is little difference in price indexes for gross and net value added. The relative price index increased rapidly over the nine-year period, and the effective rate of protection for factor income in Japan *vis-à-vis* the Netherlands increased from 57 per cent in 1975 to 95 per cent in 1980 and 128 per cent in 1984. The nominal rates of protection were 41, 50, and 91 per cent which is lower than the effective rates of protection. At Japanese weights (i.e. including rice) the relative price index for net value added is very high in 1975 because Japanese net value added at Dutch prices was very low. But for 1980 and 1984 net value added became negative and the indexes cannot be interpreted. Also gross value added appears to be very low, which results in very high relative price indexes. The reason for the different result with the Dutch weights is caused by the inclusion of rice. As will be shown below this crop has a negative value added at Dutch (shadow) prices.

Table 5.4 provides a comparison of real levels and relative trends in production, current input, and value added. In 1975 Japan has a good harvest and gross value added was 3.2 per cent higher than the trend indicated by the three-year average. In 1980, however, Japan

Table 5.4 Real comparison of production, input and value added 1975, 1980, and 1984

(current prices; billion Yen)

	Netherlands			*Japan*			*Ratio Japan/Netherl.*		
	1975	*1980*	*1984*	*1975*	*1980*	*1984*	*1975*	*1980*	*1984*
Japanese Prices									
Total Production	3,426	4,777	5,286	9,576	11,193	12,573	2.8	2.3	2.4
Current Inputs	1,678	2,389	2,481	3,770	5,394	6,217	2.3	2.3	2.5
Gross Value Added	1,748	2,388	2,806	5,806	5,799	6,356	3.3	2.4	2.3
Depreciation	145	246	300	957	1,451	1,468	6.6	5.9	4.9
Net Value Added	1,603	2,142	2,506	4,849	4,348	4,889	3.0	2.0	2.0
Dutch Prices[a]									
Total Production	2,428	3,188	2,770	4,770	5,221	4,786	2.0	1.6	1.7
Current Inputs	1,276	1,863	1,484	3,121	4,565	3,792	2.5	2.5	2.6
Gross Value Added	1,152	1,325	1,287	1,649	656	994	1.4	0.5	0.8
Depreciation	128	219	185	842	1,356	1,062	6.7	6.2	5.7
Net Value Added	1,024	1,106	1,102	807	–701	–68	0.8	[b]	[b]

Sources Appendix Table D.2 and Van der Meer and Yamad (1988: Table 4).
Notes All values expressed in market prices. a. Converted to yen by exchange rate of respective years. b. Negative and cannot be interpreted.

experienced a poor harvest and gross value added was 3.1 per cent below the trend. This shows that real comparison in agriculture may be very sensitive to the choice of a specific benchmark year. Figures for 1975 overestimate Japan's real performance, whereas those for 1980 present a downward bias. In the following, more attention will be given to 1975 and 1984 and to the trend between these years than to the year 1980 and changes over the two sub-periods. Seven interesting conclusions can be drawn. First, the most surprising finding is that the total value of production in Japan is only about twice as high in 1984 as in the Netherlands, or, more precisely, 2.4 times as high if measured at Japanese prices and 1.7 times as high at Dutch prices. Second, at Dutch prices the real comparison shows a less favourable picture for Japanese agriculture. The main reason is, as explained before, that Japanese rice has a much lower value at Dutch shadow prices (Italian prices). Third, both price bases indicate that the gap in the total value of production between both countries has narrowed since 1975. Fourth, the relative trend in current input in both countries is opposite to that in production as its real level in Japan has relatively somewhat increased. Fifth, as a result of differences in relative levels and trends of production and current inputs, gross

Table 5.5 Cost structure of Japanese and Dutch agriculture at Japanese and Dutch price bases, 1975, 1980, and 1984

	Netherlands			*Japan*		
	1975	*1980*	*1984*	*1975*	*1980*	*1984*
Japanese Prices						
Total Production	1,000	1,000	1,000	1,000	1,000	1,000
Current Inputs	490	500	469	394	482	494
Gross Value Added	510	500	531	606	518	506
Depreciation	42	51	57	100	130	117
Net Value Added	468	448	474	506	388	389
Dutch Prices						
Total Production	1,000	1,000	1,000	1,000	1,000	1,000
Current Inputs	526	584	536	654	877	797
Gross Value Added	474	416	465	346	123	203
Depreciation	53	69	67	177	261	223
Net Value Added	422	347	398	169	-137	-20

Source Table 5.4.

value added in Japan has relatively decreased. In Japanese prices it declined from 3.3 times as high as in the Netherlands in 1975 to 2.3 times in 1984, but at Dutch prices it is only 0.8 times as high in 1984. Sixth, the level of depreciation is much higher in Japan, although the gap has somewhat decreased since 1975. Perhaps the high level is affected by different national accounting practices, in particular with regard to distinguishing between current inputs and investments, but most likely is that Japan has a much higher capital output ratio. Finally, net value added in Japan has relatively declined. At Dutch prices it is even negative in 1980 and 1984.

Table 5.5 shows the shares of the main aggregates in total production. It appears that the Dutch cost structure does not change much when expressed at Japanese prices. For Japan, on the contrary, the effect of Dutch prices is dramatic. After 1975 the cost structure has worsened. At Dutch prices current costs and capital consumption can no longer be recovered from the value of production, which means that agriculture's contribution to national income is negative.

Real economic performance is indicated here by labour productivity. Fortunately labour input in hours can be used for both countries which is a much more reliable measure of labour input than the number of workers. Since total production in Japan is only about 1.7 to 2.8 times higher than in the Netherlands (depending on the price base and the year, see Table 5.4) and labour input

Table 5.6 Comparison of labour input and labour productivity in Japanese and Dutch prices, 1975, 1980, and 1984

	Netherlands			*Japan*			*Ratio Netherl./Japan*		
	1975	*1980*	*1984*	*1975*	*1980*	*1984*	*1975*	*1980*	*1984*
Hours worked (million)	674	584	558	10,439	8,149	7,697			
Japanese Prices (Yen)									
Total Production/ hour	5,083	8,180	9,473	917	1,374	1,634	5.5	6.0	5.8
Gross Value Added/ hour	2,594	4,089	5,028	556	712	826	4.7	5.7	6.1
Net Value Added/ hour	2,379	3,667	4,491	464	534	635	5.1	6.9	7.1
Dutch Prices (Yen)[a]									
Total Production/ hour	3,603	5,458	4,965	457	641	622	7.9	8.5	8.0
Gross Value Added/ hour	1,709	2,270	2,306	158		129	10.8	28.4	18.9
Net Value Added/ hour	1,519	1,894	1,975	77	-86	-9	19.7	[b]	[b]

Sources Total production, gross and net value added from Table 5.4. Labour input Netherlands from Van der Meer (1987a). Labour input Japan for 1975 and 1980 from Yamada (1987a); original data and data for 1984 estimated from MAFF, *Farm households economic survey*, various issues.

Notes a. Converted to yen by exchange rate of respective years. b. Negative and cannot be interpreted.

in hours about 14 to 15 times, there is a big difference in total labour productivity (see Table 5.6,). At Japanese prices the productiv ity ratio is about 1:6, and at Dutch prices it is 1:8. Despite the fact that labour input in hours declined more rapidly in Japan than in the Netherlands (at compound rates of 3.3 and 2.1 per cent respectively), total production per hour grew more in the Netherlands. The gap between the countries in gross and net value added per hour at Dutch prices is very big because value added in Japan is almost negligible or negative. In 1975 gross value added per hour in Dutch agriculture at Japanese prices was 4.7 times as high as in Japan and it increased to 6.1 times in 1984. For net value added the gap is bigger and has also increased since 1975.

It can be derived directly from Table 5.6 that real productivity comparisons based on conversion at official exchange rates result in an underestimation of the productivity gap between the two countries. This is because Japan's official exchange rate is much affected by the strong competitiveness of manufactured goods in export markets, whereas there are many policy measures to offset negative effects of the strong yen on agricultural incomes. Therefore, the Purchasing Power Parity of Japan's agricultural products is much lower than the exchange rate. Hence, Japan's agricultural production is much over-valued if the offical exchange rate is applied for comparisons.

Sub-sectoral comparison

It is important to know whether there are major differences in relative performance between the sub-sectors. First of all Japan may have a serious disadvantage for production of field crops because of the small acreages of its farms and the small sizes of fields. For horticulture and intensive livestock production such constraints are less serious because relatively little land is used per unit of output. Dairy farming and beef production based on on-farm production of fodder certainly have economies of scale with regard to land, but this is related basically to the number of animals per farm and per worker. These animals can in principle also be fed on purchased feed, which means that use can be made of land elsewhere. The latter occurs in areas in the US and in Japan, except Hokkaido (Van der Meer, Yamada and Egaitsu 1987). It depends on the cost of transportation of milk and fodder and which system is more economical.[3] If transportation of fodder is cheaper, these activities are similar in character to intensive livestock raising and there are few economies of scale with regard to land.

In the Netherlands, on the other hand, farm sizes form a less severe constraint for achieving high productivity in field crop production than in Japan, but arable farming in the Netherlands is probably also the part of agriculture with relatively the lowest real productivity compared to other efficient producers, e.g. the USA and Australia. Dutch livestock farming may occupy a middle position. Horticultural production in the Netherlands is probably among the most advanced in the world. This holds in particular for flowers, for which the Netherlands is the biggest exporter in the world market.

Such likely differences of real productivity between sub-sectors cannot be discerned at local prices. The sub-sector with lowest productivity at international prices may in fact have the highest productivity at local prices because of price policies. Moreover, comparison of sub-sectoral labour productivities may be strongly affected by differences in contributions of land and capital. For example, land rent takes a larger proportion of gross value added in arable farming than in the other sub-sectors.

Table 5.7 Labour productivity ratios for sub-sectors between Japanese and Dutch agriculture, 1975, 1980, and 1984

	Total agri-culture[a]	*Arable crops*	*Live-stock products*	*Horti-cultural crops*
Total production/hour				
	Ratio Netherlands/Japan			
Converted at exchange rates				
1975	3.9	4.7	3.2	3.8
1980	4.0	3.8	3.2	4.4
1984	3.0	2.7	2.5	3.8
Japanese prices				
1975	5.5	6.3	4.7	4.6
1980	6.0	9.0	4.5	6.1
1984	5.8	7.7	4.5	6.6
Dutch prices				
1975	7.9	12.5	4.7	5.3
1980	8.5	11.8	4.6	6.4
1984	8.0	10.2	4.6	6.8
Gross value added/hour				
	Ratio Netherlands/Japan			
Converted at exchange rates				
1975	3.1	4.4	3.8	3.7
1980	3.2	3.8	3.4	4.4
1984	2.8	2.8	4.1	3.5
Japanese prices				
1975	4.7	5.1	7.3	3.7
1980	5.8	11.0	6.2	5.6
1984	6.1	10.0	8.2	6.4
Dutch prices (A)				
1975	10.8	21.1	11.0	5.5
1980	28.3	[b]	10.8	7.6
1984	17.9	59.4	12.0	6.8
Dutch prices (B)				
1975	10.5	24.3	12.7	4.9
1980	19.6	257.7	10.2	6.2

Sources Van der Meer and Yamada (1988: annex Table D.8).

Notes a. The figures in the 'Total agriculture' column differ slightly from data in previous tables because of rounding errors. b. Negative gross value added in Japan. For the Netherlands detailed cost indexes could be calculated for 1975 and 1980 for the three sub-sectors, for 1984 approximations had to be made. Consequently Dutch gross value added could be expressed at Japanese prices. For Japan no cost indexes could be calculated per sector. Two approximations are applied to estimate Japanese gross value added at Dutch prices. Variant (A) assumes the same cost index for each sub-sector. For 1975 and 1980 the cost index for horticulture should be higher than average because of low energy prices in the Netherlands. For these years also an alternative variant (B) has been calculated for which the index for Dutch sub-sectors (at Dutch weights) is applied to Japanese data.

Data on value added and labour input by sub-sector are not available in the national statistics of both countries. Estimates of gross value added and real sectoral labour productivities were made for the three benchmark years by using the same data material as for the whole sector. Unfortunately data available on depreciation by sub-sector are insufficient to make reliable net value added estimates. The methods used are explained in Van der Meer and Yamada (1988: annex D). The productivity ratios are summarized in Table 5.7. It should be noted that the error margins for real comparisons by sub-sectors are higher than for the whole sector.

Total production value per hour in Japan is significantly inflated by high price levels, in particular for arable crops (Table 5.7). The productivity gap calculated at exchange rates for arable crops and livestock products seems to narrow over the period 1975–84, whereas it remains stable for horticultural crops. (This is more obvious if the year 1980 is disregarded because it was a year with a poor harvest.) At Japanese prices, however, the gap in labour productivity increases over time for arable and horticultural crops, and it remains about the same for livestock products. It also appears that the productivity gap is smallest for the livestock sector and biggest for the arable crops sector. The relative ranking is the same in Dutch prices, but here the gap for the arable crops is narrowing. This is probably the result of the absence of rice.

Gross value added per hour, converted at exchange rates, is more than three times higher in the Netherlands. There is no clear trend for the horticulture and livestock sub-sectors, but for the arable sub-sector the ratio has declined from 4.4 to about 2.8. At Japanese prices the gap in gross value added per hour is biggest for arable crops and smallest for horticultural crops. Most striking is that for all sub-sectors the gap increased significantly. For Japan no details of costs are available for sub-sectors, which means that no deflator can be applied for groups of inputs. Therefore at Dutch prices two estimates are used as a proxy: the (A) variant assumes the same price index for inputs of each sub-sector, and the (B) variant provides estimates for specific price indexes for the inputs by sub-sector. For 1984 no (B) variant could be estimated (see Van der Meer and Yamada, 1988: annex Table D.8). At Dutch prices (the (A) and (B) variants) the gap seems to be bigger for all sub-sectors than for Japanese prices. Again it appears that the horticulture sub-sector performs relatively best and the arable sub-sector worst in Japan, where in 1980 and 1984 gross value added from arable crops in almost zero. The (B) variant shows a relatively better performance for Japan's horticulture, as the price index for inputs in this sector is higher than for the other sub-sectors. If we ignore the figures for 1980 because this was a poor crop year in Japan, we come to the important conclusion that the gap in gross value added per hour, measured in Dutch prices, increased in all sub-sectors.

The findings of the relative performance of sub-sectors suggest that the constraint on farm sizes plays a role in Japan. At least it helps to explain the poor performance of the arable sub-sector. However, in international perspective Japan's performance may be even worse than depicted, because here it is compared to Dutch arable farming which probably has a relatively lower productivity performance than the other two sub-sectors. The poor performance of the arable sub-sector in Japan may be largely caused by rice production. If the price indexes from Table 5.2 are adjusted for rice[4] and are applied to the cost of production data for rice (specified in the MAFF Yearbook of Agriculture), net value added clearly turns negative. The middle ranking of the livestock sub-sector is as expected. As will be shown below, dairy farming and intensive livestock raising perform better than the livestock sub-sector on average. The average for the livestock sub-sector may be negatively affected by poor performance in beef production. But land scarcity and farm sizes are not the only factors affecting productivity. There must be other important factors of an institutional nature that can explain why labour productivity for horticulture, Japan's most productive sub-sector in terms of real gross value added per hour, is only one-fourth to one-seventh of the Dutch level, and why the gap has increased over this period. Below we shall reveal more information about relative levels for real labour productivity for some livestock products and also see that for livestock products which require little land, productivity in Japan is still far behind that in the Netherlands.

Comparisons for some livestock products

Cost of production estimates also provide a source of information that can be used for comparison of real productivities and rates of protection. Actually these sources contain more detailed information than sector accounts. They even allow for comparison of total factor productivity. But the use of these data has limitations as well. Their main weakness is their representativeness. Annual sample surveys are made in both countries but the surveyed population differs from the overall population. In Japan only family farms are surveyed, and limited companies and other corporate farms which are of increasing importance, in particular in intensive livestock raising, are excluded. The size of these farms is much bigger than that of family farms. Therefore, the averages obtained in these surveys are downwardly biased. For the Netherlands the opposite is the case, since production from small farms, providing gainful employment for less than about half a full-time person, is not included. This excludes a few per cent of production, and gives a small upward bias to the thus calculated averages.

Other obstacles for comparisons of cost of production data stem from differences in definitions and methods used. In previous reports the available data sources have been discussed in detail, and efforts were made to make cost of production tables more comparable (Van der Meer, Yamada, and Egaitsu 1987; Van der Meer and Yamada 1989). Here attention will only be given to the results.

There is much interest in Japan in the comparison of the cost of production of agricultural products with other countries. One reason is to compare economic performance with other countries, another is to gather information for policy and trade negotiations with farmers' unions and foreign trade partners. Usually such comparisons are conducted at prevailing prices and exchange rates and focus on profitability. This, however, has serious shortcomings. In the past fifteen years there have been important changes in the exchange rates between the major economic trading blocs in the world with major impact on national price levels in different countries. Therefore, the results of comparisons through exchange rates are unstable and become rapidly obsolete. Another disadvantage of cost and income comparisons at exchange rates is, similar to that of the comparison of national income, that domestic price levels may differ substantially, and that the findings may provide a biased picture of the real economic performance of a (sub-) sector.

In this study comparisons are made of 'real' cost of production and productivity in dairy milk, pigs, eggs, and broiler production. Real comparison implies that outputs and inputs are valued in both countries at the same prices. This method is closely related to the so-called 'double deflation method' of comparisons of real output and productivity which is applied above for the agricultural sector as a whole and the three sub-sectors.

Dairy farming

Dairy farming in Japan differs strongly in character between Hokkaido, where about one third of the production takes place, and all other regions of Japan, to which we shall refer here as 'other regions'. Hokkaido has relatively much land and is similar to the Netherlands as dairy farming is mainly based on on-farm feed production.

In other regions land is scarce and most feed has to be bought, even roughage. Hokkaido farmers have also specialized in raising milking cows for other areas because of the availability of land and local feed. Because of a quota system for milk, farmers in the other regions receive 18 per cent higher prices than farmers in Hokkaido. Since the Japanese national average is in fact the average of a bimodal distribution, it is not so meaningful in comparisons with Dutch data, and comparisons between the Netherlands, Hokkaido, and other regions are given instead. The data refer to the farming season 1983/4 which was the latest year for which data were available when the calculations were made. In this period the Dutch quota system for milk was not yet introduced.

If different weights are used one can expect different results from the comparisons of productivity. A country (or region) often shows the best performance if its own weights (i.e. prices) are used. This is also the case in this comparison. In Table 5.8 three kinds of productivity indicators, i.e. total productivity, net factor productivity and net value added per hour (labour productivity), are presented at three different price bases. For Japan, the three productivity indexes are lowest at Dutch prices. The average Dutch dairy farm shows relatively the best performance at Dutch prices. This is also the case for large Dutch farms. However, on small Dutch farms, productivity is the highest at Hokkaido prices, which implies that the input–output price structure in Hokkaido is rather favourable for them while the Dutch price structure is apparently more favourable for big farms.[5] For the other regions of Japan, all indexes are the highest at the other regions' prices. For Hokkaido, however, only total productivity is the highest at Hokkaido prices, but the other two productivity indexes are the highest at the other regions' prices.[6]

Apart from differences caused by weighting there are important similarities. Total productivity in Hokkaido is 72–83 per cent of the Dutch level, net factor productivity 47–60 per cent, and labour productivity 41–51 per cent, depending on weights used. The difference for the other regions is bigger, with respectively 61–76, 28–52 per cent and 22–32 per cent. The cost of production of milk is on average higher in Hokkaido than in the Netherlands, but significantly lower than in the other regions.[7] Therefore, we can conclude that the figures above show without doubt that dairy farming is more competitive and productive in Hokkaido than in the other regions.

In the Netherlands differences in productivity between large and small farms appear to be bigger than in Japan. This can be illustrated as follows. Large farms (in terms of numbers of cows) in

Hokkaido are smaller than the average large farm in the Netherlands, but slightly bigger than the average Dutch farm (Table 5.8). Large farms in the other regions correspond in size with the Dutch average. Small farms in the Netherlands have bigger sizes than the average in Hokkaido and the other regions. Although size differences in Japan between the average and large farms are bigger than in the Netherlands, the differences in productivity are in most cases smaller. This means that economies of scale are more

Table 5.8 Comparison of real productivity and cost of 100 kg milk production between Japanese and Dutch farms, 1983/4

	Dutch farms			*Japanese farms*			
				Hokkaido		*Other regions*	
	All	*Large*	*Small*	*All*	*Large*	*All*	*Large*
Number of milk cows	57.9	72.3	31.4	28.1	66.3	15.2	57.6
Hectares grass and fodder	24.5	29.6	15.2	23.4	53.3	2.2	4.8
				(All Dutch farms = 100)			
Total productivity[a]							
Hokkaido prices	100	103	89	83	87	73	83
Other regions' prices	100	103	87	82	85	76	88
Dutch prices	100	104	83	72	78	61	77
Net factor productivity[b]							
Hokkaido prices	100	108	71	60	67	43	62
Other regions' prices	100	109	71	61	66	52	78
Dutch prices	100	110	67	47	55	28	44
Net value added per hour							
Hokkaido prices	100	114	61	48	60	29	43
Other regions' prices	100	114	60	51	63	32	50
Dutch prices	100	114	60	41	51	22	36
Total cost for 100 kg milk							
Hokkaido prices	100	97	110	113	107	127	112
Other regions' prices	100	97	112	114	110	123	106
Dutch prices	100	96	118	130	120	154	120

Source Van der Meer, Yamada, and Egaitsu (1987: Table 19, with some revisions).
Note a. total productivity is the total value of production divided by total cost. b. net factor productivity is net value added divided by factor cost. Small farms in the Netherlands have usually more than 20 and less than 43 milk cows; large farms in Japan have more than 50 milk cows.

important in the Netherlands. Analysis of farm income indicates that small farms in the Netherlands are not economically viable and have no future. Yet, productivity on these farms is still higher than that on large farms in Japan.

Differences in productivity can be caused by differences in biological efficiency and labour efficiency. In practice, it is not possible to quantify both components unambiguously, because there are several possible criteria. One, for example, is milk yield per cow, but if milk is not of the same quality (fat content), or produced at different material costs, the comparison may be biased. Feed cost per kg of milk may be another criterion, but on-farm fodder production differs strongly between the other regions, on the one hand, and Hokkaido and the Netherlands on the other. Actually one can say that in the other regions purchased feed is substituted for (inputs for) on-farm fodder production, and the opposite is the case in Hokkaido and the Netherlands. However, various efficiency criteria all point in the same direction. Differences in milk yield per cow between Hokkaido and the Netherlands are small, and non-factor input per 100 kg of milk in Hokkaido is about equal to that in the Netherlands, but higher in the other regions. Grass yield per hectare and milk fat content are lower in Japan. In general, however, it seems that biological differences are minor, and they cannot explain more than a fraction of the differences in productivity and cost of production between both countries.

Labour efficiency, on the other hand, is relatively low in Japan and can explain nearly the whole difference in productivity and cost of production. One would expect that this is related to lower investment levels, but that is not the case. Real costs of buildings per 100 kg of milk are also relatively high in Hokkaido where, probably because of heavy snowfall in winter, expensive tower silos are used, but low in the other regions because of a milder climate. Real cost of machinery per 100 kg of milk are high in Japan, mainly because of high depreciation cost (which is a non-factor cost component). The conclusion is that low labour productivity levels in Japan are mainly the result of too intensive use of labour, or in fact, surplus of labour. This is related to many factors, such as insufficient experience of management, low qualification of workers, inappropriate lay-out of farms, and relatively low wage levels. Moreover, the product price level is high enough to allow labour intensive production methods.

Capital investment per unit of output is already relatively high, but its efficiency is probably low. Increases in labour productivity will therefore require a rapid reduction of labour input per unit of output, accompanied by increased efficiency in capital use rather

Table 5.9 Kilograms of milk produced per hour worked in Japan and the Netherlands, 1950/1–1985/6

Three-year average	*Netherlands* *kg/hour*	*Netherlands* *Compound growth rate (%)*	*Japan* *kg/hour*	*Japan* *Compound growth rate (%)*
1950/1	13.1		4.9	
1960/1	18.3	3.4	7.5	4.3
1970/1	31.5	5.6	16.0	7.9
1985/6	88.6	7.1	40.5	6.4
Whole period		5.6		6.0

Sources and notes Netherlands: Calculated from cost of production tables as reported in LEI/CBS, *Agricultural Statistics*, issues 1955, 1965, 1975, and 1988, and wage costs per hour for workers on dairy farms published in the same sources. Unweighted averages were taken from three main areas: clay and peat areas in the north, grass areas in the west, and sandy soil areas. Over time some changes in boundaries of these areas took place. In 1950/1 the sandy soils were represented by the provinces Brabant and Overijssel only, whereas the other areas were represented by South Holland and Friesland. Japan: Years are respectively 1951, 1961, 1970, and 1986. Data up to 1970 are from MAFF, *Time-series of Agricultural Economic Statistics, vol. 5: Cost of Production Surveys* 1974. The 1985/6 data are from MAFF, *Cost of Production Report*, 1987.

than increased levels of fixed capital stock. This does not exclude the possibility that the present capital stock has to be replaced by a capital stock of higher quality, in particular with regard to efficiency of labour use.

An interesting question is whether dairy farming in Japan has been able to narrow the gap in labour productivity with the Netherlands. Exact information on trends in net value added is difficult to obtain, but some evidence of gross (physical) labour productivity, expressed in kilograms of milk per hour worked, could be obtained from cost of production reports. These data may be biased because of changes of coverage and concepts of hours used and, in the case of the Netherlands, changes in the share of by-products. Nevertheless, the results are not without interest (see Table 5.9). It appears that after the Second World War productivity in the Netherlands has always been twice as high or even more than in Japan. The fact that labour productivity in Japanese dairy farming has lagged behind all the time is quite natural since it has a relatively short history. Dutch dairy farming has continued to improve its productivity and realized a more than six-fold increase since 1950, or an annual growth rate of 5.6 per cent for over more than three decades. Surprisingly, the speed even accelerated after 1970/1.[8]

Table 5.10 Comparison of price levels in dairy farming between Hokkaido and other regions in Japan, 1975

	(Index: Dutch average = 100)	
	Hokkaido	*Other Regions*
Hokkaido prices		
Value of production	163	190
Non-factor cost	144	144
Net value added	196	289
Labour income	261	403
Other regions' prices		
Value of production	160	186
Non-factor cost	144	144
Net value added	186	258
Labour income	272	343
Dutch prices		
Value of production	169	196
Non-factor cost	142	144
Net value added	231	371
Labour income	428	597

Source Van der Meer, Yamada, and Egaitsu (1987: Tables 15, 16 and 17).
Note Indexes at Hokkaido prices and other regions' prices are based on Dutch weights, and indexes at Dutch prices are based on Hokkaido and other regions' prices.

Japan increased productivity at a slightly higher speed than Dutch dairy farms did for the same period. However, contrary to the Dutch experience, the pace slowed down during the last fifteen years. Apparently there is a ten-year time-lag between the two countries. Whether Japan can realize the present Dutch productivity level after another ten years may depend upon how rapidly Japan can enlarge its farm size. Japanese dairy farms may continue to enlarge their size as well as their productivity to a certain extent. However, given various institutional barriers, it seems rather difficult for Japan to realize the present Dutch level in a short time.

In Japan price levels for milk and by-products are much higher than in the Netherlands (see Table 5.10). In Hokkaido they are about 60 per cent higher and in the other regions about 90 per cent. Prices for non-factor inputs are about 45 per cent higher than in the Netherlands, which means that farmers receive a considerably larger nominal protection than required for compensation of higher input prices. The effective rate of protection appears to be in the range of 86 to 131 per cent for Hokkaido for the different prices and weights. For the other regions it is much higher because of the higher nominal rate of protection and ranges from 158 to 271 per cent. The implicit percentages of support for farm family labour income are 161 to 328 in Hokkaido and 243 to 497 per cent for the other regions. It appears that the estimated rates of protection for value added and labour income are much higher at Dutch prices than at Japanese prices.

Intensive livestock raising

Comparison of intensive livestock raising is of importance for our study since this branch of agriculture uses hardly any land. Land scarcity and small farm sizes can therefore not explain differences in productivity.

A comparison of real productivity in the intensive livestock industry faces some problems, which are inherent in particular features of the industry. Intensive livestock production, and in particular, poultry raising, is characterized by relatively small net value added margins. As a consequence value added fluctuates heavily with changes in feed and output prices. However, the intensive livestock sector also has a greater capacity to adapt itself to rapidly changing market conditions than most other agricultural sub-sectors because of the relatively short life-cycles of pigs and poultry. Occasionally net value added margins may be zero or negative, and the comparison of net value added per hour may fluctuate heavily from year to year. Moreover, the comparison is very sensitive to even small differences in definition and statistical errors. Therefore, in the case of small value added margins, special attention should be given to real cost levels, physical productivity ratios, to averages over several years, or to 'normalized results'. This comparison, therefore, focuses on several technical and economic productivity criteria and structural features of pig and poultry farming in both countries.

Comparability of broiler production is low because of structural differences. Broilers in Japan are fed to 2,480 grams and in the Netherlands to 1,600. This is related to consumer preference, and results in lower feed efficiency (Van der Meer and Yamada 1989: 30–1). Also one-day-old chickens appear to be much more expensive in Japan.

Comparative price and productivity measures for pig raising, broiler, and egg production have been brought together in Table 5.11. The following conclusions can be drawn from this table. Japanese farmers operate under higher input and output prices. Non-factor cost and product price levels are much higher for pigs than for broilers, and lowest for eggs. The nominal rate of protection

Table 5.11 Summary of price and quantity of intensive livestock production in Japan compared to the Netherlands, 1983/4

	Pigs[a]		*Broilers*		*Eggs*	
	P[b]	*Q*[b]	*P*	*Q*	*P*	*Q*
Protection for Japan vis-à-vis the Netherlands						
Nominal rate of protection (%)	72		32		17	
Effective rate of protection (%)						
Dutch weights	208		1[f]		−20	
Japanese weights	304		2028[f]		−37	
Productivity ratios[c] *Japan/Netherlands* (Netherlands = 100)						
Kg product per hour labour		24		32		26
Kg product per kg of feed		99		87		100
Net value added per hour						
Dutch prices		14		4[f]		17
Japanese prices		18		76[f]		13
Net value added per unit of factor input						
Dutch prices		20		6[f]		20
Japanese prices		31		106[f]		18
Total value of production/total input						
Dutch prices		67		86		77
Japanese prices		81		99		87
Cost of production[d] (Netherlands = 100)						
Non-factor cost per unit of product						
Dutch prices/weights	147	107	133	104	120	102
Japanese prices/weights	146	107	125	97	121	103
Total cost[e]						
Dutch prices	128	147	126	117	112	114
Japanese prices	105	122	109	109	100	128

Source Van der Meer and Yamada (1989: Table 15).

Notes a. Pigs represent the consolidated data for piglets and hogs. b. P and Q indicate price and quantity indexes. c. Productivities have been corrected for double counting of weight. d. The cost of production for pigs may be about 5 per cent upwardly biased because of double counting. e. Total cost is the cost of production before deduction of by-products. f. Because of small net value added margins and considerable differences in price and production structure, ratios based on net value added give highly contradictory results. See text for explanation.

ranges from 17 per cent for eggs to 72 per cent for pigs. The particular results for 1983/4 show high effective rates of protection for pigs and negative effective protection for eggs. The latter is related to unfavourable product feed prices in this year in Japan. For broilers a very wide range is found for effective protection depending on differences in production structure, in particular the difference in fattening weight and in the cost of one-day-old chickens. The differences in labour efficiency for the three sub-sectors are about the same: Japanese farmers use three to four times more labour per kg of product than Dutch farmers. However, biological efficiency in terms of feed conversion is about the same in both countries. The 15 per cent higher feed use for broilers in Japan can at least partly be attributed to consumer preference for higher fattening weights.

Net value added per hour in pig raising and egg production is about five to seven times higher in the Netherlands. For broiler production in Japan net value added per hour at Japanese prices is 76 per cent of the Dutch level, but at Dutch prices value added is nearly zero. The result thus appears very dependent on the price base. Net factor productivity (net value added per unit of factor input), which is in many respects the best criteria for measuring the economic performance of a sector of the economy, gives the same mixed pattern as net labour productivity. The gap between both countries is smaller. For broilers productivity at Japanese prices is even slightly higher in Japan. Total productivity for broilers shows only equal performance for Japan at Japanese prices. In other cases total productivity in Japan is 13–30 per cent lower. Non-factor input per unit of product is equal or slightly higher in Japan. However, detailed analysis showed also that higher labour saving investments have resulted in higher cost of buildings and equipment in the Netherlands. The energy cost for heating is also higher in the Netherlands, which can be explained by the cooler and more humid Dutch winters. Total costs in Japan are higher in all cases.

There is a rapid increase of the share of production on corporate farms in Japan (Van der Meer and Yamada, 1989: Tables 4 and 5). This probably means that this part of the intensive livestock sector is more productive than the family farms, and it may indicate the demise of family farms in these sub-sectors. Therefore the averages shown for family farms are likely to underestimate average productivity levels and trends.

Long-term trends in gross labour productivities in intensive livestock production

Data available from the cost of production reports allow for a rough comparison of changes in gross labour productivity between both countries since 1960. The concepts applied and their representativeness may not be fully comparable over time and between countries, but the data certainly have indicative value. It should be noted again that the Japanese data do not cover the increasing share of production comprised by corporate farms. The average growth performance in Japan is likely to be better than indicated by family farms.

Table 5.12 Trends in gross labour productivity in pig raising in Japan and the Netherlands, 1959/60–1985/6

	Netherlands		*Japan*	
	kg/hour	*Compound growth rate (%)*	*kg/hour*	*Compound growth rate (%)*
1959/60	5.2		1.2	
1969/70	13.6	10.0	3.9	14.6
1979/80	31.2	8.7	10.1	9.9
1985/6	55.7	10.1	12.7	3.9
Whole period		9.5		9.5

Sources Van der Meer and Yamada (1989: Table 12). The 1985/6 data for Japan from MAFF, *Cost of Production Report* (1987), for the Netherlands from LEI/CBS, *Agricultural Statistics* (1988).

Note Japanese data refer to three-year averages 1960–2, 1969–71, 1979–81 and the single year 1985–6.

Pigs

In both countries the average growth rate of gross labour productivity in pig raising has been very high since 1960 at over 9 per cent in the Netherlands and in Japan (Table 5.12). The growth rate slowed down significantly over time in Japan, whereas in the Netherlands growth was more stable. It seems that gross labour productivity in Japan lags about fifteen years behind the Netherlands.

Eggs

Gross labour productivity in egg production increased more rapidly in the Netherlands (14 per cent per year) than in Japan (11 per cent per year) (Table 5.13). In both countries productivity growth was most rapid in the 1960s and it slowed down afterwards. In terms of gross labour productivity egg production in Japan is ten to fifteeen years behind the Netherlands. But in particular for this sub-sector the average performance on corporate farms is likely to be much closer to the Netherlands. According to a rough estimate[9] the number of kg of eggs per hour for corporate farms was 53.4 in 1985. This is 80 per cent higher than that of family farms, but still less than half of the Dutch level.

Broilers

For Japan data on broilers are available from 1969 onwards only. Since that period growth of gross labour productivity has been very

Table 5.13 Trends in gross labour productivity in egg production in Japan and the Netherlands, 1959/60–1985/6

	Netherlands		*Japan*	
	kg eggs per hour	*Compound growth rate (%)*	*kg eggs per hour*	*Compound growth rate (%)*
1959/60	3.5		3.3	
1970/71	28.7	21.2	8.4	12.2
1979/80	72.3	10.8	22.7	10.5
1985/6	112.2	7.6	29.6	5.5
Whole period		14.3		10.9

Sources Van der Meer and Yamada (1989: Table 13). The 1985/6 data for Japan from MAFF, *Cost of Production Report* (1987), for the Netherlands from LEI/CBS, *Agricultural Statistics* (1988).

Note Japanese refer to three-year averages 1961–3, 1969–71, 1979–81 and the single year 1985–6.

rapid, and faster than in the Netherlands (see Table 5.14). The Netherlands experienced a very rapid growth of productivity during the 1960s, and as a result gross productivity at the end of that period was four times higher than in Japan. Since then the gap has narrowed, but the Dutch productivity level is still three times higher. The very low price levels in recent years in the Netherlands have probably negatively affected productivity growth (LEI 1984: 52).

Table 5.14 Trends in gross labour productivity in broiler production in Japan and the Netherlands, 1959/60–1985/6

	Netherlands		*Japan*	
	kg broiler per hour	*Compound growth rate (%)*	*kg eggs per broiler*	*Compound growth rate (%)*
1959	9.8			
1970	64.6	18.7	13.5	
1979/80	136.2	8.2	33.4	9.5
1985/6	179.6	4.7	65.2	11.8
Whole period		11.8		11.1

Sources Van der Meer and Yamada (1989: Table 14). The 1985/6 data for Japan from MAFF, *Cost of Production Report* (1987), for the Netherlands from LEI/CBS, *Agricultural Statistics* (1988).

Note Japanese data refer to three-year averages 1969–71, 1979–81 and the single year 1985–6.

Comparison of Japan and the Netherlands with Taiwan and the USA

The findings from the comparison between Japan and the Netherlands for the agricultural sector as a whole can be broadened by comparing each of these countries with Taiwan and the USA. This means that the price comparisons were done at Japanese and Dutch weights. Similar calculations at US weights and Taiwanese weights were not undertaken because of considerable additional time requirements for such calculations. An approximation at Taiwanese and US weights was made by substituting weights for the groups of products and inputs of Japan or the Netherlands by those of Taiwan or the USA and reweighting the aggregate price ratios (see Appendix Tables D.3 and D.4, pp. 190–1). Indexes adjusted in that way are more suitable for converting value aggregates in Taiwan and the USA into Dutch or Japanese prices than price indexes based in Dutch and Japanese weights. The comparisons with Taiwan and the USA are less detailed than the comparisons between Japan and the Netherlands in the sense that less time could be spent on gathering price data.

Relative price levels

The relative price levels are compared among the four countries and summarized in Table 5.15. First, it appears that at Dutch weights price levels of Japan and Taiwan are relatively lower than at Japanese weights. This is probably largely because weights for rice are zero in the Netherlands. Second, at Japanese weights net value added at US prices and Dutch prices is nearly zero in 1975 and negative in 1980 and 1984. As a result price levels of net value added cannot be compared at Japanese weights. Third, the price indexes for total production reflect exchange rate fluctuations between the countries. The yen and the Dutch guilder appreciated considerably relative to the dollar from 1975 to 1980 (see Appendix Table D.2, p. 188). From 1980 to 1984 the guilder depreciated significantly and the yen only little. The Taiwanese currency, NT dollar, showed less pronounced changes because it was mainly tied to the US dollar. Japan's relative price level for total production increased significantly at Japanese and approximate US weights despite the US dollar's appreciation, but at Dutch weights the relative price level in 1984 is about the same as in 1975. The absolute level was about 2 times higher at Dutch weights and 2.5 to 3.4 times at Japanese and US approximate weights. The relative Dutch price level in 1975 and 1980 was 30 to 40 per cent higher at each weighting system, but at Dutch and US approximate weights in 1984 it dropped to below the US level, whereas at Japanese weights it remained 30 per cent higher. This again shows the dominant role of rice in the weighting systems. Also Taiwan's estimated relative price level depends much on the weighting system. At Japanese weights its price level was relatively lower than at Dutch weights in 1975 and 1980. This is because Taiwan's livestock prices are relatively high and the heavy share for livestock in the Dutch weighting system blows up Taiwan's level. At its own approximate weights for groups of products and inputs its level each year is about 5 per cent above the US level. At Japanese weights its price level increased very much in 1984. The adjustment for its own product and input groups does not change the picture though the relative level is somewhat lower.

The relative price level for net value added equals 100 plus the effective rate of protection. At Dutch weights Japan's effective rate of protection *vis-à-vis* the US price level increased from 143 to 210 per cent and declined again to 143 per cent in 1984. At Japanese weights the level is astronomically high in 1975 and cannot be measured in 1980 and 1984 because of negative value added. The Dutch level of effective protection was 55 and 60 per cent in 1975

Table 5.15 Price levels in Japan, the Netherlands, and Taiwan relative to the USA, 1975, 1980, and 1984

(USA = 100)

	Total production			*Net value added*		
	1975	*1980*	*1984*	*1975*	*1980*	*1984*
A. *At Dutch weights*						
Japan	183	219	181	243	310	243
Netherlands	130	146	95	155	160	107
Taiwan	133	150	146	104	213	202
Taiwan[a]	107	106	105	110	120	117
B. *At Japanese weights*						
Japan	254	288	343	3,067[d]	[c]	[c]
Netherlands	127	135	130	[d]	[c]	[c]
Taiwan	117	130	189	[d]	[c]	[c]
Taiwan[a]	104	112	172	[d]	[c]	[c]
C. *At approximate US weights*[b]						
Japan	245	275	331	397	530	667
Netherlands	127	134	95	128	107	100

Source Appendix Tables D.3 and D.4.

Notes a. based on Taiwan's weights of groups of products and inputs, which is a proxy for its own weights; b. same as for Taiwan as explained in note a; c. net value added in Japan is negative at US prices; d. net value added in Japan is nearly zero, which makes the results very unstable and unreliable.

and 1980 respectively, but because of the guilder's depreciation it dropped to only 7 per cent in 1984. At US approximate weights Dutch effective protection is only 28 per cent in 1975, 7 per cent in 1980 and zero in 1984. Taiwan's effective rate of protection measured at Dutch weights increased dramatically from nearly zero in 1975 to over 100 per cent in 1980 and 1984. At its own approximate weights there was a slight increase from 10 per cent in 1975 to about 20 per cent in subsequent years. This contrast is mainly caused by the different weight of livestock in Taiwan.

Real labour productivities

For the estimation of labour productivities a common standard for measuring labour input is needed. Unfortunately, employment figures appear to be unreliable because of extensive part-time labour in agriculture.[10] In particular in Japan, Taiwan, and the USA many farm workers have off-farm employment as well. Moreover, in all countries there are many unpaid family workers and older people who engage only part-time in farm work, in particular in the peak seasons. It appears that methods of recording the labour input of these people differ much among countries and even between agencies in each country. Consequently, the comparability of the results is low. Moreover, little consideration is given to the fact that part of the full-time workers have very long working hours. Therefore we have a preference for using hours worked as a standard. For Japan and the Netherlands such data have been estimated for the farm sector by Yamada (1987a) and Van der Meer (1987). These estimates cover all kinds of labour (even labour by contracting services in the Netherlands), with the minor exception of persons employed by agricultural limited companies in Japan, which are of increasing importance in intensive livestock farming. For Taiwan, labour input data in working days are available (Chen, 1987). Unfortunately, labour hours per day are not available. By assuming seven hours per working day as an average total labour input in hours was calculated. Probably seven hours is too little for peak seasons, but too high for slack seasons, and may therefore be close to reality. For the USA hours worked are reported in the national accounts up to 1979, when the series was discontinued and replaced by a series in full-time equivalents (US Department of Commerce 1981, September issue and 1982, July issue). The latter can be used to extrapolate the series from 1979 to 1984. Unfortunately the US series of hours worked is downwardly biased since it excludes some groups of family workers. Farm operators who spend most of their time in off-farm employment and unpaid family workers are not included. This may imply a considerable underestimation. Another suspect feature is that the recorded employment in agricultural services, forestry, and fisheries is very high compared to employment on farms if related to the share in GDP. This suggests that some farm labour input is actually registered under agricultural services. Therefore altogether US labour input in hours on farms is probably underestimated. The magnitude is unknown, but may range somewhere between 10 and 25 per cent. We did not correct the figure, but should remember this bias when comparing the labour productivity level in the US with the other countries.

The real labour productivities for total production and gross and net value added are summarized in Table 5.16. As mentioned already net value added in Japan is negative at Dutch and even more at US prices. At US prices even gross value added turned negative in 1980. But also at Taiwanese prices Japan's performance

Table 5.16 Real labour productivities in Japan, the Netherlands, Taiwan, and the USA, 1975, 1980, and 1987 (yen per hour)

	Total production per hour			*Gross value added per hour*			*Net value added per hour*		
	1975	*1980*	*1984*	*1975*	*1980*	*1984*	*1975*	*1980*	*1984*
Dutch prices									
Japan	457	641	622	158	80	129	77	–86	–9
Netherlands	3,603	5,458	4,965	1,709	2,270	2,306	1,519	1,894	1,975
Taiwan[a]	555	959	850	417	586	548	393	562	525
USA[a]	5,084	6,141	5,873	2,694	2,650	2,977	1,990	1,651	2,250
Japanese prices									
Japan	917	1,374	1,634	556	712	826	465	534	635
Netherlands	5,083	8,180	9,473	2,594	4,089	5,028	2,379	3,667	4,491
Taiwan[a]	1,116	1,775	1,899	945	1,420	1,477	915	1,382	1,438
USA[a]	9,810	12,600	20,560	6,720	8,830	16,020	6,270	8,230	15,050
Taiwanese prices									
Japan	420	613	890	95	159	270	22	20	125
Netherlands	3,669	5,639	7,655	1,200	2,546	3,858	1,011	2,221	3,443
Taiwan	458	700	941	303	445	599	279	414	569
US prices									
Japan	362	477	476	104	56	–78	15	–131	–260
Netherlands	2,774	3,749	5,204	1,124	1,451	2,263	981	1,185	1,840
USA	4,007	4,578	6,216	2,083	2,247	3,183	1,653	1,288	2,275

Source Appendix Table D.5.

Notes Values converted by deflators based on Dutch and Japanese weights. a. weights adjusted according to share of groups of products and inputs. For possible bias in labour input in Taiwan and the US, see text.

is poor as evidenced by the fact that net value added per hour is close to zero. Taiwan's agriculture is more productive than Japan's at all price bases and for all years. For total production per hour the difference is about 10–50 per cent. The lowest difference is found at Taiwan's own prices. For gross value added the gap is considerable. At Japanese prices it ranges between 70 and 100 per cent, whereas at Taiwanese prices Taiwan's gross value added per hour is about two-and-a-half to three times higher, and at Dutch prices the gap is even bigger in recent years. For net value added per hour the gap is much higher at Taiwan's prices, but even more than 100 per cent at Japanese prices. So clearly Taiwan has taken over the leadership role in productivity in Asian agriculture from Japan. Table 5.16 shows that one main reason for Japan's poor performance is its excessive use of inputs and capital goods. This excessive use is attractive for farmers at actual inflated product price levels, but it reduces real net value added at international prices. Another main reason is that labour input per unit of total product is too high as evidenced by the fact that total product per hour is lower than in Taiwan despite the higher level of capital consumption (depreciation) in Japan. High product prices allow surplus labour to remain in agriculture.

The other interesting comparison is between the United States and the Netherlands. In terms of total production per hour US productivity is higher than in the Netherlands, in particular at Japanese prices, which reflects the role of prices of rice and other grains, and at Dutch and US prices for 1975. In other cases the difference ranges between 12.5 to 25 per cent which is perhaps not significant given the downward bias in US labour input figures. For gross value added differences are bigger, in particular at Japanese prices, but also at Dutch and US prices. For net value added the gap tends to be smaller because depreciation is relatively more important in the USA than in the Netherlands. At US prices net value added per hour is 70 per cent higher than in the Netherlands in 1975, 9 per cent in 1980 and 24 per cent in 1984. At Dutch prices net value added per hour is 40 per cent higher in the US in 1975, 7 per cent lower in 1980 and 15 per cent higher in 1984. The annual output fluctuations and major changes in exchange rates and accompanying fluctuations in prices and cost structure make the result of the comparisons rather unstable. Because of this and taking into account the under-reporting of labour input in US agriculture, no significant difference in real net productivity per hour can be found for 1980 and 1984 between both countries.

The difference between the Netherlands and the USA on the one hand and Japan and Taiwan on the other, is big. In terms of net labour productivity Taiwan's level is about a quarter to a fifth or even less of the level of the Western countries, if measured at Dutch or Taiwanese prices and a third at Japanese prices. The gap appears to increase mainly because of increased input use, similar to that in Japan.

Comparison with other studies

In this section our estimates of real output and rates of protection in Japan, the Netherlands, and the USA will be compared with findings in other studies. Most relevant are the already mentioned studies by the FAO (1986) and Van Ooststroom and Maddison (1985) (O–M). Rates of protection can also be compared with a study by Anderson, Hayami, and Honma (1986) (A–H–H) and a subsequent update by Hayami (1988).

First the question should be raised to which extend the results are comparable from the point of view of coverage. The FAO and O–M studies basically aim at estimating purchasing power parities (PPP). Relative price levels can be derived from the PPPs by dividing by the exchange rate, and real output ratios are derived

Table 5.17 Total value of agricultural production at current prices in sector accounts and other studies for Japan, the Netherlands, and the USA in 1970, 1975, and 1980

	1970		*1975*		*1980*	
A. *Japan* (billion yen)						
Sector accounts	4,935	(100)	9,576	(100)	11,193	(100)
FAO	5,272	(107)	9,398	(98)	11,175	(100)
Van Ooststroom–Maddison	–	–	8,728	(91)	–	–
B. *Netherlands* (million Dfl)						
Sector accounts[a]	13,444	(100)	20,691	(100)	27,951	(100)
FAO	10,992	(82)	17,904	(87)	23,759	(85)
Van Ooststoom–Maddison	–	–	17,881	(86)	–	–
C. *United States* (million US$)						
Sector accounts[b]	51,900	(100)	94,100	(100)	137,900	(100)
FAO	47,787	(92)	91,350	(97)	133,519	(97)
Van Ooststroom–Maddison	–	–	93,066	(99)	–	–

Sources Sector accounts from US Department of Commerce, *Statistical Abstract* (1985) and *Survey of Current Business* (1986, July issue); LEI/CBS, *Agricultural Statistics* (1987); MAFF *Social Accounts* (1984). FAO (1986: Tables 5.1 and 5.4); and Van Ooststroom and Maddison (1985: Table 1).

Notes The implicit values in the FAO study were calculated by multiplying the PPP by the value at international prices. a. including value added tax; b. total value of farm output minus gross rental value of farm houses.

simultaneously without correction for undercounting. At the beginning of this chapter it was already indicated that FAO production statistics, on which the FAO and O–M studies are based, cover less production than the national accounts do, but exactly how much less is not clear. Our study also starts with an estimate of relative price indexes (= PPP/exchange rate), but we apply the indexes to sector account aggregates by which the problem of under-coverage is avoided. In Table 5.17 the values of production officially reported in the sector accounts for agriculture are compared with the values calculated in the FAO and O–M studies. It appears that the FAO study overestimates total production in Japan for 1970, whereas it is about equal for other years. The FAO study underestimates total value of production for the Netherlands by 13 to 18 per cent, and for the US by 3 to 8 per cent. The O–M study underestimates total production for 1975 in Japan by 9 per cent and in the Netherlands by 14 per cent, but the difference for the US is only 1 per cent. Since neither of the studies indicates its coverage it remains unclear as to which extent deviations are caused by prices and volumes.

The study by Anderson, Hayami, and Honma (1986), updated by Hayami (1988), has a more limited scope and coverage. It aims at estimating nominal rates of protection and covers only twelve commodities which, according to Hayami (1988: 4), account for 60–70 per cent of the value of agricultural output in cash of the countries under study. This is much less than in the other studies. An important feature of these studies is that not a single horticultural crop is included. Protection for horticultural crops is relatively low, which is quite a source of bias for Taiwan and the Netherlands. Because of this it should be expected that these two studies tend to overestimate rates of protection.

For the coverage of input a comparison is only possible for the O–M study as the FAO study does not estimate inputs. By using the PPP from the O–M study we estimated the implicit value of current inputs. It appears to be 1 per cent higher in Japan than reported in the sector account, but 62 per cent lower in the case of the Netherlands. For the US the O–M estimate of intermediate input is almost 6 per cent higher than the value in the sector account for agriculture (Appendix Table D.5, p. 192 and Van Ooststroom and Maddison 1985: Table 5).

There are no methodological obstacles for comparing the results of our study on price levels with those of the FAO (1986) and Van Ooststroom and Maddison (1985). Comparison shows that differences between our estimate at Japanese weights (Table 5.15) and the FAO and O–M estimates (Table 5.18) are small. Much lower

Table 5.18 Relative price levels of total production in other studies

(USA =100)

	1970	*1975*	*1980*	*1984*
A. *Total production*				
At international prices and national weights (FAO)[a]				
Japan	216	254	296	–
Netherlands	112	134	140	–
At US prices and national weights (O–M)[b]				
Japan	–	235	–	–
Netherlands	–	120	–	–
At border prices and national trade weights (A–H–H)[c]				
Japan	157	169	185	191
Netherlands	127	127	127	108
Taiwan	92	115	152	135
B. *Current inputs*				
At US prices and national weighs (O–M)[b]				
Japan	–	222	–	–
Netherlands	–	114	–	–

Sources a. FAO (1986: Table 5.1); b. Van Ooststroom and Maddison (1985: Table 11); c. Anderson, Hayami, and Honma (1986: 26) and Hayami (1988).

Notes The relative prices from the O–M study were obtained by dividing PPP of currencies to the dollar by the exchange rate to the dollar. Those from the A–H–H and Hayami studies were obtained by adding 100 to the nominal rates of protection and dividing the indexes for Japan, and Netherlands, and Taiwan by the corresponding US index for the same year. See Table 5.15 for our corresponding estimates for the Netherlands and Japan.

are price levels for Japan at Dutch weights, which is the result of the zero weight for rice for Dutch agriculture.

The O–M study also provides a PPP for inputs used. But a major part of the inputs – seed and feed – are valued at output prices, which may be a source of error. In fact seed is usually much higher priced than common farm products. In Japan feed is available at international prices instead of at the high price level for domestic crops as is the case in the EC countries. This partly explains why the Japanese price level in the O–M study is as high as 222 per cent of the US level, and our estimate only 140 or 160 per cent depending on the weights used (Table 5.18 and Appendix Table D.2, p. 188). Their estimate for the Netherlands of 114 per cent of the USA level corresponds fairly well to our findings of 115 and 124 per cent at Dutch and approximate US weights respectively. In addition it should be mentioned that our input price indexes are based on a much larger and more representative sample.

From a methodological point of view the results of the studies by Anderson, Hayami, and Honma (1986) and Hayami (1988) are not comparable with ours, because they compare wholesale prices with border prices, whereas we compare farm prices in different countries. Our study is oriented to measurement of real output, productivity, and rates of protection within the agricultural sector proper. The study by Anderson, Hayami, and Honma focuses on border protection, which may be quite different from the explicit and natural protection enjoyed within the agricultural sector. Another problem is that exported and imported goods may differ much in quality and price from the average at the farm gate, partly because of trade disruptions. In fact border prices often are not independent from protectionist policies, and differences in border prices for different countries, reported by Anderson, Hayami, and Honma (1986: 128–44), seem to support such suspicion, at least for Japan.

The relative price indexes from the A–H–H study given in Table 5.18 should be compared with our price estimates in Table 5.15 based on each country's own weights. The price level for Japan derived from A–H–H appears to be low compared to our estimates despite the fact that our study includes many products with lower rates of protection. In particular our estimates at Japanese weights, which include rice, are much higher and since rice is also included in the estimate by Anderson, Honma, and Hayami this result should be comparable. Apparently, the use of border prices is the main reason for the difference. In situations where there are serious trade obstacles the use of border prices may result in considerable biases since the border prices are not representative for international prices for standard qualities. The A–H–H estimate for the Netherlands seems to be low for 1980 and perhaps too high for 1984. Taiwan's price level estimated at Dutch weights (Table 5.15) corresponds fairly well with the A–H–H estimates except for 1975, but those at Japanese weights are lower in 1975 and 1980 and higher in 1984. Our estimates at approximate Taiwan weights are lower except for the mixed weights with Japan.

In Table 5.19 results of the three studies are summarized. Comparative estimates of real total production and value added in Japan and the USA are presented as a percentage of the Dutch level. The FAO and O–M studies probably overestimate real production in Japan because presumably the FAO data source has a lower coverage of Dutch production. This is the effect of the omission of several products, in particular flowers and ornamental plants and trees. This may be one reason explaining the relatively

Table 5.19 Comparison of real total production and real value added

Netherlands = 100

	1970	*1975*	*1980*	*1984*
A. *Total production*				
At international prices and national weights (FAO)[b]				
Japan	251	236	195	–
United States	1,765	1,725	1,557	–
At US prices and national weights (O–M)[c]				
Japan	–	212	–	–
United States	–	1,574	–	–
At Dutch prices				
Japan	–	196	164	173
United States	–	1,459	1,316	1,250
At Japanese prices				
Japan	–	280	234	238
United States	–	1,996	1,801	2,293
At approximate US prices				
Japan	–	202	178	126
United States	–	1,493	1,428	1,262
B. *Gross value added*				
At US prices and national weights (O–M)[c]				
Japan	–	185	–	–
United States	–	1,260	–	–
At Dutch prices				
Japan	–	143	50	74
United States	–	1,630	1,367	1,364
At Japanese prices				
Japan	–	332	243	227
United States	–	2,678	2,525	3,366
At approximate US prices				
Japan	–	143	54	[a]
United States	–	1,917	1,813	1,487
C. *Net value added*				
At Dutch prices				
Japan	–	79	[a]	[a]
United States	–	1,444	1,092	1,213
At Japanese prices				
Japan	–	302	203	195
United States	–	2,727	2,624	3,545
At approximate US prices				
Japan	–	24	[a]	[a]
United States	–	1,741	1,601	1,308

Sources b. FAO (1986: Tables 5.4 and 6.2); c. Van Ooststroom and Maddison (1985: Tables 1 (a) and 6). Other data are our calculations at Dutch, Japanese, and approximate US prices from Appendix Table C.6.

Notes a. net added in Japan negative, ratio cannot be compared.

low level for the Netherlands in the FAO and O–M studies. The estimates based on Japanese prices give a much more favourable picture for Japan and the US because of the high prices for rice and other grains. At Dutch prices real value of production of Dutch agriculture *vis-à-vis* Japanese agriculture is 8 to 10 per cent lower than at international prices, whereas at Japanese prices the opposite is the case with 28 to 31 per cent. In both cases the results are upwardly biased for the country whose prices are used. This is actually as expected. This shows the risk of using occasional national prices as a base for real comparison.

An interesting finding is that all estimates except those at Japanese prices, indicate a relative increase of Dutch real total production and gross and net value added.

The relatively high level of real total production in the US and Japan in the FAO study, and to a lesser extent in the O–M study as well, is affected by the magnitude of the under-count of values as found in Table 5.17. If this is taken into account, it appears that the differences in real total production between these studies and our estimates at Dutch weights are small. Apparently the Dutch price level and price structure correspond more closely to the international prices than those of Japan. In binary comparisons two results are always found if weighting systems of both countries are used. A weighted average of prices and real output of two countries is often preferred, but that is only justified if one is not interested in the rest of the world. A weighted average of Dutch and Japanese prices would most likely result in an upward bias in real output for Japan *vis-à-vis* its real output measured at international prices. This is strengthened because of the bigger weight of Japan. A weighted average of the US and Japan would be less affected because of the much bigger weight of the US.

A comparison of our gross value added estimates with the estimates of the FAO and O–M studies is hardly useful, because the data sources they used lack the necessary information on inputs required for proper revaluing of inputs. Our study shows that estimation and comparison of real gross value added is possible by use of detailed national data sources. It shows also the importance of comparing net value added, because of the relative importance of depreciation of purchased capital goods. Our preference for comparison of net value added is strengthened by the impression that there are considerable differences between countries with regard to capital consumption, distinction between current inputs and capital goods, and in norms for depreciation.

Finally, it should be noted that Table 5.19 shows a wide range of results in real comparisons on real total production. Differences in data sources, weights, and annual fluctuations in prices and quantities may have considerable effect on findings. Estimates of gross and net value added are even more sensitive since errors and statistical deviations in real total production may double and triple in real gross and net value added. Real estimates on output and productivity can be quite helpful for international economic analysis. Unfortunately, international data sources are not sufficient for this. Our findings show that detailed national data sources are required for reliable results.

National and international prices

Japan's negative value added estimates at Dutch and US prices for 1980 and 1984, seem to conflict with growth rates reported in national statistics and in the analysis of long-term growth as given by Yamada (1987a), and they therefore require an explanation. This contradiction can be explained as follows. Analyses of economic growth and productivity imply comparisons of quantities of inputs and outputs over time. This is always done at constant national prices and, consequently, results depend on the price bases used. The use of prices of another country could give strongly different results. At national prices value added in agriculture may show positive growth, whereas at international prices there may be stagnation or even negative growth. This can be illustrated with the example in Table 5.20, where at national prices net value added grows at 2 per cent, while at international prices growth is negative (–1.2 per cent). If output prices are more upwardly biased than input prices, which is common in countries with protectionist agricultural policies, the calculated real growth rates at national prices are usually higher than real growth at international prices. At national prices it may be profitable to use inputs which would not be economical at international prices. By this mechanism even real net value added and real productivity at international prices may become negative, as is found for Japan in 1980 and 1984.

Related to this is the difference between the nominal and effective rate of protection. The former is defined equal to the index for gross output minus 100, the latter is the implicit price index for value added minus 100. From Table 5.20 it can also be seen that the effective rate of protection is much higher than the nominal rate of protection.

In this respect the following observations can be made with regard to Japan's agricultural development. High rice price levels are nothing new to Japan.[11] Nevertheless before 1960 the nominal rates of protection and the shares of non-factor input in gross

Table 5.20 Example of real growth at national and international prices

	At constant national prices		*National*[a] *price level (index)*	*Constant international prices*	
	Year 0	*Year 1*		*Year 0*	*Year 1*
Gross ouput	100	105	200	50.0	52.5
Purchased inputs	50	54	150	33.3	36.0
Net value added	50	51	ca. 300[b]	16.7	16.5
Growth rate	+2%			−1.2%	

Notes The effective rate of protection is the implicit price index for value added minus 100. a. The international price level is assumed to be 100 for both years. b. The implicit price index for net value added is 300 in year 0 and 309 in year 1.

output were undoubtedly not high enough to allow for the possibility of negative real value added at international prices. The divergence between growth rates at national constant prices and international prices must have taken place after 1960, when real rice prices in Japan increased relatively to the international level and by which the use of inputs became much more attractive at local prices. This domestic price gap was further enlarged by investment subsidies, interest subsidies, and tax benefits. In particular the extensive mechanization, which took place on small farms during the past twenty-five years, would not have been economically viable at much lower product price levels.

Japan's case shows that if the focus of productivity studies is on the national prices only, it is not possible to evaluate the contribution of agriculture to the development of the national economy satisfactorily. At national price levels productivity in agriculture may seem comparable to that in other sectors, but measured at international prices there may be a considerable gap in productivity. This point is of particular relevance to Japan, where the levels of real productivity in manufacturing are close to that in other industrial countries, while real productivity in agriculture is far behind.

Growth rates and real comparison of agricultural production in Japan, the Netherlands and the USA

A real comparison for a particular benchmark year can be used not only for comparing productivity in that year, but, combined with growth rates, also for comparing trends in real output and productivities over time. As indicated above, real comparisons for

Table 5.21 Real comparison of production, input, gross value added of Japan, the Netherlands, and the USA (unit: billion yen; indexes)

Volume Ratios (%)

A. *Comparison at current prices*

	Japan/ Netherlands[a]		*Japan/ Netherlands*[b]		*Japan/ USA*[c]		*Netherlands/ USA*[c]	
	1975	*1984*	*1975*	*1984*	*1975*	*1984*	*1975*	*1984*
Total production	280	238	196	173	13.5	10.0	6.7	7.9
Current input	225	251	245	256	20.0	23.8	8.3	9.2

B. *Volume at national constant prices* (1975 = 100)

	Netherlands 1984	*Japan 1984*	*USA 1984*
Total production index	137	106	114
Current input index	118	124	124
Gross value added index	159	93	105

C. *Volume estimates for 1984 at constant price series of the other country via volume ratio* (1975 = 100)

	Netherlands 1984		*Japan 1984*	
	at Japanese 1975 prices	*at US 1972 prices*	*at Dutch 1975 prices*	*at US 1972 prices*
Total production index	125	135	120	84
Current input index	111	137	123	147
Gross value added index	137	130	115	–

Sources Data in part A ratios at Japanese and Dutch prices from Table 5.4 and for the data at US prices our calculation for this study and Appendix Table D.2; the volume indexes under B from the sources cited under Table 5.17.

Notes See also Van der Meer and Yamada (1988: 58, footnote 5). The constant price data for the Netherlands at Japanese prices in C were calculated by dividing Japanese constant price data at the 1975 price level by the volume ratios at Japanese prices in part A. The Japanese constant price data at Dutch prices in C were obtained by multiplying Dutch constant price data at the 1975 price level by the volume ratios at Dutch prices under A. The constant price data at national prices can be obtained by multiplying the current values for 1975 by the volume index.

Similarly Dutch and Japanese constant price series were obtained at US prices. For Taiwan no constant price series are available for 1982–4. The index at approximate weights of Taiwan and the US were not used because of the mixed character of the implicit deflators. Gross value added under C is obtained by deducting current input from total production. a. at Japanese current prices; b. Dutch current prices; c. US current prices.

different benchmark years may conflict with growth rates estimated from national accounts series.

In this section our real comparisons for different benchmark years are confronted with growth rates at national constant prices over the period between 1975 and 1984. For each benchmark year we have sets of volume ratios in Japanese and in Dutch prices of Japanese and Dutch production, inputs, and gross value added.

Further, we use volume series for both countries which are obtained directly from the sector accounts for agriculture. By dividing Japanese constant price estimates by the volume ratios at Japanese prices for the benchmark years, Dutch volume estimates are obtained through constant Japanese prices.[12] Thus, Dutch growth over the period 1975–84 calculated from constant price series at Japanese prices can be compared with the growth calculated from constant price series at Dutch prices. For Japan similar estimates of alternative constant price series, measured at Dutch prices, can be obtained by multiplying the Dutch volume series by volume ratios at Dutch prices. And, finally, growth in Japan and the Netherlands can be estimated at US prices also. The results of these comparisons are given in Table 5.21 and contain several interesting statistical inconsistencies.

First, it appears that growth of total production in Japan was more rapid if measured through Dutch prices (under C) than at Japanese prices (under B), but at US prices it declined. Dutch growth of total production through US or Japanese prices was slower than measured in the Dutch sector accounts. Total production growth at US prices was more rapid than at Japanese prices. Second, for Japan the alternative estimate of growth of volume of inputs at Dutch prices differs little from growth actually recorded in the national accounts, but at US prices there is a dramatic increase. Whereas use of Japanese prices results in a lower alternative growth estimate for inputs in the Netherlands, US prices also indicate a stronger increase for the Netherlands. Third, alternative gross value added estimates (calculated indirectly as total production minus input) also show major discrepancies. Gross value added in Japan measured at Dutch prices grew by 15 per cent whereas a decline of 7 per cent is recorded in the national accounts. However, at US prices the discrepancy in volume growth between total production and inputs results in negative gross value added at constant prices.

For the Netherlands growth of gross value added at national prices is 59 per cent, but lower at US and at Japanese prices (only 30 and 37 per cent). In the case of the US prices this is mainly caused by much higher growth of current input.

In Chapter Four we found that differences in price weights can have major effects on growth rates. The discrepancies in real comparisons and growth rates found in Table 5.21 also indicate important implications of the use of particular weights. The discrepancies in Table 5.21 can have two major sources. The first is that growth rates are much affected by differences in price structures used. A second is the sensitivity of the real comparison for differences in price and production structure in both countries, as evidenced by the differences in volume ratios measured at Japanese and Dutch prices. The magnitude of such differences depends on differences in the cost and output structure. Comparisons between countries with more similar productivity levels and structure, e.g. Belgium and the Netherlands, would most likely give much smaller statistical inconsistencies. Although much smaller in magnitude statistical errors can be the source of discrepancies as well. Finally, it is likely that estimates of the level of national account aggregates are less reliable than estimates of growth rates.

Conclusion

In this chapter we have made a detailed comparison of real output and productivity in agriculture in Japan and the Netherlands for 1975, 1980, and 1984. It appears that labour productivity (net value added per hour) at Japanese prices is about five to seven times higher in the Netherlands than in Japan, and that the difference has increased. At Dutch prices net value added in 1980 and 1984 is even negative. Further analysis for the sub-sectors' arable production, livestock, and horticulture shows that in terms of gross value added the productivity gap is biggest for arable production and smallest for horticulture. This supports the general belief that land scarcity and small farm-sizes are obstacles for achieving high productivity in Japan, but there must be other important factors as well. For horticulture, which is not very land intensive, gross value added per hour is four to seven times higher in the Netherlands and the gap has also been increasing over time. For livestock products, some of which are hardly using land, there are considerable gaps in productivity as well.

The comparison with Taiwan shows that Japanese agriculture has lost its technological leadership in Asia. The main reasons for this are the higher labour intensity and the excessive consumption of current inputs and capital in Japan. At US prices net value added in Japanese agriculture in 1980 and 1984 and gross value added in 1980 are negative.

Comparison of our findings with other studies shows that detailed comparison of real output and productivity requires the use of national data sources, because information available in international sources is not sufficient.

Finally this chapter shows that growth rates at constant national prices may differ considerably from growth rates at constant international prices. This is empirically illustrated by contradictions between the results of our real comparisons for Japan, the

Netherlands, and the USA for the period 1975–80 and the growth rates for these countries at constant national prices. The same mechanism can also be used to show how (net) value added at international prices for Japan's agriculture could become negative, despite positive growth rates at constant national prices. However, a full explanation of Japan's agricultural development process in which this occurred requires analysis of historical, political, and institutional factors. Such analysis is the aim of the next chapter.

Chapter six

The eclipse of Japanese agriculture

In previous chapters we established several criteria to assess productivity in contemporary Japanese agriculture. It appeared that in international perspective the level and growth rate of productivity has been lagging behind in recent decades. Here we sum up the main findings first. In Chapter Two it was shown that Japan is the only industrial country where labour productivity in agriculture grows slower than in industry. This is even the case in the period 1975–85 when labour productivity growth in industry slowed down considerably. In Chapter Three it appeared from an estimated inter-country functional relationship that Japan's agricultural labour productivity falls short of its predicted level. In real terms Japan's agricultural productivity is far behind other industrial countries and resembles more the level in Newly Industrializing Economies. An in-depth comparative analysis of agricultural development in Japan and the Netherlands in Chapter Four shows that productivity growth in Japan's agriculture in recent decades is comparatively poor and that the gap with the Netherlands increased. In the comparison in Chapter Five of real output and productivity in Japan, the Netherlands, Taiwan, and the USA, it was found that Japanese net value added at US and Dutch prices turns negative in 1980 and 1984, and that in 1980 at US prices even gross value added was negative. This means that from an international perspective Japan's agriculture provides a negative contribution to real national income. Sub-sectoral analysis showed that not only the arable crops sector, which includes rice, but also the livestock and horticultural sectors lag far behind the Dutch level and that the gap has increased since 1975. And last but not least, despite a much lower general level of economic development in Taiwan, agriculture in Taiwan has a higher real labour productivity than in Japan. At the same time indicators show that Japan's level of agricultural protection is among the highest in the world and much higher than that of most other industrial countries (FAO

1986: 26), even before the strong appreciation of the yen in the mid-1980s. This contrast of high prices and low productivity performance is consistent with our inverse U- shape hypothesis as explained in Chapter Two.

This chapter analyses reasons for Japan's poor performance. There are two major reasons. The first reason is the adverse effect on agriculture of the rapid industrial development during the past two decades; the second is the response to this situation by the government with a particular set of agricultural policies. Their supplemental effect on productivity has negatively affected Japan's agricultural performance. In this chapter, these two factors will be discussed first. Thereafter the political and institutional background, the dynamic effect of high prices, and technological and structural aspects will be discussed.

Rapid industrial growth

The rapid growth of productivity in Japanese industry in the post-war period, in particular from 1950 to 1973, is unique among industrial economies and has had a strong bearing upon agricultural development. In the 1950s there was still a backlog in agricultural and industrial productivities because of disruptions caused by the war. Consequently, in the recovery period productivity growth was high in both sectors. Since shortages of inputs disappeared in this period agricultural productivity could also increase rapidly, and the development of Japan's agriculture was still favourable. But as the backlog gradually disappeared in the 1950s productivity growth in agriculture slowed down and started to lag behind productivity growth in industry which grew rapidly at the same time. The growth rate of GDP per worker in industry for the period 1960–75 was 8.3 per cent compared to 4.8 in agriculture (Table 6.1).

This gap in labour productivity resulted in increasing pressure on agriculture. Income differences between agriculture and industry tended to increase, and young and enterprising people started to move from agricultural to industrial employment, because of better income prospects; labour in agriculture became scarce. This shift from a labour surplus situation, which was very pronounced after the war, to one of labour shortage took place rapidly, and consequently, wages for unskilled labourers increased rapidly as well. This is regarded as a turning point in Japanese economic development (Minami, 1973, see also Lewis, 1954). Because of the labour shortage, labour-intensive activities in agriculture with low (marginal) labour productivity were no longer attractive, and some

Table 6.1 Growth rates of GDP, employment, and productivity by sector in Japan, 1950–85 (%/year)

	Total	*Industry*	*Services*	*Agriculture*[a]	
				b	c
GDP					
1950–60	9.5	15.2	9.0	4.4	
1960–75	8.8	11.1	8.5	–0.1	
1975–85	4.7	5.1	4.7	0.1	
1950–85	7.8	10.5	7.5	1.2	
Employment					
1950–60	2.3	4.6	6.4	-1.9	-3.3
1950–75	1.0	2.6	2.6	–4.7	–4.3
1975–85	1.1	0.8	2.0	-2.7	–4.0
1950–85	1.4	2.6	3.5	-3.3	-3.9
GDP per worker					
1950–60	7.0	10.2	2.4	6.4	7.9
1960–75	7.7	8.3	5.8	4.8	4.4
1975–85	3.6	4.3	2.7	2.9	4.1
1950–85	6.3	7.7	3.9	4.7	5.4

Sources OECD, *National Accounts*, and *Labour Force Statistics*, and Ohkawa and Shinohara (1979). Data for agriculture from Yamada (1987a) and updates for 1982–5. Employment from the Statistical Bureau (1987).

Notes GDP at factor cost in 1975 prices. Agriculture does not include forestry and fishing; industry consists of mining, manufacturing, electricity etc., and construction; and services the remaining subsectors. a. based on three-year averages for gross value added and single year data for labour input; b. employment in number of workers; c. employment in number of hours worked.

disintensification took place. However, during the period 1960–75 the growth of gross value added per hour in agriculture was still 4.4 per cent per annum because employment in number of hours declined by 4.3 per cent per year. This implies that rapid industrial growth in this period affected agricultural productivity growth positively by absorbing surplus labour from agriculture. Perhaps it also contributed to productivity growth in agriculture by providing modern inputs. The high support price for rice probably already had negative effects in this period, but these were not yet dominant. However, the situation soon worsened. Industrial growth slowed down, although it was still considerable with an annual rate of 5.1 per cent. Agricultural GDP, however, hardly grew and productivity growth dropped to 4.1 per cent because the decline in agricultural employment had become slower. In fact after 1960 there was a sharp decline in comparative advantage for agriculture because the decline in agricultural employment was not rapid enough to compensate for the slow growth of GDP, while the reverse was the case in most other developed countries. Alternatively it can be said

Table 6.2 Changes in shares of agriculture, forestry, and fisheries in employment and in GDP for selected developed countries (%)

	Employment					*GDP*			
	Early year[a]		*1939*	*1960*	*1985*	*Early year*[a]	*1939*	*1960*	*1985*
Japan	75	(1885)	44	30	9	64	23	14	3
Netherlands	36	(1850)	17	10	5	13	7	6	6
Sweden	62	(1870)	29	16	5	39	13	8	4
Denmark	55	(1850)	29	16	7	27	12	9	6
Germany, FR	55	(1850)	27[b]	13	6	28	9[b]	4	3
France	53	(1856)	36[c]	22	8	23	14[c]	10	5
UK	27	(1861)	6[b]	5	3	8	3[b]	3	3
Italy		–	–	33	11	–	–	11	6
USA	49	(1889)	24	10	3	23	7	5	3
Australia	30	(1861)	20	12	6	11	13	8	6

Sources 1960 and 1985 data are basically from OECD; pre-war data are taken from various materials and linked to be continuous by country at 1975 prices. Detailed sources are given in Van der Meer (1983b).

Notes a. Early year for each country is shown in parentheses; b. 1938; c. 1936.

that, given the rate of decrease in agricultural employment, gross value added did not grow fast enough to keep agriculture competitive.

Structural transformation in post-war Japan was significant. The share of agriculture in total employment was almost half in 1950. It decreased to 30 per cent in 1960, but that level was still as high as the pre-war level of Western countries (Table 6.2). Subsequently, it declined further to 9 per cent in 1985. This change shows rapid social and structural transformation. However, Japan's decline in agricultural employment is not a record in the Western world. The decline of employment in agriculture, forestry, and fisheries in France, the Federal Republic of Germany and Italy in the period 1950–85 was as high or higher than in Japan (van der Meer 1988). Of course the shift in numbers was much more impressive in Japan than in other industrial countries, except Italy. In terms of the share of agriculture in GDP economic transformation in Japan was more rapid. It declined from 20 per cent in 1950 to only 3 per cent in 1985: Japan is now one of the countries in the world with the lowest share of agriculture in GDP. This clearly shows Japan's highly unbalanced post-war growth experience. The discrepancy between a 9 per cent share in employment and a 3 per cent share in GDP may not be considered as unbalanced from a national perspective because of the large share of part-time workers and the favourable level of farm household income. From an international perspective, however, it shows the need for a further significant decline in the

Table 6.3 Changes in basic characteristics of farm households in Japan, 1960, 1975, and 1987[a]

	1960	*1975*	*1987*
Farm households (1,000)			
Full-time	2,078 (34)	616 (12)	631 (15)
Part-time			
Mainly engaged in farming	2,036 (34)	1,259 (26)	632 (15)
Mainly engaged in other jobs	1,942 (32)	3,078 (62)	3,021 (70)
Total	6,057	4,953	4,284
Arable land (1,000 ha)	6,122	5,530	5,340
Land area per farm (ha)	1.01	1.12	1.25
Farms by size of area (1,000)			
Less than 1 ha	4,243 (70)	3,458 (70)	2,928 (68)
1–5 ha	1,754 (29)	1,429 (29)	1,276 (30)
Larger than 5 ha	60 (1)	66 (1)	80 (2)
Workers engaged in farming (1,000)			
Only in farming	13,096 (74)	6,498 (48)	5,619 (50)
Mainly in farming	1,446 (8)	1,334 (10)	558 (5)
Mainly in other jobs	3,114 (18)	5,778 (42)	5,171 (45)
Total	17,656	13,610	11,348
Farm household income (1,000 yen)[b]			
Farm income	225 (50)	1,146 (29)	1,012 (13)
Non-farm income	} 224 (50)	2,268 (57)	4,503 (64)
Grants, pension		546 (14)	1,485 (21)
Total	449	3,961	6,999

Source MAFF, *Statistical Yearbook*, various issues.
Notes a. Percentage shares are in parentheses; b. Data for 1987 is for 1986.

agricultural labour force. In other industrial countries there is also need for such structural adjustment, but it is less urgent than in Japan since the gap between shares in employment and GDP is much smaller. In most other industrial countries, except Italy, industrialization took a longer time and social transformation has proceeded more gradually. Japan caught up very rapidly in industrial productivity by utilizing its advantages as a late-comer, in particular by borrowing technology from earlier developed countries. The considerable gap resulting from unbalanced growth was one of the main factors leading to strong protection for agriculture. This actually had an adverse effect on agriculture's productivity performance, as we shall see later, and contributed to the impalance.

A major effect of Japan's rapid industrial growth and the spread of industrialization to most areas was that job opportunities increased almost everywhere. This permitted many farmers to become part-time farmers. It was enhanced by the development of mechanization of rice production, and stimulated by government policies, in particular the high price policy for rice. Due to various factors, including the negative effect of policies to be explained later, most farmers tended to keep their farm land and continued farming even though farming was no longer a necessary source of income for them. Even many full-time non-farm workers continue farming, in particular in rice cultivation. They or their family members can do this, for example, on Sundays, by using special machines for tiny paddy fields developed by Japanese manufacturers. Table 6.3 shows the dominant characteristics of part-time farmers in Japan. As will be argued later on the impact of the emergence of this large number of part-time farmers on productivity growth is strongly negative.

Post-war agricultural policies and growth of productivity

Agricultural policies in the post-war period, and in particular after 1960, developed partly in response to the effects of rapid industrial growth on agriculture. However, especially in the first decades after the war, agricultural policies were still much affected by the near-famine situation of the early post-war years and the loss of food supplies from the former colonies. Food production and food security were over-riding aims, and economic efficiency for agriculture, although not completely ignored as we shall see below, was definitely an issue of lower priority. Moreover, as we shall discuss later in this chapter, the political structure did not enhance a gradual shift in priority from food production to efficiency, but to farm income support. In retrospect it is useful to analyse on the one hand how the political structure set conditions for farm policies and how the political process generated them, and on the other what the probable effects were of these policies on agricultural development. The political aspects have been extensively discussed by Hayami (1988), Anderson, Hayami, and Honma (1986). Johnson, Hemmi, and Lardinois (1985) and Hillman and Rothenberg (1988) and will also be given attention in this chapter, but our main aim is to analyse the effects of policies on agricultural development with special emphasis on economic efficiency and productivity.

Since the gap in productivity between industry and agriculture was a major reason for designing the particular farm policies, an important counter-factual question is whether other policies could have achieved higher growth rates of productivity. A first question is whether productivity increases in agriculture and industry have the same limiting boundaries. In fact, rates of technological progress and rates of physical and human capital formation define the upper limit for productivity increases. Such an upper limit is probably higher in industry. Industrial technology can be imported and adjusted more easily than agricultural technology. The latter is more location-specific and requires more efforts to adapt it to local conditions. The organization of agriculture in small family farms with self-employed labour is in itself no obstacle for high productivity, as evidenced by the experiences of the Netherlands and other West European countries, but this does not mean that maximum growth rates are the same as for a sector based on large capitalist enterprises. The characteristic of agriculture, that demand for its output tends to grow slowly, implies that rapid growth of productivity requires reduction of production capacity, which, given the organization of agriculture in small family farms, may be more bound by social structure. There are in any case few examples in the world where labour productivity in agriculture grew at rates higher than 5 per cent for a long time and they are found among industrial countries, whereas there are several examples of prolonged labour productivity growth at rates of close to 10 per cent in industrial development.

Japan's agricultural policies

Johnson, Hemmi, and Lardinois (1985) rightly distinguish two groups of agricultural programmes: one originates in agrarian Japan and the other in modern Japan. The Staple Food Control Programme of 1942, the Land Reform Programme of 1946 and the Agricultural Co-operative Programme of 1948 belong to the former group, while programmes under the Basic Agricultural Act of 1961 belong to the second group. The first group stemmed from the severe food shortage experienced during and after the Second World War. When food shortages disappeared in the late 1950s adjustment to the conditions of rapid industrial growth became an important issue for agricultural policy. The 1961 Act intended to increase labour productivity by transforming the structure of the agricultural sector. This included adjustment of agricultural production to changing demand, reduction of the number of farms, and establishment of viable farms with sufficiently high productivity to provide incomes equal to that of urban workers.

Apparently agricultural policies swung between the first and second kinds of programmes, i.e. between the extremes of increasing food production (or food security) and increasing productivity (orienting production on comparative advantage). From 1960 to 1973 policies emphasized increased productivity, but with the so-called world food crisis in 1973 – especially the soybean export embargo in the USA – and the establishment of 200-mile fishing zones, the emphasis shifted towards increasing food production, which assumedly would improve food security (Johnson, Hemmi, and Lardinois 1985: 18–19). In the 1980s, however, over-production of grains became apparent in the world market again, and the policies gradually swung towards increasing productivity. One of the major themes of the 'Basic Guidelines of Government Policy in the 1980s is the adoption of the target of increasing Japanese agricultural productivity to the level of EC countries.

However, the government's swing towards improving productivity did not invoke a significant change in productivity improvement, in spite of the fact that it was fully recognized that the 1961 Act had failed. The reason for the failure originated in the political structure, to which we shall refer below. The government could not abolish, or even effectively reduce, the strongly negative effects of the supply oriented programmes on economic efficiency. The most influential policies, which have the most adverse effects, are the rice policies based upon the 1942 Staple Food Control Programme. The original purpose of the law during war-time has disappeared completely, but the law remains a legal framework for protection of rice production.

Rice policies

Among the various government policies in Japan rice policies have been most harmful for achieving productivity increases. The negative value added for rice at international prices indicates that rice is a crop for which comparative advantage is relatively low in Japan. But government support is very high, even much higher than necessary for maintaining self-sufficiency, and several policies have been designed to control surplus production. The high price level for rice forms a major reason for the inflated land prices, which in even the remotest areas are among the highest in the world. As a result specialization in products more profitable in real terms is jeopardized. Japan now has expensive policies by which rice land is kept under-utilized, while it is importing increased amounts of vegetables of which more could be grown in Japan if resources were reallocated. Since rice is particularly easy to grow by part-time farmers rice price policies form a main reason for this slow transformation of Japanese agriculture. If rice prices were reduced by half it would be much less attractive, if not infeasible, for many part-time farmers to continue growing rice, and many would give up farming. Even half the present price level is considerably higher than the rice price in most other countries and the rice price at which Japan would remain self-sufficient in rice. However, such a change in policy would have two important consequences. First, it would result in land price decreases by which other crops such as vegetables and fodder crops would become more profitable. Second, such a change would provide better opportunities to enlarge the scale of operations of more productive farmers.

Political structure and farmers' organizations

Hayami (1988) and many others have pointed at the strong political power of agricultural interests in the Japanese political system. In all the countries interest groups try to influence government policies to their advantage. This is often detrimental to the interest of other groups in society. It may even be detrimental to the economic development of the lobbying group itself if it prevents or delays necessary structural adjustment and stimulates inefficient production processes. Japanese agricultural interests form a typical example.

The origin of the present farm policies in Japan and the political power base of the rural sector is found in the organization of food production and the various institutional changes during and after the war. Farmers' organizations which the government designed and used for implementing policies became powerful organizations. Moreover, the rural votes weigh much heavier than urban votes because the adjustment of electoral districts lagged behind the changes in population distribution. The fact that the continuously ruling Liberal Democrat Party depends much on rural votes and funding from rural business interests has been an obstacle for adjusting the number and sizes of election districts, as well as for designing farm policies in which consumers' interests are given more weight.

In this particular political framework the farmers' organizations have among others, identified it as their interest to organize and represent as many people as possible. In practice this means that they do not favour policies that result in the reduction of the number of farm households, and they use conservative nationalist ideologies and agrarian fundamentalism for legitimation of their stand. The Ministry of Agriculture, Forestry, and Fisheries, which is highly dependent for its powerbase on the farmers' organizations, takes the same stand. It records, as 'farm households' all households engaged in agricultural production activities, even if the amount produced is insignificant, and as 'farm labour' all persons engaged in farm work, even if the number of hours spent is insignificant. Most importantly agricultural policies basically aim to preserve all farm households, regardless of whether they are engaged full-time or part-time in farming.

In the past co-operatives have played important roles in Japanese agricultural development. In this respect the situation seems similar to that in the Netherlands. After the Second World War, however, development of co-operative systems in both countries diverged very much. In Japan the agricultural co-operative system is favoured by the government with privileges, regulations, backing of marketing cartels, and in several cases even with monopoly rights. In addition the co-operative system is assigned to implement several government policies for which it receives funds from the central and prefectural governments. The co-operatives also provide many services to non-farm people, such as retail trade, credit, and insurance. In particular in rural areas these services tend to be dominated by the agricultural co-operative system. Activities not directly related to provision of inputs for farming or to marketing and sale processing for farm produce, form in many cases a major source of income for co-operatives.

Because of its size the Japanese co-operative system has major vested interests itself which may conflict with the interests of farmers, and especially with the interests of full-time farmers (Hayami 1988). In particular, institutional rents stemming from its privileged position may create such conflicts, but on the other hand, the distribution of these rents also forms an important basis for maintaining political power. Because of its many functions, its mass membership, its political affiliations, and the huge business and institutional resources it controls, the co-operative system is one of the major power groups in Japanese society. A politician who loses the favour of this group has a limited chance of re-election, certainly in rural districts (*Far Eastern Economic Review*, 17 November 1988).

The situation in the Netherlands represents a sharp contrast with Japan. The co-operatives in the Netherlands are not centralized, are largely single purpose, and are much less engaged in politics. They do not receive government funds, and have no privileges other than a small tax advantage. As a result of mergers, co-operatives have become big competitive enterprises which differ only slightly from private enterprises. Little in these reminds one of the former small village-based co-operatives in which community spirit was a major organizational force.

Two important questions emerge from the concentration of power of Japanese co-operatives and farmers' organizations. One is whether the co-operatives leave sufficient room for competition which is necessary for boosting efficiency and squeezing margins in agribusiness and services related to agriculture. The other is whether pre-occupation with serving such a wide spectrum of farmers is conducive for productivity increases in agriculture. We think both questions should be answered negatively.

The role of supporting services and industries for agriculture

Our comparisons in Chapter Five show much higher input prices in Japanese agriculture than in the Netherlands. Contrary to Japan's exporting manufacturing industries, the agribusiness industries in Japan have not been exposed much to foreign competition. Many of these industries were created after the Second World War. Several of them have a high natural rate of protection because of consumers' preference, or because they produce goods and services that are almost non-tradeables. Many of them started with protection from import substitution policies just as other manufacturing industries. Shinohara (1982) gives a positive evaluation of Japan's substitution policies. His main argument is that the support was only temporary and that later on these industries had to face competition in international markets. This may be true for the export industries, but generally not for the agribusiness industries. The latter industries often had the support of farmers' organizations which in many cases resulted in continued protection. Moreover, since protection is usually given for final products, the support given by farmers' organizations also enabled them to share in the protection which was actually intended for agriculture.

The high price level of agricultural inputs in Japan suggests low efficiency in these businesses. This was confirmed for the compound feed industry in our comparative research on the dairy industry (Van der Meer, Yamada, and Egaitsu 1987: 62). Tentative results of a comparative research on real productivity in manufacturing industries in Japan and the USA by Szirmai and Pilat (1989) give more general support to this. The study shows that in recent years food processing industries in Japan have relatively low real labour productivities compared to those in the United States, whereas exporting manufacturing industries have comparable or sometimes even higher real labour productivities than in the United States.

In transport and distribution the cost level depends much on the amounts handled and geographic concentration. In general there is a strong inter-relationship between productivity in agriculture and productivity in supporting agricultural industries and services. It is unlikely that agricultural industries and services can achieve a high productivity (from an international perspective) if their customers are large numbers of small-holders, thinly spread over a large area. On the other hand industries and services based on big and specialized farms, concentrated in a certain area, can achieve high productivity by economies of scale in handling and transportation. Efficient suppliers of farm inputs will enhance farm development by promoting specialization of farms.

For a co-operative, organized and operating in a traditional way, it is usually difficult to support specialization by offering smaller margins for big farms as it may upset the equality ideal of the traditional co-operative movement. In a competitive marketing situation, however, co-operatives are forced to do so because they would otherwise lose their best customers. In Japan such dangers are not so great. The land reform after the war eliminated bigger farms, and created a large number of small homogeneous farms. Moreover, the near monopolist or oligopolist power of agricultural co-operatives backed up by political influence makes it very difficult for outsiders to under-cut the market position of the co-operatives. Since the co-operatives have the aim of keeping as many families in farming as possible they use their power to fight against the private companies that try to serve big farms. In most other developed countries economies of scale in farm production, which form an important engine for specialization and increase in farm-size, are to a significant degree supported by differences in efficiency in marketing. But in Japan the co-operative system has tried to offset the effects of economies of scale in marketing by implicitly subsidizing marketing cost for sub-marginal farmers at the expense of more efficient farmers. Only in intensive livestock production is the co-operative monopolist position challenged seriously by private companies, who provide not only feed but also breeding stock, animals for production, sales contracts, and credit. By this, farmers become independent from co-operatives, but dependent on private agribusiness. In this sub-sector co-operatives seem to be losing ground.

Compared to the case in the Netherlands, the specializing farmer in Japan receives in general less benefit and incentive from his input suppliers, because of the inefficiency of his suppliers, and often he meets institutional obstacles for rationalization maintained by the suppliers. As a result, a Japanese farmer pays a higher margin for the services and products he buys than his Dutch colleague. The inefficiency and low productivity of the suppliers is in turn to a large extent caused by the fact that the Japanese farmers have such small farms, which are geographically not efficiently concentrated.

Part-time farming

Other farm policies in Japan are also responsible for retarding specialization and farm-size increases. The high price levels allow even very inefficient farmers to stay in business, and several other policies have been conducive for the emergence of part-time farming. The tax system penalizes farmers who sell their land. Land rent control by law was recently abolished in order to promote the policy of small farmers renting out their land to bigger farms. This policy can still only be put into effect through administrative guidance, however. It should be noted here also that the scattered pattern of land holding forms an obstacle for increasing farm sizes and achieving economies of scale. It is also impractical for bigger farmers to rent a significant amount of land, because of the considerable contract cost in dealing with many small land owners. Even if a considerable area was rented from small-holders, economies of scale remain small without land consolidation. this means that considerable increase of farm sizes through rental contracts as advocated by Hayami (1988) is difficult to achieve in the short run.

Prospects for considerable farm-size increases by purchase are also dim. Agricultural price support and land policies have pushed up land prices continuously. Most Japanese are convinced that it is wise to keep assets, not only because they give protection against possible inflation, but also because interest rates on savings are low, and sale of land and termination of farming is subject to a huge tax payment. On the other hand part-time farming in Japan is supported by investment subsidies.

In the Netherlands investment subsidies are of much less importance than in Japan, and most significantly, only provided to so-called viable farms. Part-time farming has never received significant support. In the early post-war period when cost of production calculations were partly used as a base for farm price policies, these calculations did not cover small sub-marginal farms. Instead there have for a long time been considerable retirement subsidies for small farmers in the Netherlands with the explicit condition that they have to sell their land to other farmers or to an intermediate government agency which takes care of reallocation of the assets for the purpose of farm-size enlargement. Such policy measures could have had a significant effect on the pace of structural change in Japan, but instead Japan subsidized its small farmers.

In Japan part-time farming forms an attractive opportunity to supplement the income of families who have their main sources of income outside agriculture. The government gives equal support to part-time and full-time farmers. Part-time farming can give significant additional tax benefits, even to people whose income is largely obtained from non-agricultural sources. Part-time farmers are politically powerful, even though they depend mainly on non-agricultural income. They consider government support for their additional income as a kind of social benefit, and are easily mobilized to rally against any plan that may reduce their benefits. But they are likely to have little direct interest in policies that boost productivities or favour structural adjustment. Therefore, part-time farmers who are organized by the powerful co-operative system, form an obstacle for restructuring of the farm sector, resource allocation, and productivity growth.

In the Netherlands part-time farming is not seen as desirable and therefore not supported. Full-time farmers are considered more dedicated and dynamic than part-time farmers and more sensitive to the long-term effects of policies and the dangers of 'over-production'. Mainly for these reasons agricultural policies in the Netherlands always focused primarily on full-time farms that can provide adequate income to a farm family. Germany, on the other hand, forms an example of a country where, similar to Japan, part-time farming is widespread and government-supported. It is most prevalent in backward areas with structural problems. Therefore it may have merit in terms of social considerations, but it is hard to advocate on economic grounds.

Excessive use of inputs

In previous chapters we referred to increasingly excessive use of inputs in Japanese agriculture. Here we shall discuss the mechanism by which this occurred because it is crucial for understanding the development of Japan's post-war agriculture. This mechanism helps to explain the inverse U-shaped relationship between the price level and productivity growth discussed and tested in Chapters Two and Three. For this first the net factor productivity ratios at constant prices in periods 0 and 1 should be considered:

$$\frac{TP_0 - NFI_0}{FI_0} \text{ (1) in period 0 and } \frac{TP_1 - NFI_1}{FI_1} \text{ (2) in period 1.}$$

Productivity growth is represented by (2)–(1) / (1) and can be the result of changes in volume of total production *TP*, non factor input *NFI* and factor input *FI*. It can be shown that at a given level of technology and prices (i.e. a given production function) the productivity ratio reaches a maximum at the point on the production function where income maximization is achieved.[1] Therefore price distortion will negatively affect real productivity (measured at international prices) unless the input/output price ratio is constant. The measurement of productivity growth, which may encounter a basic statistical problem because of changes in price weights for each of the aggregates between period (1) and (2), is ignored for a while. It is not our first concern here.

First, it should be pointed out that in practice the ratio will not be optimal with regard to market prices. In fact there may be a considerable spread among farms. Many farms (or all of them) may not realize the maximum because of institutional obstacles for achieving optimal allocation. These obstacles may be found in the tax system, in legislation, and in the social and economic environment. Of great practical importance for agriculture is that subjective valuation often results in shadow prices quite different from market prices, and that consequently the subjective optimum for the farm differs from the normative optimum at market prices (Ellis 1988; Johnson and Quance 1972).

Of primary interest for analysis are changes in the numerator (factor input) and the denumerator (net value added). We shall look at factor input first. Land input contributes little to changes in factor input because it is usually rather stable and its share in factor input is small. In developed countries labour is the most important factor input in agriculture. The volume of farm labour may decline because of reallocation to other sectors. Most labour in agriculture is self-employed family labour, supply and demand of which differs considerably from supply and demand for paid labour. The rate of reallocation of farm family labour depends much on relative labour income expectations in agriculture and other sectors. This means that agricultural productivity is affected by employment opportunities in other sectors. This is obvious from the experiences in industrial economies after 1973. Because growth rates of employment in non-farm sectors declined the pace of reallocation of agricultural labour also declined and growth of labour productivity in agriculture was negatively affected (Van der Meer 1988). Usually the effect of a decline in labour input on the volume of factor input is partly offset by an increase in capital cost, stemming from investment by which the remaining labour in agriculture increases its working capacity.

Investment in agriculture depends largely on (subjective) private profitability expectations and can be affected by various forms of investment subsidies and taxation. Partly it may also be carried out by government, as in the case of land consolidation. Investment in agriculture need not reduce labour input by way of substitution. For a good understanding at this point a distinction should be made between labour input in terms of number of farm workers available for work regardless of their working hours, and labour input in terms of hours actually worked. In particular the number of self-employed family workers is not necessarily affected directly by investment. Investment may just reduce the burden of work or increase the profitability of farming, while marginal productivity of labour input in hours may decline. In principle part-time farming may be enhanced by investment subsidies and keep people in agriculture. These subsidies may improve profitability and productivity of the first hours of labour input, while decreasing the marginal profitability and productivity per hour. As a result part of the available hours of family labour may in fact be set free for off-farm employment and total family income may increase.

Investment usually not only affects the amount of factor input but also the amount of non-factor input and, hence, net value added. Investment cost consists of interest cost, which is part of factor cost, and depreciation, which is non-factor cost. But there is also associated cost of operation, such as cost of fuel and maintenance. In developed countries investment in machines usually has little effect on total production and net value added in constant prices may decline as a result of increased profitability of investment. Consequently, government investment support may result in a decline of net value added in real terms, while enhancing part-time farming. On balance the effect on the productivity ratio may be negative if labour input does not decline fast enough to compensate for the effects of increased capital cost and non-factor input on the ratio.

So far the analysis assumes that the product price level does not change. Changes in relative prices can have a strong effect on the measurement of productivity changes. Higher product prices will increase the profitability of investment and input use. Labour may be kept in agriculture far beyond its presumed employment level at lower price levels because high product prices offset the push factor. Current input and investment are also likely to be used more than at lower price levels. From the constant price perspective of period 0 this will lead to a relative decrease in productivity, because productivity reaches a maximum at the point of income maximization on the production function, and this is no longer the same point as for the price conditions of the base period. From a later perspective, i.e. the price conditions of period *t*, productivity is likely to have increased, as did income. A long period of product price increases may therefore result in declining productivity from an earlier Laspeyres point of view (weights of the early period), and in increasing productivity from a later Laspeyres point of view (weights of the later period). Chain-linked series will show an in-between result. The mechanism described here can also show why in a country like Japan with high and increasing product price levels a growth of real value added can be recorded because growth is measured at high domestic constant prices, whereas a decline may be recorded from the perspective of other countries with low or decreasing price levels.

Japan's experience over the past decades with excessive growth of inputs can be well understood by this mechanism. Yamada (1987a) showed that growth of net value added measured at 1955 prices (1955 prices were still close to international price levels) was much slower than measured at 1975 prices. In the previous chapter this was further analysed in comparison with the Netherlands. It appeared that after 1960 investment in Japan increased more rapidly than in the Netherlands, and in recent decades the use of capital contrasts poorly with the Netherlands. The level of investment in Japanese agriculture can be further analysed in comparison with other Western countries.

Over-investment in Japanese agriculture

Gross fixed capital formation in agriculture, expressed as a percentage of value of production at current prices, has increased rapidly in Japan (Table 6.4); until 1960 it was comparable to levels in Europe,

Table 6.4 Gross fixed capital formation as a percentage of total production

	Total production at current prices						*Total production at international prices*[a]		
	1950	*1960*	*1970*	*1975*	*1980*	*1985*	*1970*	*1975*	*1980*
Japan	5.3[b]	11.4	22.1	25.6	32.4	28.4	44.7	65.0	95.9
Netherlands	4.8	4.2	8.7	8.7	13.2	9.5	9.7	11.7	18.5
Denmark	NA	NA	8.9	15.1	14.0	8.9	8.6	19.0	19.2
France	5.6	8.0	10.2	12.5	11.6	9.7	11.7	19.5	17.4
Germany FR	7.8	17.4	16.5	14.2	16.1	15.5	20.3	20.9	25.0
Italy	10.1	17.8	13.2	14.6	16.2	16.0	17.8	19.9	24.6
UK	NA	NA	8.9	11.0	10.9	7.2	9.2	13.2	15.3
EC-6	7.2	12.5	12.3	12.8	14.0	12.6	15.0	18.6	21.0
EC-9	NA	NA	NA	12.6	13.6	11.7	NA	17.6	20.0
USA	11.5	8.7	12.6	12.9	13.4	9.2	12.6	12.9	13.4

Sources FAO (1986: 26); Eurostat, *Sector Accounts Agriculture - Forestry 1987*, and previous issues; US Department of Commerce, *Survey of Current Business*, July 1987 and previous issues; MAFF (1987) *Social Accounts for Agriculture and Farm Households*.

Notes Data for EC countries are obtained from our own calculations after linking total production and gross fixed capital formation series. EC-6 was established in 1958, consisted of Belgium, France, Germany FR, Italy, Luxemburg, and the Netherlands. EC-9 was formed in 1973 and comprised EC-6, Denmark, Ireland and the UK. a. percentages at current prices multiplied by each country's relative price index for total production calculated by the FAO (1986: 26); b. data for 1952; NA = not available.

but over the past decade it was twice as high as in the EC. This percentage, however, is not a good indicator of the real gross fixed investment/output ratio among countries. It is downwardly biased in countries with high product price support. For the years 1970, 1975, and 1980 gross fixed capital formation can also be expressed as a percentage of total production at international prices calculated by the FAO (1986). This percentage may be upwardly biased in so far as price levels for investment are higher than in other countries, but differences in price levels for investments are likely to be much smaller than differences in price levels for agricultural products. This is confirmed by the inter-country deflators for capital goods (depreciation) estimated in the previous chapter. In any case the result in Table 6.4, though perhaps somewhat upwardly biased, shows a dramatic high level of real investment, increasing from 45 per cent in 1970 to 96 per cent in 1980. This means that at international price levels the total value of production is hardly sufficient to generate this level of gross fixed investment. This finding is in agreement with the high level of depreciation for the agricultural sector as a whole and for rice production in particular found in the previous chapter. Obviously there is a considerable waste of capital goods, induced by high output prices and generous investment support. We conclude therefore, that increasingly excessive use of capital goods and current inputs is a first and major factor explaining Japan's poor agricultural performance.

Technology and its effect on productivity

Technology is the major factor explaining productivity. The best technologies determine the maximum productivity that could be obtained at the so-called technological frontier.[2] However, there are always gaps between maximum productivity, the productivity of the farms using the best practice, and the productivity of the average farms, and the productivity of poorly performing farms. Many factors may be responsible for a backlog in actual productivity. Such factors can be too small farm sizes, fragmented landholdings, government policies, lack of necessary inputs during war periods, financial obstacles for adequate investment, obstacles in legislation, lack of experience of workers, and failing dissemination of knowledge among potential users of new technology. Several of these factors have been discussed in the previous section and some will be discussed later, but first attention will be given to the distinction of land-saving and labour-saving technologies and the factors that effect their relative level in Japan and other developed countries.

Table 6.5 Government expenditure on research and development (R & D) in agriculture, forestry, and fisheries, 1979

	Total government R&D expenditure (mill. $[a])	*Per hectare[b] ($[a])*	*Per worker ($[a])*	*Per capita ($[a])*	*In % of gross value added at current prices[c]*	*In % of real final output[b] in international dollars[d]*
Japan	551	100.66	90	4.8	1.30	3.64
Netherlands	90	42.25	321	6.4	1.71	1.00
Denmark	20	6.86	94	3.9	0.69	0.50
France	189	5.94	101	3.5	0.78	0.64
Germany FR	115	8.79	74	1.9	0.68	0.60
Italy	56	3.13	19	1.0	0.25	0.26
UK	201	16.72	307	3.6	2.43	1.54
EC-6	467	6.40	69	2.4	0.67	0.56
EC-9	716	7.66	91	2.8	0.85	0.75
USA	663	1.59	189	2.9	0.90	0.57

Sources OECD, (1984: 87, 166, 229); OECD, *Labour Force Statistics 1969–1980;* OECD, *National Accounts Statistics 1972–1984*; Real final output from the FAO (1986), but adjusted for under-counting by Van der Meer and Yamada (1988: 51). Land from sources used in Appendix B.

Notes a. Government expenditure expressed in the OECD's International dollars (obtained from ICP method). b. R&D expenditure per hectare and R&D expenditure as a percentage of final output are upwardly biased because they include expenditure for forestry and fisheries. c. Gross value added at current prices for 1979. d. Real final output 1980 expressed in per cent of the FAO's International dollars for agriculture (farm sector only).

Government policies to promote technology

In the nineteenth century Japan's agriculture was characterized by relatively scarce land, high land prices, and abundant cheap labour. Such conditions were conducive to the development of land-saving technologies (Hayami and Ruttan 1985). These technologies, which can also be referred to as biological technologies, could be partly borrowed from Europe but adjusted and further developed for local ecological situations and consumer preferences. Since the nineteenth century, Japanese governments have promoted the development of such technologies considerably and successfully, and since the natural environment, irrigation, other infrastructure, the input/output price relations, and the economic environment were relatively favourable, Japan's agriculture developed itself as the technological leader in Asia (Hayami *et al.* 1975).

After the Second World War the Japanese government continued its supportive role in land-augmenting investment and in research. In a comparative survey of 1979 (OECD, 1984) it appeared that Japan's expenditure on research and development (R&D) for agriculture (including forestry and fishery) was very high compared to other countries. It was even more than in the EC–6 countries together, 83 per cent of the expenditure of the USA, and 77 per cent of the EC–9 (Table 6.5). Per head of population it was second after the Netherlands, but considerably higher than in other EC countries and in the USA. Per worker, government expenditure is comparable with the EC, but it is affected by the higher share of employment in agriculture (including forestry and fisheries) in Japan which can partly be attributed to the fact that employment in Japan includes large numbers of part-time workers. On an hourly base it is probably much higher in Japan. Japan has a very high R&D expenditure per hectare. It spends per hectare more than twice as much as the Netherlands, the second ranking country, about fifteen times more than the EC–9 and sixty times more than the USA.

Expressed as a percentage of gross value added Japan's expenditure on R&D is third after the Netherlands and the UK, and clearly higher than in the EC and the USA. However, since Japan's gross value added is much inflated because of high price support for farm products this percentage underestimates expenditure as a percentage of real production. For comparison, expenditure on R&D is also expressed as a percentage of real final output in international dollars. This may overestimate Japan's percentage somewhat because forestry and fishery is included in R&D expenditure but not in real final output, though the bias is not likely to be of great importance. The result shows that relative to the size of its agriculture as indicated by real final output Japan is spending by far the most of these OECD countries.

Given Japan's lasting efforts to boost biological technology and land productivity and its general quality of research it is no surprise that in this field differences with other developed countries are of minor importance. This can be observed by comparing crop yields with other countries, in so far as differences in input/output price ratios or in growing conditions are not reasons for major differences in yields. Our comparative research for the livestock sector showed that milk yield per cow and non factor input per 100 kg of milk is not much different from the Netherlands. Japan's feed efficiencies for pigs and poultry are also close to Dutch standards. Even though there is probably still a small gap, its bridging cannot have much effect on the differences in labour productivity and in total factor productivity. Therefore, low land productivity, low biological efficiency and lack of related technological knowledge are not major factors explaining the poor performance of Japan's agriculture, but low efficiency in labour use is a major factor.

Labour saving technology and unique aspects of Japanese mechanization

In recent decades Japan has become one of the most advanced countries in the world in engineering. It is producing and exporting many types of machines, transport equipment, and even agricultural machinery. Japan has also developed many kinds of labour-saving equipment for agriculture. Given the widespread availability of labour-saving equipment and machinery in Japan one wonders whether there can be a gap in basic labour-saving technology in agriculture between Japan and the advanced Western countries. During our comparison of prices of inputs in Japan and the Netherlands and in particular of capital goods, of which the results were presented in Chapter Five, several interesting differences were observed between both countries.

The basic problem in comparing prices of agricultural machinery and tractors in both countries is that there are huge differences in sizes and qualities of machines and tractors. Very little of the kind of machinery used in Japanese agriculture is also used in Dutch agriculture because it is basically inefficient in labour use under Dutch conditions. On regular dairy and arable farms in the Netherlands no Japanese tractor is used at all. Although the engineering and technical characteristics of Japanese tractors are among the best in the small-size classes, the use of tractors of these sizes is nowadays limited even in Dutch horticulture where the acreages are small.[3] Horticulturists do most of their work with bigger tractors (about 40 HP) and small-sized Japanese or Italian two-wheel and four-wheel tractors are used only for very small areas (e.g. seedbeds) or special jobs. The small Japanese four-wheel tractors are said to be no cheaper than Italian tractors (rather more expensive), but less noisy. There is considerable import of these Japanese tractors in the Netherlands, but there are mainly used for maintenance of public parks, lawns, and road borders, and also for experimental stations.

In general the capital value of tractors in Dutch horticulture is relatively small, and that of small two-wheel tractors is almost negligible, compared to all kinds of specialized machinery for soil preparation, climate control, transport systems, crop harvesters, and machines for product handling. Many types of these special machines have been developed jointly by horticulturists and specialized construction firms in the Netherlands. There is even an important export of such machinery which indicates that unit prices of such machinery in the Netherlands are low compared to other countries.

The latter point indicates a general feature of agricultural mechanization. Agricultural machinery is usually developed jointly by farmers and small construction firms. If new designs are successful they are copied by bigger construction companies for larger scale production. Then it depends on the quality of mechanical engineering, cost levels, and on the applicability in other countries whether such companies can export machinery. The best machinery is usually produced in areas with advanced agriculture and advanced mechanical engineering.

It is not surprising that Japan has an advanced position in small-scale mechanization for rice farming. Its rice agriculture and mechanical engineering are both technically advanced. Yet its small scale mechanization is in many cases not suitable abroad: for developing countries it is usually too sophisticated and too expensive, and for industrial countries it is not suitable because it is designed for farms too small and too labour-intensive to be economical. Outside rice agriculture some components, such as small tractors with related equipment, may be applicable to some extent, for example, in horticulture in Western countries.

Agricultural mechanization in the USA and Western Europe is basically designed for specific features of agriculture in these areas. The quality of farm machinery from a user's point of view depends on the embodied agricultural technology and the engineering skills in these countries, and has to be assessed in relation to the farm sizes for which it is designed. In the past, there were considerable differences between farm mechanization in the USA and West European countries. As labour intensity – the amount of labour per unit of output – in European agriculture has come closer to the American level, the differences in European and American types of mechanization have become smaller. Most of the machinery developed in these countries cannot be applied profitably on small Japanese farms. The machines and tractors are too big, too sophisticated, and too expensive for these farms. Bigger farms, mainly found on Hokkaido, make extensive use of imported machinery.

Japanese manufacturers have started to copy such machinery. They have sufficiently high engineering skills to do so, but they also have several set-backs. First of all they do not have a highly developed agriculture in which advanced equipment can be developed and tested. Consequently, so far the quality of Japanese large-scale mechanization is said to be behind the quality of imported large-scale machinery. Second, the Japanese market for large-scale farm machinery is limited, and this forms a set-back for low-cost production and distribution systems. Finally, the recent appreciation of the yen versus the US dollar and European currencies has reduced the competitiveness of the Japanese agricultural machinery industry.

An important question is how to evaluate the quality of Japanese farm machinery. From an engineering point of view the quality is good and prices reasonable, but from a farm economic point of view these machines are not suited to realize high labour productivity. Under Dutch prices farms could not survive with such labour intensive technologies. In Japan they can because of higher farm product prices. Without these high prices, such labour-intensive farms and related equipment would also rapidly disappear in Japan, and induce production of more labour-saving farm mechanization. There is no doubt that the trend in Japan is in the same direction as in the other developed countries, but the gap in labour intensity is still enormous. So from the point of view of labour-scarce high-productive agriculture Japanese machinery is of a 'low quality', whereas it is of 'high quality' from a manufacturer's and engineering point of view.

Lagging adjustment to new economic conditions and labour efficiency

Labour intensity in Japanese agriculture cannot be explained by lack of basic knowledge on labour-saving machines, equipment, and construction. This, however, does not mean that Japanese farm workers have similar knowledge of such capital goods, their use, and related labour-saving production methods as have their colleagues in Western countries. The average qualification of Japanese farm workers with respect to these matters may be relatively low. The farm work-force consists of a considerable share of part-time workers who do not specialize in agriculture, and older people and women with low formal education. Moreover, production systems have to be developed in joint practice with qualified workers who operate or supervise them.

In Japan there are some livestock and horticultural farms with the most modern capital goods, sometimes directly imported or copied from systems in use in North America or Europe. But a contrasting feature of these capital goods, apart from the fact that their prices are usually much higher, is that they are usually operated by much more labour than for example in the Netherlands. A dairy farmer in Hokkaido who had extensively invested in modern equipment and buildings and had visited modern farms in Europe gave as his opinion, when we visited him in 1986, that the farm lay-out of these European farms was more labour efficient.

This is most likely related to lack of knowledge because of less experience, not only on the part of farm workers but also on the part of construction companies. This lack of experience is also related to the fact that lower wage rates in the past did not induce such an intensive search and interest among farmers, researchers, and makers of capital goods for labour-saving techniques as in Western countries. The actual situation is lagging in view of rapidly changed circumstances. But, nowadays, even after considerable wage increases and currency appreciations, wage rates for farm labour are still much lower than in the Netherlands, which also helps to explain lower labour efficiency and lack of knowledge about labour-saving production techniques.

Farm size and land fragmentation

The reasoning so far has ignored the fact that in many cases farm sizes and fragmentation of landholding do not necessarily form a major bottleneck for the introduction of labour-saving techniques. This is certainly a very important obstacle for most farms. But it would be wrong to generalize. For a growing part of agricultural output in Japan land is not the major bottleneck for achieving economies of scale. In horticulture and in the intensive livestock sector, including dairy farming based on purchased fodder, relatively little land is required for introducing labour-saving techniques, and farm size in hectares is therefore hardly a bottleneck for achieving high labour productivity. Obstacles for creating farms of sufficient sizes in these sectors are at least relatively small compared to rice farming. In 1986 horticultural farms in the Netherlands had on average only 2.5 hectares of horticultural crops, and intensive livestock farms 4 hectares, while land on these farms is in many cases not directly related to intensive livestock production.[4] Yet it was found in our comparison between Japan and the Netherlands that labour intensity in Japan in these subsectors was also three to seven times higher than in the Netherlands. Here is obviously a backlog of labour-saving technology which is hardly caused by acreage constraints, but rather by a lack of structural adjustment.

For land-intensive production – rice, field crops, and pasture-based livestock raising – small sizes and fragmentation of landholding form a serious obstacle to the introduction of labour-saving production methods. Despite significant over-investment in labour-saving equipment, Japanese farmers produced little more than 10 kg paddy per hour in the early 1980s in contrast to US farmers who produced about 500 kg.[5] In wheat production a Japanese farmer produces about 27 kg per hour compared to nearly 400 kg produced by an American farmer.[6] For the Netherlands comparable data are not readily available. The last annual cost of production calculation for wheat was published in 1962. This showed a gross labour productivity of 31 kg per hour, which was already more than for Japan twenty years later. Our rough calculations suggest that it increased to about 300 kg per hour in 1988.

Need for structural changes

These huge gaps between Japan on the one hand and the USA and the Netherlands on the other cannot be narrowed to a significant degree without increasing farm and field sizes in Japan tenfold. Japan has achieved almost a six-fold increase of labour productivity of rice production in the period since 1950, and nearly a twenty-fold increase in production of wheat, but the price is very expensive by any international standard.[7] It could only develop because of high support prices and it depends on continuous high levels of support. Introduction of production systems with significantly higher real productivity implies considerable cost reduction, and is impossible without important structural changes. The use of more fertilizer, or more productive animals and crop varieties is not so dependent on structural change. With respect to such biological technologies there is in general, as argued before, not so much difference between Japan and Europe. But declining margins can usually only be offset by introducing production systems on much larger scales. These systems are based on lumpy investments, and only feasible if significant structural changes are taking place simultaneously.

Farm size and economies of scale

Why is enlargement of farms so slow in Japan? Many people seem to think that land scarcity and unfavourable topography limit farm sizes. This may be the case in some areas, but there are many areas in Japan where there is no significant physical obstacle for a considerable enlargement of fields and farms. The question therefore is why scale-sensitive activities are not concentrated in such areas and why such increases in scale do not occur, while leaving areas with more constraints to activities that are less sensitive to economies of scale.

Hayami (1988:96) argues on the basis of cost of production reports that during the first decades after the war economies of scale were of little importance to Japan, but that they have increased since the late 1960s. The facts are correct, but they may blur some other aspects of importance. The post-war land reform has considerably reduced the possible emergence of economies of scale. The question whether a 3 hectare grain farm has more economies of scale than a 0.3 hectare farm is hardly relevant because of scattered land-holdings on the one hand and because these sizes are so small if compared to the scale of production in other industrial countries. From an international point of view the range of farm sizes over which economies of scale are of real importance is not included in the comparison. The real potential of large-scale production has never served as a policy target for established viable farms when labour became expensive and the need for labour-saving techniques apparent. Moreover, several policies have in fact mitigated emerging economies of scale even over the actual range of farm sizes. At lower price levels income differences between small and larger farmers would be more pronounced because of lower cost of land and different opportunities among farms to reduce costs. Also the nearly monopolist/oligopolist position of co-operatives has reduced opportunities for bigger farmers to obtain economies of size from their potentially better market efficiency.

Slow structural transformation

Slow structural transformation is a cause as well as a result of a lack of economies of scale. This can be shown as follows. If few farmers are willing to give up their land, others cannot enlarge the size of their operation and the increase of economies of scale is delayed, or, perhaps more precisely, the range of farm sizes over which economies of scale can emerge remains limited. If, on the other hand, economies of scale are strong, then bigger farmers can buy assets from sub-marginal farmers at prices sufficiently attractive for the latter to give up farming. (Provided that the tax system does not form a major obstacle.) For the smaller farmers there is a choice between giving up farming and concentrating fully on non-agricultural income earning, or becoming part-time farmers. In Japan many small farmers opted for part-time farming. We have already discussed reasons for the emergence of part-time farming, and implications for agricultural development. Here we shall investigate whether structural transformation in Japanese agriculture is slow or rapid.

Table 6.6 shows that the number of farms declined slowly from 1955 in Japan. Although agricultural production in the Netherlands grew very rapidly, the number of farms declined from 1955

Table 6.6 Changes in farm structure in Japan and the Netherlands, 1955–87

	Number of farms (thousand)		*Area per farm (hectares)*		*Labour input (million hours)*	
	Japan	*Netherlands*	*Japan*	*Netherlands*	*Japan*	*Netherlands*
1955	6,043	261[a]	0.99	8.9	25,610	1,524
1975	4,953	163	1.12	13.3	10,439	674
1987	4,284	132	1.25	15.7	7,697[b]	558[b]
growth rate (%)						
1955–75	–1.0	–2.3	0.6	2.0	–4.0	–4.0
1975–87	–1.2	–1.7	0.9	1.4	–3.3[b]	–2.1[b]

Sources Farms: Netherlands from LEI/CBS (*Agricultural Statistics* 1988: 20; 1971: 33; 1960: 54), and Japan from MAFF, *Yearbook 1986/87* and Statistical Bureau, *Japan Statistical Yearbook 1984*. Land: Japan from Yamada (1987a) and data for 1987 projected from MAFF, *Agricultural Statistical Yearbook 1986/87*: 56, and for the Netherlands from Van der Meer (1986) extended with LEI/CBS (*Agricultural Statistics* 1987: 20). Labour: Japan from Yamada (1987a) and extended on the basis of MAFF, *Farm Household Economic Survey*, and Netherlands from Van der Meer (1987a).

Notes a. Published data before 1970 are not comparable and were estimated by linking older series to the 1970 level. b. 1984 instead of 1987.

to 1975 by 38 per cent in the Netherlands and by 18 per cent in Japan and over the period 1975–87 by 19 and 14 per cent respectively. Farm sizes in Japan increased slowly and, in view of the range where important economies of scale can be expected, this increase was of little significance for rice and field crops. As a result sales for most farms in the Netherlands developed sufficiently rapidly to provide incomes to at least one full-time worker. This is one of the reasons why part-time farming has never become important in the Netherlands, farm policies are another one.

There are several possible measures for structural transformation: decline of labour, decline of the number of farms, reallocation of land to other farms, and growth of production per farm. Since 1950 Japan's economy grew faster than any of the other OECD economies, but its gross value added from agriculture grew less, except for the period 1950–60. Yet the decline of employment in its agriculture, forestry and fisheries was even slower than in the EC–6 countries, in particular France, Germany, and Italy (Van der Meer 1988). Compared to the Netherlands in terms of hours of labour input for the farm sector only, employment only declined faster in Japan over the period 1975–87 (Table 6.6).

Conclusion

Japan's unprecedented growth of labour productivity in industry in the post-war period tended to increase the difference in income between agriculture and industry. This resulted in a rapid decline of the agricultural work-force and increasing wage rates for unskilled labour. Obviously, under such conditions rapid structural adjustment of the agricultural sector is required, with the creation of modern farm units which can reap the gains of mechanization and economies of scale. Government policies for speeding up structural reform can be crucial for achieving rapid productivity growth. However, the actual political conditions were unfavourable for such policies. On the one hand, there was the general fear in Japan of food shortages which resulted in policies to promote production and self-sufficiency for food rather than structural adjustment. The main example are rice policies which prevent allocation of resources to products for which Japan has a comparative advantage. On the other hand, the political power of farmers' organizations formed a force for over-protection of the agricultural sector and an obstacle for structural adjustment. The revealed consequences of over-protection in Japan confirms the inverse U-shape hypothesis in Chapters Two and Three. Japan's policies for promoting self-sufficiency were not successful in the long run because of failure to achieve more rapid structural change and productivity growth.

In comparative international perspective Japan's agricultural sector peformed relatively poorly despite high investment rates and high outlays for research. There is not a major gap in agricultural technological knowledge between Japan and other industrial countries, but a backlog of technical progress in Japan awaiting changes in policies and farm structure. The main reasons for Japan's poor performance are a backward economic structure and relatively slow structural adjustment. The government and the co-operatives have aimed continuously to keep as many people in farming as possible. This has gradually resulted in a farm sector and farmers' organizations mainly consisting of part-time farmers. Not only have agricultural interests a strong power within the political system, but within the farmers' organizations the interests of inefficient small farms tend to dominate. There are many obstacles for enterprising farmers who want to expand the size of their farms. As a result, gains from economies of scale equal to those in West European countries cannot be reaped.

Chapter seven

Prospects for Japan's agriculture

The further development of Japan's agriculture toward the year 2000 depends on three major factors: general economic development, trends in world agriculture and trade, and changes in agricultural policies. The first two factors are largely exogenous to agriculture, since Japan's agriculture has little effect on general economic growth, and although Japan is a major importer of agriculture products in the world, the volume of its agriculture production is only a small part of world production. But it depends to an important extent on government trade and agricultural policies how both factors bear upon Japan's agriculture. These policies are the outcome of an interactive process in which mainly domestic, but increasingly international forces also come together.

The economic setting

At present Japan's economy is probably entering a new development stage which affects the outlook for agriculture. In the past decades five main factors contributed to high industrial growth rates:

(1) the availability of an educated labour-force which could absorb new skills;
(2) rapid bridging of the technological gap with the most advanced industrial countries by adapting imported technology;
(3) high saving and investment rates;
(4) import substitution policies; and
(5) most of the time an under-valued exchange rate which substituted for lagging domestic demand.

Some of these factors are rapidly losing their importance.

The challenge

In several branches of industry productivity levels are no longer different from the other advanced nations (Szirmai and Pilat 1989). Therefore future growth rates of output and productivity are likely to be much lower than in the recent past, and dependent on the pace of generation of new technologies. This means that agriculture has better chances to bridge the gap in labour productivities with industry than in the past. If we assume, for example, that Japanese industry may realize not far from 4 per cent growth in labour productivity per year, then agriculture can only catch up if labour input declines by more than 4 per cent per year, or alternatively, if net value added would grow by a higher rate than the decline in employment would fall short of 4 per cent. The experience over the past ten years suggests that such a decline in employment or increase in net value added will be difficult to achieve under the present policies.

But keeping up with Japanese industry may not be enough. Competitiveness in Japanese agriculture depends not only on labour productivity growth in Japanese agriculture and industry, but especially also on the relative performance of agriculture in the main western countries. It is not unlikely that in western countries productivity growth in agriculture will continue to exceed that in industry. That requires Japanese agriculture to do the same in order to prevent further loss of comparative advantage. A continued decrease in comparative advantage would seriously further undermine the competitive position of Japanese agriculture. There are several compelling reasons why agricultural productivity in Japan has to grow faster than in the past. The first of these is increased international competition. In the past the political power of farmers' organizations was a dominant factor in designing agricultural policies. However, foreign trade considerations and urban interests are becoming more important factors. With increasing competition from abroad Japan's agriculture may shrink more and more, the self-sufficiency rates will further decline, and the remaining parts of agriculture will become increasingly artificial behind a barrier that is under continuous attack from abroad as well as from domestic interest groups.

Since Japan became a developed country with a significant share in world trade it has had less chance to maintain a structurally undervalued currency and a structural surplus on its current account. It is simply not accepted by other powerful countries and not expected to endure by currency speculators. The same applies to policies for import substitution. What has been notified under

GATT rules in the past may, to some extent, be defended successfully, but it is unlikely to be accepted by other countries for a *nouveau riche* such as Japan to build new barriers. More likely is that barriers to imports in Japan will be reduced in order to protect export industries against restrictions in foreign markets. A process has already started in which agriculture and its related industries are losing their extreme forms of protection. Therefore rapid increases in productivity are required for survival of Japanese agriculture.

The potential for increasing productivity is not lacking. As we have argued in the previous chapter, there is a backlog of potential productivity increases awaiting institutional change and changes in the production structure. In particular, for horticulture and most of the livestock sector this is not so difficult to achieve from a technical point of view. The analysis in the previous chapter suggests that higher growth of productivity will depend on rapid reduction of farm labour input while maintaining output, and reduction of the use of non-factor input and capital consumption per unit of product. This will most likely require rapid reduction of inefficient part-time farming, reduction of excessive use of inputs, and enlargement of farms to sizes that can achieve economies of scale. These are compelling requirements for achieving rapid growth of productivity. It is simply a matter of 'to be or not to be'. Policies to pursue this fall into two groups: policies that form a prerequisite, and supportive policies. Considerable reductions in output prices, in particular for rice, and withdrawal of investment and interest subsidies for inefficient small farms seem to be crucial. A change in land policies and land taxation may be indispensable as well. These three elements seem to be prerequisites, but in addition there are many possible supportive policies. Special tax regulations for farmers who wish to give up and some kind of pension or subsidy for farmers who sell their farm, as practised in the Netherlands and some other European countries, could accelerate structural change. In addition, policies to make industries and services related to agriculture more competitive and efficient would be conducive for farm development.

Changing the institutional and political environment

Since a structurally overvalued exchange rate is not likely to be feasible in the long run, future economic growth will become more dependent on the leading role of domestic consumer demand. So far the purchasing power of Japanese consumers has been low compared to their money incomes. Two important drains on this power are responsible for this. One is the extremely high level of rural and urban land prices, the other stems from the low productivity of many local industries and services. Structural changes to solve this will affect agriculture and its related industries, although not in a negative way only.

Land policies

The role of land in general Japanese economic and agricultural development is most remarkable. In the course of economic development in Western countries the share of (urban and agricultural) land in factor income has shown a secular decline. Schultz (1953) already observed this thirty-five years ago. This was contrary to the pessimistic expectations of classical economists who believed that the share of rent incomes would increase and in that way reduce profits and real income of wage earners. It cannot of course be concluded that Japan's experiences confirm the development pattern expected by the classical economists, but in no other developed country is rent income economically and politically as important as in Japan. It may be added that policies and institutions in other developed countries have not contributed so much to pushing rental incomes up. Rents form a substantial cost for many other products, and the share of consumer income spent on rent is most likely higher than in any other industrial country.

The causes of the high prices are manifold and complex and their analysis is beyond the scope of this book. Agricultural price policies, tax policies, and various institutional obstacles for better land allocation and for land-saving innovations are certainly among them. Of interest here is that farm policies contribute to high prices, and that farm-size adjustment is harmed by high land prices. The first point is obvious. Prices for farm products always affect land prices. The negative effects are that land has become so expensive that considerable enlargement of the land area of farms is difficult to finance, but also because part-time farmers keep their land as asset holders, awaiting ever further increases of land values. As we saw in the previous chapter, policies have rather favoured that behaviour and as such impeded requisite structural transformation.

Changes in land policies are of great importance for modernizing agriculture. But, although generally deemed necessary, they are as difficult to introduce as changes in farm policies, because wealth based on land values and rent incomes are quantitatively very important for many people who are politically well represented. Significant changes in land policies could even have tremendous financial effects. In recent years groups with vested interest in land, such as land development and construction companies have become among the most influential power groups in the ruling Liberal Democrat Party. These and the farmers' lobbies can by the nature of their interest not favour any reform that will bring land prices down. Much will depend on the question of whether other interest groups in the political system can balance the political power of rent-seeking groups.

Political structure

A factor of special relevance for agricultural policies is the changing political structure. In the past, consumer purchasing power could grow rapidly because of high economic growth rates. Under such conditions high food prices did not seriously limit the growth of purchasing power and did not meet strong resistance. Moreover, many people, remembering the food scarcity of the Second World War period, believed that food security could be achieved and should be promoted by high agricultural support prices. This belief is declining, although it is still widely endorsed. More consumers have started to realize that farmers have become more wealthy than the average Japanese wage and salary earner, that there is over-production of several products, and that food prices in Japan are much higher than abroad. At the same time, trading partners, not so successful in competing with Japan in manufacturing, have put continuous pressure on Japan to open its agricultural markets for at least some products. The combined effect of these forces may be that the ruling party, the Liberal Democratic Party, which has thus far relied heavily for support on agricultural interests, will probably gradually reorient its agricultural policies. But so far other interest groups have not cashed-in, and policies remain dominated by the rent-seeking interest groups.

The main pressure for changing farm policies comes from manufacturing interests who want to make trade concessions for agricultural products in order to avoid import restrictions in Western countries. In the near future there will most likely be increasing pressure for more market orientation and less protection. This will have a negative effect on agricultural incomes at least in the short run. But there are positive effects as well, which may have a stronger impact in the long run. One effect will be that the production structure, more than in the past, will reflect comparative advantages of regions and sub-sectors. Another effect will be that inefficient producers will increasingly give up their resources allowing more productive producers to obtain their land, perhaps at lower prices. Both effects will influence agricultural productivity positively.

Supporting industries and services

In the previous chapter we summed up evidence that some input producing and output processing industries and agricultural services are relatively inefficient if compared to Japan's exporting manufacturing industries. This causes farmers to pay too much for their inputs, and consumers too much for the final product because margins between farmers and consumers are too big. Several of these industries were started only in the post-war period under import substitution policies. In some cases these policies may not have resulted in establishing viable industries which can meet the efficiency standards of other advanced nations. Lack of foreign and domestic competition may explain this. The gradual opening of the Japanese economy will probably enhance productivity in these sectors. Higher efficiency and lower prices will not only increase purchasing power of consumers, but will also have a positive effect on agriculture. As we have argued in the previous chapter, competitive industries and services are more conducive for agricultural development. Here farmers', or better full-time farmers' and consumers' interests are parallel. Dismantling of various formal and informal market regulations and abolition of protection for such industries will in general be an advantage for agriculture, although not necessarily in the short run.

Chapter eight

Relevance of Japan's post-war development experience for developing countries

Many factors explaining the poor performance of Japan in agricultural productivity are specific for Japan. Yet, the fact is that to some extent Korea and Taiwan share Japan's experience of relatively poor performance of agriculture compared to other sectors. Other countries in Asia have not had similar experiences yet, except perhaps Malaysia with its rice sector. But it is not difficult to imagine that in a not too far future similar problems of unbalanced sectoral productivity growth could occur in other developing countries in a process of rapid industrialization. This is especially true in parts of Asia and parts of China, also Java, and even Thailand. The depicted pattern of unbalanced growth will probably only become visible in countries where employment in agriculture starts to decrease rapidly. That means that it is most likely to occur in countries and areas that already have a sizeable non-agricultural sector and moderate or low population growth.

A first question here is whether there are common reasons for the relatively lagging performance in labour productivity in agriculture in Japan and other East Asian countries. The next question to be raised is what policies are optimal for mitigating the adverse effects of rapid industrial growth for agricultural development, or, in other words, how can such serious forms of unbalanced growth be avoided without of course slowing-down the speed of industrialization?

Japan was the first developed country in Asia. It had already experienced considerable growth in agriculture before the Second World War, and growth in industry was even more spectacular. This was followed by a strong decline caused by war damage and post-war disruption, and a rapid recovery in the 1960s. Around 1960 Japan had reached again its pre-war long-term growth trend. But then agriculture was subject to serious pressure because its productivity growth rates fell far short of those in industry. Japan's comparative advantage in agriculture, which was low already, declined rapidly and relative incomes in agriculture were put under pressure. In several respects the development in Taiwan and Korea during the past fifteen years has been similar to that of Japan from the late 1950s onwards. One difference is the time-lag, another is that industrial productivity in Japan was already much higher in 1960 than in Taiwan and Korea in 1975, whereas in agriculture the productivity gap with Korea was much smaller and with Taiwan almost insignificant. In fact the Japanese economy was more unbalanced with respect to inter-sectoral productivity differences in 1960 than that of Korea and Taiwan fifteen years later. Therefore it is remarkable that protection in both countries has been raised so rapidly and by so much already (see Table 5.15 p. 115 and Hayami 1988:6). Both economies are similar to Japan in that part-time farming, particularly in rice, has increased rapidly.

The experiences of Western countries suggest that lagging growth of labour productivity in agriculture, and the related decline in comparative advantage, is a natural phenomenon in rapidly industrializing countries. It is a temporary phenomenon related to the general pattern of economic growth, and leads to temporary sectoral imbalances. However, the decline in comparative advantage in present day developing countries is much more rapid than in nineteenth century Europe, because of much higher growth rates of output and productivity in industry. Rapid growth in non-agricultural sectors has the advantage that demand for labour in non-agricultural sectors is also more rapid and, consequently, the agricultural labour force can decline more rapidly. On the other hand this presupposes increasing inter-sectoral differences in income which act as the engine for rapid social and structural transformation. It is this aspect which causes political resentment and pressure on the government to support farm income. If the government responds to this pressure it weakens the incentive for rapid structural adjustment. The specific inverse U-shaped relation between price level and productivity growth in agriculture may justify some protection, but Japan's experience shows that over-protection is counter-productive because in a dynamic perspective it worsens the situation. It therefore seems desirable for governments to study how rapid growth of labour productivity in agriculture can be achieved simultaneously with rapid industrialization. The choice of an optimal price level as discussed is only one thing, but many other policies can be very effective as well. Structural reform is often a pre-condition for the introduction of labour-saving production processes in land scarce situations with small farms and scattered landholdings. The emergence of large numbers of part-time farmers, in particular if they are organized in a politically powerful organization, can be a serious obstacle for structural reform which is necessary for creating viable farms. Viable farms can be defined as farms of a sufficiently large size to capture the potential benefit from economies of scale. Investment subsidies for this group of farms can be beneficial because these subsidies increase their relative competitiveness without leading to excessive use of capital, but the same subsidies given to part-time farmers encourage inefficiency and discourage required structural reform.

Japan was the first non-Western country that experienced considerable technical change and productivity increases in agriculture. This experience is in many respects an example for developing countries that want to achieve agricultural development. After 1960 Japan's agricultural development has not been successful. Japan has not been able to transform its agricultural structure sufficiently rapidly, but instead started to rely on a policy of high subsidization and price support which was in many respects counter-productive. This is an important experience from which developing countries which are experiencing rapid industrial growth may learn. Rapid growth requires considerable structural transformation. Without considerable structural change agriculture cannot in many cases achieve sufficiently high productivity growth.

Appendix A

Data for international comparison of growth of labour productivities used in Chapter Two

Country classification

The country classification and development status of countries are given in Table A.1.

Definition of sectors

The A-sector includes agriculture, fisheries, and forestry (ISIC 1). The I-sector comprises mining, manufacturing, electricity, gas and water, and construction ISIC (2, 3, 4 and 5). The S-sector comprises trade, restaurants and hotels, transport, storage and communication, financial institutions, insurance, real estate and commercial services, government, social and personal services, and activities not adequately defined (ISIC 6, 7, 8 and 9). The text refers to the A, I, S, and I&S sectors briefly as 'agriculture', 'industry', 'services', and 'non-agriculture'. The averages in the tables are unweighted averages. The figures for the S+I sectors together for individual countries are weighted, which may result in some apparent contradictions between group averages for industry and services on the one hand, and I+S on the other. Individual countries do not show such contradictions despite the low reliability of figures for the S-sector for several countries.

Data sources

GDP and Employment: calculated from World Bank, *World Tables*, third and fourth editions, and World Bank, *World Development Reports*, various issues. Data for Taiwan from the Council for Economic Planning and Development, *Taiwan Statistical Data Book*, 1987. Labour data after 1980 are not published in the World Bank sources and were obtained from OECD, *Labour Force Statistics*, 1988; FAO, *Production Yearbook*, various issues; ILO,

Table A.1 Country classification and development status

Country	*Status*	*Country*	*Status*	*Country*	*Status*
Latin America		*Asia and the Pacific*		*Africa South of the Sahara*	
Argentina	mi	Bangladesh	li	Angola†	mi
Bolivia	mi	Fiji*	mi	Botswana	mi
Brazil	mi	Hong Kong†	mi	Cameroon*	mi
Chile	mi	India	li	Centr. Afr. Rep.	li
Colombia	mi	Indonesia	mi	Congo	mi
Costa Rica	mi	Korea	mi	Ethiopia	li
Dominican Rep.	mi	Pakistan	li	Gambia, The	li
Eduador*	mi	Philippines	mi	Ghana	mi
El Salvador	mi	Singapore	mi	Ivory Coast	mi
Guyana	mi	Sri Lanka	li	Kenya	mi
Honduras	mi	Taiwan	mi	Liberia*	mi
Jamaica	mi	Thailand	mi	Mali*	li
Mexico	mi			Mauritania	mi
Nicaragua	mi			Mozambique†	li
Panama	mi	*Industrial economies*		Niger	li
Paraguay*	mi			Nigeria	mi
Peru	mi			Senegal	mi
Uruguay	mi	Australia	hi	Sierra Leone*	li
Venezuela	mi	Austria	hi	Sudan*	li
		Belgium	hi	Tanzania*	mi
Middle East and Mediterranean		Canada†	hi	Togo*	li
		Denmark	hi	Uganda*	li
		Finland	hi	Zimbabwe*	mi
		France	hi		
Algeria	mi	Germany, West	hi		
Cyprus	mi	Italy	hi		
Egypt	mi	Japan	hi		
Greece	mi	Netherlands	hi		
Morocco	mi	Norway	hi		
Portugal	mi	Spain	hi		
Syria*	mi	Sweden	hi		
Tunisia*	mi	United Kingdom	hi		
Turkey	mi	United States	hi		
Yugoslavia	mi	Hungary	hi		

Note Development status: li = low income countries; mi = middle income countries; hi = high income countries. The period of analysis is 1960–85 with the following exceptions: for countries marked with * the period starts in 1965; and for countries marked with † the period ends in 1980.

Yearbook of Labour Force Statistics, various issues; and ADB, *Key Economic Indicators*, 1987. For a few countries data series had to be projected because of lack of reliable data for recent years. Index pressure on land = ratio of actual population to potential population. Actual population from the World Bank's *World Tables*, potential population from FAO (1983). The potential refers to the situation with low input use in agriculture, given the actual irrigation.

Irrigation contribution to food supply is the percentage calculated at low inputs from Table 2.4 of the same FAO study.

The distortion index for the 1970s was taken from the World Bank's *World Development Report 1983*: 60–1.

The price level for agricultural production is defined as the ratio of the Purchasing Power Parity and the Exchange Rate, both expressed in local currency units per US dollar, and taken from FAO (1986: Table 3.1).

Appendix B

Inter-country data for 1963, 1975, and 1985 used in Chapter Three

In the first section of Chapter Three the method and data used for the international comparison of agricultural productivity in 1963, 1975, and 1985 have been explained already. In this appendix we supplement that information and give detailed data sources.

Our productivity indicator is gross value added per worker. These data are not readily available, thus we had to estimate them ourselves. The data used for analysis are presented in Table B.1 to Table B.4 (pp. 172–8).

Sources and notes

Total production (Table B.1)

Total production is calculated by multiplying the product quantity of each commodity by its unit price, and aggregating the values for all product per country in each year. The quantities of products for 1961–5 average (all countries) and each year of 1984–6 (except for Taiwan) are taken from the *FAO Production Yearbook*, various issues. Product quantities for Taiwan for 1975 and 1985 are from the Department of Agriculture and Forestry, *Taiwan Agricultural Yearbook*, Taipei, various issues. The 1975 international unit prices in terms of 'International dollar' and the value of total production for 1975 are taken from FAO (1986: 28 and 31) (except for Taiwan). The definition of the International dollar is explained in Chapter Three and in note six of that chapter with use of formulas. For 1984–6 averages are calculated.

Gross value added ratios (Table B.1)

Ratios of gross value added to total production were taken from agricultural sector accounts at 1975 national prices for 1963, 1975, and 1985. If 1975 price data were not available, another constant

Table B.1 Estimates of total production, gross value added ratio, and gross value added in agriculture in 1975 prices, 1963, 1975, and 1985 (million 1975 International dollars)

Country	*Total production*			*Gross value added ratio (%)*			*Gross value added*		
	1963	*1975*	*1985*	*1963*	*1975*	*1985*	*1963*	*1975*	*1985*
Asia									
East Asia									
Japan	8,297	12,484	12,982	71.6	61.1	55.0	5,941	7,628	7,140
Korean Rep.	1,657	3,244	4,070	88.7	81.6	74.0	1,469	2,647	3,011
Taiwan	1,438	2,237	2,843	75.3	66.1	58.7	1,083	1,479	1,669
Other Asian countries									
Indonesia	5,786	9,981	14,162	97.1	91.4	85.9	5,619	8,208	12,165
Philippines	2,656	4,400	5,387	92.2	89.7	85.9	2,449	3,947	4,628
Thailand	3,597	5,939	8,565	78.0	75.5	77.6	2,805	4,484	6,647
India	31,436	47,294	55,606	93.0	91.7	86.4	29,236	43,369	48,044
Pakistan	3,535	6,652	9,498	89.4	90.5	90.8	3,161	6,020	8,624

Europe									
North West Europe									
Sweden	1,838	2,055	2,326	46.7	48.7	51.9	858	1,001	1,207
Belgium-Lux.	2,149	2,884	3,063	64.0	46.1	52.4	1,375	1,330	1,605
Denmark	3,025	3,115	4,118	47.7	47.7	53.0	1,443	1,486	2,183
Netherlands	3,386	5,297	7,186	51.7	50.8	53.7	1,751	2,691	3,859
France	17,047	21,450	25,337	72.6	62.1	60.0	12,376	13,320	15,202
Germany FR	11,965	14,920	16,897	57.5	54.3	53.9	6,880	8,101	9,107
Ireland	1,451	2,048	2,405	66.9	66.9	58.5	971	1,370	1,407
UK	8,132	9,409	11,776	45.8	45.8	55.1	3,724	4,310	6,489
South Europe									
Greece	2,101	3,620	3,888	77.2	80.5	75.0	1,622	2,914	2,916
Italy	11,246	15,209	15,532	80.3	73.2	68.6	9,031	11,133	10,655
Portugal	1,458	1,750	1,653	47.6	47.6	50.3	694	833	831
Spain	6,416	10,547	12,275	64.7	59.4	54.3	4,151	6,265	6,665
EC total	68,377	90,249	104,131	64.4	59.6	58.5	44,018	53,752	60,920
Americas–Oceania									
Australia	7,036	9,425	10,800	63.2	63.2	66.8	4,447	5,957	7,214
USA	70,847	91,350	107,100	49.9	49.9	55.4	35,353	45,584	59,334
Canada	7,599	9,865	12,885	63.6	55.9	47.2	4,833	5,514	6,082
Argentina	8,763	11,377	13,564	71.3	71.3	74.7	6,248	8,112	10,132
Brazil	14,454	21,721	30,039	87.7	87.7	87.6	12,676	19,049	26,314
Mexico	5,343	8,331	12,376	65.9	65.9	67.7	3,521	5,490	8,378

price series or, if necessary, current price data were taken. The ratios for Asian countries in 1963 and 1975 were from APO (1987). For the 1985 ratios of Asian countries, national data such as MAFF (1985) for Japan, Ministry of Agriculture and Fisheries (1986) for Korea, Department of Agriculture and Forestry, *Taiwan Agricultural Yearbook*, 1986 for Taiwan, and Rijk and Van der Meer (1984) for Thailand were utilized. If no national data were available, the ratios in APO (1987) were extrapolated by use of the Asian Development Bank (1987) and FAO production indexes. The ratios for Greece, Portugal, Spain, Australia, Argentina, Brazil, and Mexico were taken from FAO (1988). Other EC countries from Eurostat, *Economic Accounts for Agriculture*, various issues. USA from the US Department of Agriculture, *Agricultural Statistics*, various issues, Sweden and Canada from FAO (1986) and OECD (1988a). If no information was available for a particular year, the ratio for the closest previous or later year is taken instead.

Gross value added (Table B.1)

Gross value added is estimated by multiplying the calculated total production by the corresponding gross value added ratio.

Number of agricultural workers (Table B.2)

Except for Ireland, Argentina, Brazil, and Mexico, agricultural labour (for crop growing and livestock raising) data are estimated. The labour data for the above four countries include fisheries and forestry. Data for Ireland from OECD (1988b), the other data for 1963 and 1975 from World Bank, *World Tables*, while the 1985 data are extrapolated by use of the *FAO Production Yearbook*.

Data for Japan from the Statistical Bureau (1987), for Korea from the Bank of Korea, *Economic Statistics Yearbook*, various issues, for Thailand from Corsel (1986). The other Asian countries for 1963 and 1975 from APO (1987) (with revision of the 1975 data of the Philippines). For 1985 *FAO Production Yearbook 1985* is used for extrapolation from the 1975 data except for Taiwan. For Taiwan, the Council for Economic Planning and Development (1987) is utilized. The definition of agricultural labour is not clear for the data of Indonesia, Philippines, India, and Pakistan for all the years.

For the other countries mixed data sources are used. The Dutch data are from Van der Meer (1987a). Most of the agricultural data sources include forestry and fisheries as well. Estimation of labour data for agriculture only is done as follows. For Australia, France,

Table B.2 Estimates of agricultural labour and land, 1963, 1975, and 1985

Country	*Agricultural workers (1,000 persons)*			*Agricultural land (1,000 ha)*		
	1963	*1975*	*1985*	*1963*	*1975*	*1985*
Asia						
East Asia						
Japan	10,823	5,870	4,490	6,061	5,572	5,379
Korean Rep.	3,991	4,831	3,292	2,087	2,272	2,224
Taiwan	1,635	1,493	1,167	874	920	892
Other Asian countries						
Indonesia	22,900	27,400	28,600	28,170	30,716	32,730
Philippines	5,317	6,744	7,989	6,611	7,628	8,507
Thailand	10,674	12,601	14,426	9,631	16,197	19,339
India	122,436	147,936	173,239	148,763	155,068	156,133
Pakistan	7,860	9,910	12,188	21,670	24,410	25,549
Europe						
North West Europe						
Sweden	359	199	150	3,114	2,867	2,788
Belgium-Lux.	259	139	106	1,819	1,688	1,511
Denmark	254	177	153	3,055	2,913	2,834
Netherlands	422	276	254	2,303	2,172	2,077
France	3,706	2,074	1,509	34,354	32,260	32,122
Germany FR	2,694	1,624	1,256	14,200	13,300	12,841
Ireland	363	238	169	4,632	5,715	5,708
UK	1,050	655	615	12,402	12,028	11,960
South Europe						
Greece	1,519	1,212	952	8,900	9,118	9,211
Italy	5,294	3,162	2,217	19,932	17,809	17,522
Portugal	1,377	1,071	957	4,862	3,410	3,290
Spain	3,605	2,536	1,753	33,009	31,921	30,416
EC total	20,542	13,165	9,830	139,467	132,334	129,492
Americas–Oceania						
Australia	428	381	392	475,942	499,439	485,665
USA	5,098	3,233	3,161	466,039	422,553	405,226
Canada	661	456	463	63,150	68,867	70,400
Argentina	1,595	1,456	1,324	174,598	178,250	178,750
Brazil	12,677	12,808	12,519	162,134	216,385	241,780
Mexico	6,292	6,982	7,553	98,728	98,339	99,249

Germany, and Sweden the agricultural share in total employment of agriculture, forestry and fisheries is obtained from OECD statistics (1988a, tables for employment by kind of activity). For other countries, agricultural labour is estimated by deducting a percentage for forestry and fisheries equal to the percentage of

Table B.3 Average horse power per tractor and total tractor horse power, 1963, 1975, and 1985

	Average horse power (Hp)			*Total horse power (1,000 Hp)*		
	1963	*1975*	*1985*	*1963*	*1975*	*1985*
Asia						
East Asia						
Japan	15	15	20	9,115	27,590	49,206
Korean Rep.	35	35	30	7	704	5,083
Taiwan	30	15	20	53	393	541
Other Asian countries						
Indonesia	30	28	30	124	254	361
Philippines	30	29	31	144	351	605
Thailand	30	28	30	61	680	3,750
India	30	27	30	792	6,137	18,233
Pakistan	30	40	42	194	1,564	6,579
Europe						
North West Europe						
Sweden	30	39	46	4,861	7,293	8,740
Belgium-Lux.	30	40	53	1,965	4,227	6,201
Denmark	30	45	53	4,386	8,350	8,815
Netherlands	35	44	46	3,306	6,897	8,832
France	35	46	53	31,365	62,447	80,878
Germany FR	25	34	42	26,793	48,639	62,370
Ireland	30	38	42	1,564	4,309	6,636
UK	35	42	46	16,837	20,348	24,175
South Europe						
Greece	30	38	39	1,250	3,548	6,825
Italy	30	38	38	10,589	31,232	46,631
Portugal	30	37	39	390	1,681	3,159
Spain	30	37	39	3,394	14,005	24,570
EC total	–	–	–	101,839	205,683	279,092
Americas–Oceania						
Australia	40	53	64	11,322	17,606	21,248
USA	35	47	58	169,941	210,043	271,208
Canada	40	54	62	22,725	33,798	40,821
Argentina	30	44	55	4,170	7,920	11,220
Brazil	30	37	42	2,781	9,891	32,340
Mexico	30	37	41	2,160	3,651	6,437

forestry and fisheries in gross value added in OECD statistics (1988a). This means that the same productivity is assumed for agriculture, and forestry and fisheries. The labour data, including forestry and fisheries, are taken from OECD (1988b), except for Greece, for which data are taken from the *FAO Production Yearbook*.

Agricultural land area (Table B.2)

Agricultural land area includes permanent pasture. Data for Asian countries for 1963 and 1975 from APO (1987) with addition of permanent pasture from the *FAO Production Yearbook*, which is also used for all data for 1985. For 1985, MAFF, *Agricultural Statistical Yearbook of Agriculture, Forestry and Fisheries*, 1987, is used for Japan, Economic Planning Board, *Korea statistical yearbook*, 1987, for Korea, and Department of Agriculture and Forestry, *Taiwan Agricultural Yearbook*, 1987, for Taiwan. Data for other countries are taken from Eurostat, *Agriculture Statistical Yearbook, 1986* and the *FAO Production Yearbook*, 1985.

Tractor horse power (Table B.3)

As an indicator of machinery capital, tractor horse power is estimated for 1963, 1975, and 1985. Data on the number of agricultural tractors (riding type) are available in the *FAO Production Yearbook*, various issues. However, time-series of the numbers do not necessarily represent the value or capacity of machinery capital correctly because of two reasons. The first is that there is an increasing trend in the horse power per tractor, in particular in industrial countries. Consequently, the trend of the number probably underestimates the trend in capital stock. The second reason is that in some countries two-wheel tractors are used in agriculture. The ratio of numbers of the two types of tractors are not necessarily the same among countries. In particular, in countries like Japan a large number of two-wheel tractors is used for cultivation of the fragmented paddy fields. Thus neglect of two-wheel tractors implies underestimation.

The problem is that there are no comparable international statistics which systematically indicate changes in tractor horse power in time-series. Furthermore, the number of two-wheel tractors is no longer compiled in the recent FAO data. But use of national data for many countries is impractical. Therefore we utilized past estimates of horse power. One from Yamada (1975) and another from Hayami and Ruttan (1985). In the former the horse power for all Asian countries in 1963 and 1970 is estimated while in the latter horse power is estimated for forty-four countries for 1960, 1970, and 1980. Both estimates, although not necessarily highly reliable, are used in this study, given time limitation.

The method applied here is to estimate the average horse power per tractor by country for each year, and multiplying it by the number of tractors. For 1963 (actually the 1961–5 average) this

Table B.4 The actual price indexes and gaps from their regional optimum level, 1980

	Country actual price index 1980 (1)	*Regional optimum level* (2)	*Gaps from optimum level 1980* (3) = (1) – (2)
Asia			
East Asia			
Japan	2.96	2.37	0.59
Korean Rep.	2.19	2.37	–0.18
Taiwan	1.29	1.19	0.10
Other Asian countries			
Indonesia	1.25	1.19	0.08
Philippines	0.86	1.19	–0.33
Thailand	0.76	1.19	–0.43
India	0.94	1.19	–0.25
Pakistan	0.90	1.19	–0.29
Europe			
North West Europe			
Sweden	1.58	1.40	0.18
Belgium-Lux.	1.43	1.40	0.03
Denmark	1.37	1.40	–0.03
Netherlands	1.40	1.40	0.00
France	1.50	1.40	0.10
Germany FR	1.55	1.40	0.15
Ireland	1.21	1.40	–0.19
UK	1.40	1.40	0.00
South Europe			
Greece	1.58	1.19	0.39
Italy	1.52	1.19	0.33
Portugal	1.62	1.19	0.43
Spain	1.30	1.19	0.11
Americas–Oceania			
Australia	0.96	1.40	–0.44
USA	1.00	1.40	–0.40
Canada	1.09	1.40	–0.31
Argentina	1.23	1.19	0.04
Brazil	0.76	1.19	–0.43
Mexico	1.19	1.19	0.00

Note See Chapter Three for explanation.

method is applied for riding tractors and two-wheel tractors separately, but for other years (except for East Asian countries), only the number of riding tractors is utilized with an upwardly adjusted estimate of the average horse power per riding tractor (to include horse power by two-wheel tractors). For East Asian countries the horse power of the two types of tractors are estimated for each bench year. The average horse power per riding type of tractor for 1963, 1975, and 1985 is estimated by rule of the thumb from estimates for 1960, 1970, and 1980 in Hayami and Ruttan (1985) and the number of the tractors in the *FAO Production Yearbook*, various issues. The estimated average horse power per riding tractor for 1975 and 1985 (except for Japan, Korea, and Taiwan) includes the additional horse power of two-wheel tractors.

Gaps of the relative price index by country from its regional optimum level (Table B.4)

The relative price index is defined as the ratio of purchasing power parity for agricultural products to the exchange rate. It is estimated in FAO (1986). Its regional optimum levels are estimated by use of the equation (3) in Chapter Three (p. 64).

Comparison of the output data in the present and previous studies (Table B.5)

The production data used in this study for 1975 are compared with previous studies by Van Ooststroom and Maddison (O–M) (1985)

Table B.5 Output data comparison with previous studies for 1975 (US = 100)

	Total production		*Gross value added ratio*			*Gross value added*		
	This study[a]	*O–M & S–O–V*[b]	*This study*	*O–M*	*S–O–V*	*This study*	*O–M*	*S–O–V*
Japan	13.7	13.4	61.1	52.9	60.7	16.7	14.7	16.6
Korea	3.6	3.6	81.6	64.2	–	5.8	4.8	–
Indonesia	9.8	11.3	91.4	91.2	91.1	18.0	21.2	20.9
Thailand	6.5	6.4	75.5	85.3	88.2	9.8	11.4	11.5
India	51.8	52.8	91.7	76.9	77.1	95.1	83.7	82.8
France	23.5	24.5	62.1	52.5	64.4	29.2	26.6	32.2
Germany	16.3	17.2	54.3	32.0	59.5	17.8	11.3	20.8
Netherlands	5.8	6.3	50.8	60.6	50.2	5.9	7.9	6.5
UK	10.3	10.7	45.8	51.4	48.1	9.5	11.4	10.5
USA	100.0	100.0	49.9	48.5	49.2	100.0	100.0	100.0
Argentina	12.5	12.5	71.3	82.6	80.0	17.8	21.4	20.4
Brazil	23.8	25.4	87.7	76.4	78.0	41.8	40.0	40.3
Mexico	9.1	9.7	65.9	67.5	71.4	12.0	13.5	14.1

Notes O–M stands for Van Ooststroom and Maddison (1985), and S–O–V for Stanneveld, Van Ooststroom and Van der Meer (1984). a. Estimates by FAO (1986); b. S–O–V used the O–M data.

and Stanneveld, Van Ooststroom and Van der Meer (1984). In Table B.5, the total value of production and gross value added are expressed as a percentage of value in the USA. The latter study applied the O–M estimates of total production data at 1975 US prices, but gross value added ratios were different. The 1975 data of total production used in this study, which are taken from FAO (1986) are by and large at similar levels. The largest gap was observed for Indonesia, at about 15 per cent, and the second was for the Netherlands, at about 8 per cent, but for the remaining countries it was at most a few per cent.

In the case of gross value added ratios, gaps are not small. This study uses the FAO's sector account data (1988, unpublished) for Argentina, Brazil, and Mexico, which are very different from the two other studies. For other countries the gaps between this study and Stanneveld, Van Ooststroom and Van der Meer are not so large in general, because national data are used. But between this study and Van Ooststroom and Maddison, sizeable gaps exist for several countries. For Germany, for instance the gross value added ratio was 54.3 in this study, while it was 32.0 in Van Ooststroom and Maddison. For Japan both total production and gross value added ratio are larger in this study than in Van Ooststroom and Maddison, thus their relative level of Japan's gross value added is larger than in this study. On the contrary, for the Netherlands both variables were smaller in this study than the other, so that the Dutch relative position of gross value added became smaller in this study than in the others. As a result, the ratio between Japan and the Netherlands was 2.8 in this study, 1.9 in Van Ooststroom and Maddison, and 2.6 in Stanneveld, Van Ooststroom and Van der Meer.

In spite of these gaps, the relative sizes of gross value added by country are roughly the same in the three studies. Thus the estimated results are probably without a large error or bias, though there exists a possibility of underestimation for the Netherlands relative to the others.

Check of underestimation by use of FAO data (Table B.6)

In the text we discussed the underestimation of the FAO production data, due to smaller statistical coverage than national data. The extent of such underestimation may be checked by comparing coverage with national sources.

Coverage and definitions differ from national accounts concepts. The first problem is that agricultural statistics from which FAO production statistics are obtained are often under-reported. This is

Table B.6 Check of underestimation by FAO data, 1975

	PPPs	*Total production*				*Ratio of (4) to (3) (%)*
		At current value		*At 1975 prices (mill. International dollars)*		
		Data source	*Value*	*Deflated by PPPs*	*This study (FAO estimate)*	
	(1)		*(2)*	*(3) = (2)/(1)*	*(4)*	*(5)*
Japan	752.8	FAO	9,720 bill.yen	12,912	12,484	96.7
Korea	762.5	FAO	2,645 bill. won	3,469	3,244	93.5
Thailand	13.31	APO	91,910 mill. baht	6,905	5,939	86.0
India	7.74	FAO	342,175 mill. rupee	44,209	47,294	107.0
Netherlands	3.38	FAO	20,691 mill.Dfl.	6,122	5,297	86.5
USA	1.00	FAO	92,878 mill.S	92,878	91,350	98.4
Mexico	14.8	FAO	153,776 mill. peso	10,390	8,331	80.2

Sources FAO (1981 and 1986) and AP (1987).
Note PPP is purchasing power parity of local currency to the US $.

common for developing countries and therefore national accounts statisticians often use upwardly adjusted data. Moreover, many smaller products are not well covered by the FAO. In other cases production not recorded in FAO statistics figures significantly in national statistics. Mushrooms and asparagus, for example, are important products in the Netherlands and Japan in 1975, but not reported in the FAO source. Of particular importance for the Netherlands is that flowers and ornamental plants and trees are not included at all. In the Netherlands at current prices these products constituted about 9.7 per cent of the total value of production in 1975, 12.4 per cent in 1980 and 13.2 per cent in 1984. In Japan the share of such products is not so high but with about 2.5 per cent still significant. A final problem is that the FAO does not distinguish differences in quality of products. Such a distinction is important for the Netherlands because of significant production for export of seed, seed potatoes and eggs for hatching. Because of these deficiencies in FAO data it is not clear which part of production is actually covered with the direct method of real comparison. Every country has a certain possibility of underestimation although in most cases not so large as for the Netherlands.

Another method to check the extent of underestimation is to compare our estimates of total production with a deflated real value of total production. For this we deflated current value of total production by PPPs taken from FAO (1986). Table B.6 shows the results. The extent of underestimation is 13.5 per cent for the Netherlands and 1.6 per cent for the USA. In EC countries national accounts are net of value added tax, i.e. 4 to 5 per cent in the case of the Netherlands, so that the Dutch figures confirm in total some 10 per cent of underestimation by the omittance of flowers, mushrooms, asparagus, etc. For developing countries the results are mixed. The underestimation is as large as 20 per cent for Mexico, while overestimation is 7 per cent for India. For Korea the difference was small. The results suggest that data reliability is lower for developing countries than developed countries. The Dutch estimates here probably have a relatively larger underestimation than those of the other developed countries.

Appendix C

Time-series data for Japan and the Netherlands 1880–1985 used in Chapter Four

Data sources and notes

Output and input data for Japan (Table C.1)

The 1880–1938 data (except for hours worked) in 1934–6 prices from Ohkawa and Shinohara (1979) and hours worked from Yamada (1982a) are linked to the 1950–75 data (except for the number of workers) in Yamada 1987a. The 1985 data (except for labour and land) from MAFF, *Agricultural Statistical Yearbook*, 1987 (in 1980 prices) are linked with the 1950–75 data in 1980. The number of workers for 1950–85 and working hours in 1985 are estimated from Statistical Bureau (1987). Land area in 1985 from MAFF, *Agricultural Statistical Yearbook*, 1987.

Output and input data for the Netherlands (Table C.1)

The labour data are from Van der Meer (1987a). Land data, 1950–80, from Van der Meer (1986), and for earlier years linked from CBS *70 Jaren* (1969) and Van Zanden (1985). Final output, non-farm current input and gross value added 1880–1938: Van der Meer and Van Ark (1987) and preliminary research results by Knibbe (forthcoming); 1950–85 LEI/CBS, *Agricultural Statistics 1988* and previous issues. Depreciation: LEI/CBS, *Agricultural Statistics 1988* and previous issues. Capital: unpublished data, April 1983, provided by A.J. Oskam and our update for 1985.

Real value added series in alternative common prices (Table C.2)

The J1 and N2 series are time-series at 1975 international prices for Japan and the Netherlands, although the latter are converted to yen by the exchange rate in 1975 (1 Dfl. = 117.36 yen). To get the J2 series, values of products and inputs by sub-groups in 1975

Table C.1 Final output, value added and inputs of agriculture in Japan and the Netherlands in 1975 national prices, 1880–1985

	1880	*1913*	*1920*	*1938*	*1950*	*1960*	*1975*	*1985*
Japan (billion yen)								
Final output	2,061	3,530	4,279	4,799	4,463	5,879	8,987	9,502
Gross value added	1,953	3,211	3,897	4,070	3,731	5,644	5,789	5,460
Net value added					3,612	5,331	4,960	4,382
Number of workers (1,000)	15,596	15,861	13,919	13,292	14,639	12,094	5,914	4,490
Hours worked (mill. hrs.)	21,902	29,671	29,690	25,890	28,320	20,361	10,499	6,996
Land area (1,000 ha)	4,749	5,708	5,998	6,124	5,858	6,072	5,572	5,379
Capital[a]					8,383	10,412	16,898	19,665
Non-farm current Input	108	319	382	729	732	1,235	3,198	4,042
Depreciation					119	313	829	1,078
The Netherlands (million Dfl.)								
Final output	1,715	3,425		5,019	6,847	10,714	18,769	26,676
Gross value added	1,475	2,437		3,905	4,369	5,081	9,530	14,219
Net value added					3,846	5,488	8,318	12,488
Number of workers (1,000)	501	570		613	593	468	276	254
Hours worked (mill. hrs.)	1,441	1,632		1,721	1,672	1,296	674	550
Land area (1,000 ha)	1,970	2,075		2,237	2,337	2,326	2,172	2,089
Capital[b]					22,380	23,090	32,927	41,765
Non-farm current input	240	988		1,114	2,478	4,633	9,239	12,457
Depreciation					523	643	1,212	1,731

Notes a. Gross capital value; b. Net capital value.

Table C.2 Real value added in Japanese and Dutch agriculture in alternative common 1975 prices, 1880–1985

	1880	*1913*	*1938*	*1950*	*1960*	*1975*	*1985*
Japan							
J1 In 1975 Japanese prices (bill. yen)							
Gross value added	1,953	3,211	4,070	3,731	5,644	5,789	5,460
Net value added				3,612	5,331	4,960	4,382
J2 In 1975 Dutch prices by Use of price ratios, then converted to yen by exchange rate (bill. yen)							
Gross value added	861	1,575	1,936	1,736	2,660	2,506	2,602
Net value added				1,632	2,385	1,779	1,656
J3 In the 1975 International dollar (mill. dollar)							
Gross value added	2,573	4,231	5,363	4,916	7,437	7,628	7,194
Net value added				4,759	7,025	6,536	5,774
Netherlands							
N1 In 1975 Japanese prices by use of price ratios (bill. yen)							
Gross value added	283	468	750	839	1,224	1,816	2,469
Net value added				769	1,138	1,654	2,237
N2 In 1975 Dutch prices, converted to yen by exchange rate (bill. yen)							
Gross value added	173	286	458	512	714	1,118	1,669
Net value added				451	638	976	1,466
N3 In the 1975 International dollar (mill. dollar)							
Gross value added	416	688	1,103	1,234	1,717	2,691	4,015
Net value added				1,086	1,536	2,349	3,526

Japanese prices are converted into 1975 Dutch prices by use of the price ratios at Japanese 1975 weights for respective sub-groups. These values are aggregated, and reconverted into yen by the exchange rate in 1975 (1 Dfl. = 117.36 yen) for comparability. This procedure implies that the effect of the exchange rate is neutral. For the NI series, values of products and inputs by sub-groups in 1975 prices are converted into 1975 Japanese prices by use of the price ratios at Dutch 1975 weights for respective sub-groups and aggregated. And to get the J3 and N3 series, time series of value added in 1975 international prices are converted to series in 1975 International dollars (FAO 1987) by multiplying the ratios of value added in 1975 in terms of 1975 International dollar to that of 1975 national prices. Data sources for Table C.2 are Appendix Table C.1 and Umemura *et.al.* (1966), Yamada (1987a), Van der Meer and Yamada (1988), LEI/CBS, *Agricultural Statistics*, various issues.

Appendix D

Data for comparisons among Japan, the Netherlands, Taiwan, and the USA for 1975, 1980, and 1984 used in Chapter Five

Method

An international comparison of real output and effective rates of protection can be made in principle by revaluing output and input of different countries at the same prices. This, however, requires the availability of all physical input and output data and corresponding prices used for estimating value added at current prices. In practice it is impossible to find data for all products and all qualities. For products which are not available in one of the countries, assumptions have to be made about valuation. The problems on the input side are even more complicated. Numerous different items are used, of which often little information is available.

In this study we tried to solve these problems by using agricultural sector accounts and basic data from agricultural price statistics. The method is to estimate relative price ratios for groups of inputs and products from a representative set of price and quantity data. The method was first developed for a comparison of Japan and the Netherlands and will be explained below. Subsequently, it was applied also for Taiwan and the USA to broaden the comparison.

The agricultural price indexes in Japan and the Netherlands, just as in most countries with a developed administration, comprise a large number of output and input items which are considered representative for price changes over time. For each product and input listed in both countries a relative price ratio (yen/Dfl.) was calculated. Each item included in the price index calculations has a weight, and items are distinguished in more or less homogeneous groups with weights (approximately) corresponding to the share of their values in the total production. Some corrections of weights had to be made for double counting of intermediate products in the price statistics (farm to farm sales). The weights are used for aggregating the yen/Dfl. price ratios for items within groups and

Table D.1 Method of calculation of real output and Purchasing Power Parity at Dutch weights and Japanese prices

	Value of production Dutch agriculture (in Dfl.)		*Weighted yen/Dfl price ratios at Dutch weights*		*Value of production Dutch agriculture in Japanese prices (in yen)*
Output groups	Y^D_1	×	R_1	=	$Y^{D(J)}_1$
	Y^D_2	×	R_2	=	$Y^{D(J)}_2$
	Y^D_3 +	×	R_3	=	$Y^{D(J)}_3$ +
Total output	Y^D	×	R	=	$Y^{D(J)}$
Input groups	X^D_1	×	Q_1	=	$X^{D(J)}_1$
	X^D_2	×	Q_2	=	$X^{D(J)}_2$
	X^D_n +	×	Q_n	=	$X^{D(J)}_n$ +
Total input	X^D	×	Q	=	$X^{D(J)}_1$
Gross Value Added	$Y^D - X^D$	(×)	I_{GVA}	(=)	$Y^{D(J)} - X^{D(J)}$
Depreciation	Z^D –	×	S	=	$Z^{D(J)}$ –
Net Value Added	$Y^D - X^D - Z^D$	(×)	I_{NVA}	(=)	$Y^{D(J)} - X^{D(J)} - Z^{D(J)}$

Table D.2 Basic data sector accounts, land and labour input

	Japan (billion yen)			*Netherlands (million guilders)*		
	1975	*1980*	*1984*	*1975*	*1980*	*1984*
Total production	9,576	11,193	12,573	20,691	27,951	37,426
Current inputs	3,770	5,394	6,212	10,879	16,331	20,042
Gross value added	5,806	5,799	6,356	9,812	11,620	17,384
Depreciation	957	1,451	1,468	1,089	1,920	2,498
Net value added	4,849	4,348	4,889	8,723	9,700	14,886
Land input (1,000 ha)	5,572	5,461	5,396	2,172	2,119	2,079
Labour input (mill.hrs)	10,439	8,149	7,697	674	584	558
Exchange rate to US$	296.79	226.74	237.52	2.53	1.99	3.21
	Tawain (million NT$)			*United States (million US$)*		
	1975	*1980*	*1984*	*1975*	*1980*	*1984*
Total production	10,375	156,855	213,436	94,100	137,900	154,300
Current inputs	35,385	57,234	77,691	45,300	70,200	75,400
Gross value added	68,990	99,621	135,745	48,900	67,700	79,000
Depreciation	5,435	6,743	6,757	10,100	18,900	22,500
Net value added	63,555	92,878	128,994	38,800	48,800	56,500
Land input (1,000 ha)	917	907	8,927	422,553	414,524	406,741
Labour input (mill.hrs)	1,778	1,412	1,361	6,968	6,830	5,895
Exchange rate to US$	38	36	39.6			

Sources Exchange rates for Japan and the Netherlands from World Bank, *World Tables* (1987), for Taiwan from Asian Development Bank (ADB), *Key Indicators* (1982) and Asian Productivity Organization (APO), *Comparative Information*, (1987).

Labour input in hours: Japan for 1975 and 1980 from Yamada (1987a); original data and data for 1984 estimated from MAFF, *Farm Household Economic Survey*, various issues. Netherlands from Van der Meer (1987a). Taiwan's labour input in days for 1975 and 1980 from Chen (1987). Data for 1984 were estimated by multiplying the 1978–82 average of days per worker taken from Chen (1987) by the estimated agricultural employment in 1984 that was derived by use of the Council for Economic Planning and Development, *Taiwan Statistical Data Book* (1987). For comparison with other countries seven hours/day was assumed. USA 1975 and 1980 from US Dept. of Commerce, 'The national income and product account of the USA 1929–1976', Supplement to the *Survey of Current Business*, Sept. 1981 and July 1982 issues. Data for 1984 estimated by extrapolating with the number of full-time labour equivalents in the July 1986 issue. These sources do not include work by operators who devote the majority of their working hours to non-agricultural activities and non-paid family workers. These figures, therefore, are underestimates of labour input.

Land input: Japan from Yamada (1987a) and expanded for 1984 from MAFF, *Agricultural Statistical Yearbook* (1986). Netherlands from Van der Meer (1986). Taiwan taken from Chen (1987) and Department of Agriculture and Forestry *Taiwan Agricultural Yearbook* (1987). USA derived from USDA, *Agricultural Statistics*, 1987 and previous issues. Total production, current input, gross value added, depreciation and net value added: Japan from MAFF, *Social Accounts of Agriculture and Farm Households*, 1984. Netherlands from CBS, 'De toegevoegde waarde in de land- en tuinbouw en het agrarisch inkomen' [Value added in agriculture and agricultural income], in *Maandstatistiek van de landbouw*, various issues. Total value of production data for Taiwan are obtained from the Department of Agriculture and Forestry, *Taiwan Agricultural Yearbook* (1985), whereas data on current input for 1975 and 1980 are taken from Chen (1987); current input for 1984 was estimated by applying the ratio of current input to total production in 1978–82, as given by Chen (1987). Depreciation for agriculture in Taiwan was not available. It was roughly estimated as follows. Depreciation for Agriculture, Forestry, and Fishery (AFF) was estimated as the difference between GDP in AFF (from ADB, *Key Indicators*, 1987) and NDP in AFF (from the Council for Economic Planning and Development, *Taiwan Statistical Data Book*, 1987). The share for agriculture in depreciation for AFF was taken in proportion to agriculture's share in total production of AFF. USA from US Dept. of Commerce, *Statistical Abstract*, 1985 and *Survey of Current Business*, July 1986. The rental value of houses which is included in the US farm accounts was deducted from total production (gross farm product) and current inputs (intermediate products purchased). Gross value added (gross farm product) is assumed to be net of rental value of houses.

for the groups. Since both countries have different weights, because of different input and output structures, two sets of price ratios can be constructed. Items missing in one country are assumed to be represented by the other items in the same group. An exception was made for rice, Japan's most important crop. The Italian rice/wheat price ratio was used to estimate a shadow price for rice in the Netherlands. A price ratio for capital goods (used for comparing depreciation) was obtained by taking unit prices for capital goods from handbooks on farm machinery, buildings and constructions. Since no weights are available in the statistics, weights were chosen on subjective grounds after checking cost of production data.

Table D.3 Comparison of inter-country price indexes: Japan, the Netherlands, and Taiwan

	Taiwan *Japanese weights* *index Japan = 100*			*Taiwan* Dutch weights index Netherlands = *100*			*Netherlands* *Japanese weights* *index Japan = 100*			*Japan* *Dutch weights* *index Netherlands = 100*		
	1975	*1980*	*1984*	*1975*	*1980*	*1984*	*1975*	*1980*	*1984*	*1975*	*1980*	*1984*
Total production	46	45	55	102	103	154	50	47	38	141	150	191
of which:												
Arable crops	33	28	31	104	154	217	37	32	27	136	237	287
Horticulture	39	38	55	35	30	52	72	68	56	121	139	175
Livestock	79	79	92	121	121	180	68	69	55	148	139	180
Current input	90	69	77	131	97	143	83	85	61	131	128	167
of which:												
Fertilizers	59	37	63	78	51	117	76	66	43	99	124	182
Seed and seedlings	31	20	22	102	102	152	77	83	63	390	283	339
Agrochemicals	106	51	49	135	60	79	91	88	61	131	118	154
Feed	115	91	99	142	110	156	77	83	63	127	120	159
Energy	36	38	45	74	60	83	77	71	66	135	160	183
Maintenance	57	59	61	NA	NA	NA						
Livestock for use	NA	NA	NA	NA	NA	NA						
Auto cost	NA	NA	NA	NA	NA	NA						
Gross value added	23	27	36	70	126	180	28	11	16	152	180	218
Depreciation	80	78	76	100	87	125	88	93	72	114	113	162
Net value added	11	11	24	67	133	189	17	b	b	157	195	228
Adjusted group weights[a]												
Total production	41	39	50	83	73	110						
Current input	91	72	81	123	95	139						
Gross value added	32	31	41	73	76	109						
Net value added	31	30	40	71	75	109						

Sources Data for Japan and the Netherlands from Van der Meer and Yamada (1988, Table 2). Data for Taiwan, our calculation following the same method.
Notes a. These alternative indexes are calculated by using Taiwanese weights for subgroups of total production and current inputs. These indexes are approximations of Taiwanese weights. b. negative net value added.

Table D.4 Comparison of inter-country price indexes: Japan, the Netherlands, and the USA

	Netherlands Dutch weights index USA = 100			*Japan Japanese weights index USA = 100*		
	1975	*1980*	*1984*	*1975*	*1980*	*1984*
Total production	130	146	95	254	288	343
of which:						
Arable crops	122	119	94	332	361	529
Horticulture	132	166	102	197	267	250
Livestock	131	143	93	173	198	163
Current input	115	139	90	140	157	146
of which:						
Fertilizers	77	112	62	130	137	139
Seed and seedlings	177	186	125	259	332	431
Agrochemicals	153	130	82	184	152	140
Feed	113	132	87	143	171	147
Energy	154	194	133	235	293	240
Maintenance	122	139	81	106	75	73
Livestock for use	173	188	118	274	185	205
Auto cost	108	135	86	54	55	73
Gross value added	152	156	102	537	1,274	-1,062
Depreciation	133	141	78	104	95	105
Net value added	155	160	107	3,067	b	b
Adjusted group weight[a]						
Total production	127	134	95	245	275	331
Current input	124	150	95	160	162	149
Gross value added	129	118	94	323	393	503
Net value added	128	107	100	397	530	667

Sources Data for Japan and the Netherlands from Van der Meer and Yamada (1988, Table 2). Data for the USA, our calculation following the same method.

Notes a. These alternative indexes are calculated by using US weights for sub-groups of total production and current inputs. These indexes are approximations of US weights. b. negative net value added.

The method for revaluing groups of outputs and inputs is illustrated in Table D.1. The values of groups of outputs and inputs at Dutch prices are revalued into yen by multiplication by the corresponding weighted price ratio yen/Dfl. Dutch gross value added in Japanese prices is found by deducting input from output in Japanese prices. Net value added is found after deducting depreciation as well.

Table D.5 Comparison of productivities in Japan, the Netherlands, Taiwan, and the USA

(unit: yen; 1,000 yen)

	At Japanese prices			*At Dutch prices*			*At Taiwanese prices*			*At United States prices*		
	1975	*1980*	*1984*	*1975*	*1980*	*1984*	*1975*	*1980*	*1984*	*1975*	*1980*	*1984*
A. Japan												
Total production/hour	917	1,374	1,634	457	641	622	420	613	890	362	477	476
Gross value added/hour	556	712	826	158	80	129	95	159	270	104	56	–78
Net value added/hour	465	534	635	77	–86	–9	22	20	125	15	–131	–260
Total production/ha	1,719	2,050	2,330	856	956	887	788	915	1,270	678	712	679
Gross value added/ha	1,042	1,062	1,178	296	120	184	178	237	385	194	83	–111
Net value added/ha	870	796	906	145	–128	–13	41	30	178	28	–196	–370
B. Netherlands												
Total production/hour	5,083	8,180	9,473	3,603	5,458	4,965	3,669	5,639	7,655	2,774	3,749	5,204
Gross value added/hour	2,594	4,089	5,028	1,709	2,270	2,306	1,200	2,546	3,858	1,124	1,451	2,263
Net value added/hour	2,379	3,667	4,491	1,519	1,894	1,975	1,011	2,221	3,443	981	1,185	1,840
Total production/ha	1,577	2,254	2,543	1,118	1,504	1,332	1,139	1,554	2,055	861	1,034	1,397
Gross value added/ha	805	1,127	1,350	530	625	619	372	702	1,036	349	400	608
Net value added/ha	738	1,011	1,205	471	522	530	314	612	924	304	327	494

C. Taiwan												
Total production/hour	1,116	1,775	1,899	555	959	850	458	700	941			
Gross value added/hour	945	1,420	1,477	417	586	548	303	445	559			
Net value added/hour	915	1,382	1,438	393	551	524	279	414	569			
Total production/ha	2,163	2,763	2,897	1,076	1,492	1,298	889	1,089	1,436			
Gross value added/ha	1,832	2,210	2,253	808	912	836	588	692	913			
Net value added/ha	1,774	2,150	2,194	762	858	800	541	645	868			
D. United States												
Total production/hour	9,810	12,600	20,560	5,084	6,141	5,873				4,007	4,578	6,216
Gross value added/hour	6,720	8,830	16,020	2,696	2,650	2,977				2,083	2,247	3,183
Net value added/hour	6,270	8,230	15,070	2,122	1,768	2,266				1,653	1,288	2,275
Total production/ha	162	208	298	84	101	85				66	75	90
Gross value added/ha	111	145	232	44	44	43				34	37	46
Net value added/ha	103	136	218	35	29	33				26	27	33

Sources See Table D.6.

Table D.6 Real productivities in Japan, the Netherlands, Taiwan, and the USA: ratios (Netherlands = 1,000)

	At Japanese prices			*At Dutch prices*			*At Taiwanese prices*			*At United States prices*		
	1975	*1980*	*1984*	*1975*	*1980*	*1984*	*1975*	*1980*	*1984*	*1975*	*1980*	*1984*
A. Japan												
Total production/hour	180	168	172	127	117	125	114	109	116	130	127	91
Gross value added/hour	214	174	164	92	35	56	79	62	70	93	39	a
Net value added/hour	195	146	141	51	a	a	22	9	36	15	a	a
Total production/ha	1,090	909	916	766	635	666	692	589	618	787	689	486
Gross value added/ha	1,295	942	873	558	192	298	479	338	372	557	208	a
Net value added/ha	1,179	788	752	307	a	a	132	49	193	93	a	a
B. Taiwan												
Total production/hour	219	217	200	154	176	171	125	124	123			
Gross value added/hour	364	347	294	244	258	233	253	175	155			
Net value added/hour	385	377	320	259	291	265	276	187	165			
Total production/ha	1,371	1,225	1,139	963	992	974	781	701	699			
Gross value added/ha	2,277	1,961	1,670	1,524	1,459	1,351	1,577	986	882			
Net value added/ha	2,404	2,127	1,820	1,616	1,644	1,509	1,726	1,054	939			
C. United States												
Total production/hour	1,930	1,540	2,170	1,411	1,125	1,183				1,444	1,221	1,194
Gross value added/hour	2,591	2,159	3,186	1,578	1,167	1,291				1,853	1,549	1,407
Net value added/hour	2,636	2,244	3,356	1,397	933	1,147				1,685	1,087	1,237
Total production/ha	103	92	117	75	67	64				77	73	65
Gross value added/ha	138	129	172	84	70	70				99	93	76
Net value added/ha	140	134	181	74	56	62				84	82	67

Sources Data at local prices from Table D.2. Data for Japan and the Netherlands at each other's prices from Van der Meer and Yamada (1988). All other data are our calculations for this study.

Note a. negative value added in Japan.

The ratios R and Q are calculated by direct aggregation, the ratios I_{GVA} and I_{NVA} are implicit price ratios obtained by dividing the right-hand terms at Japanese prices by the left-hand term at Dutch prices. These ratios correspond with what is usually called the Purchasing Power Parity (PPP). If these ratios are divided by the exchange rate E (yen/Dfl) the relative price indexes between the Netherlands and Japan are found.

The nominal rate of protection for a country is usually estimated as the ratio of domestic prices and c.i.f. or f.o.b. prices. The corresponding nominal rate of protection at farm gate prices for Japanese farmers compared to Dutch farmers is $R/E - 1$. It indicates the difference in farm price level between the two countries. $I_{GVA}/E - 1$ and $I_{NVA}/E - 1$ are the effective rates of protection for factor income gross and net of depreciation in Japan compared to the Netherlands. The effective rate of protection indicates the implicit price support for factor input, while taking into consideration the differences in product and input prices.

Since these indexes were calculated at Dutch weights the results are biased towards the Dutch cost and output structure. Similar calculations were made at Japanese weights which gave of course different results. This method can also be used for products if detailed cost of production tables are available (see Van der Meer, Yamada and Egaitsu 1987).

Data sources

Sources of prices for Japan and the Netherlands and the methods used for comparison are described in detail in Van der Meer and Yamada (1988, annex A). For the comparisons with Taiwan and the United States the same Dutch and Japanese prices and weights were used. For Taiwan price data used for calculation of price indexes were provided by Mrs Yueh-eh Chen. In addition prices were taken from Department of Agriculture and Forestry (1986, August). For the USA prices were obtained from USDA, *Agricultural Statistics*, various issues.

Sources of data on quantities of products and inputs and other data are given under Table D.2 (p. 188).

Years selected for comparison were 1975, 1980, and 1984. The motivation for this was as follows. The year 1975 is the major benchmark year for international comparative studies of real productivity and purchasing power. Fortunately this is also a base year for the price index calculations in Japan and the Netherlands which means that weights are available. Because of year-by-year fluctuations we decided to take two more years: 1980, because it is the next base year for the price statistics, and 1984 which was the last year for which data were available when the comparative part of this study started. Since 1984 is not a base year we used the 1980 price index weights. The year 1983/4 was also the year for which productivities for livestock products were compared.

Notes

Chapter two: Sectoral productivity performance in international perspective

1. The A-sector comprises farming, fisheries, and forestry (ISIC 1). The I-sector comprises mining, manufacturing, electricity, gas and water, and construction (ISIC 2, 3, 4, and 5). The S-sector comprises trade, restaurants and hotels, transport, storage and communication, financial institutions, insurance, real estate, and commercial services, government, social and personal services, and activities not adequately described (ISIC 6, 7, 8, and 9).
2. Factoral terms of trade are calculated as the (implicit) price index of gross value added in agriculture divided by the (implicit) price index of gross value added for other sectors (industry or services, or industry + services). The implicit indexes are obtained by dividing gross value added in current prices by gross value added in constant prices.
3. This section is mainly based on Van der Meer (1983a and 1983b). The analysis was further expanded in Van der Meer (1987b).
4. Exceptions were experiences of countries with vast land (and mining) resources, such as Australia, and the USA after the civil war.
5. The period 1913–50 is commonly used by economists in periodization of economic growth. But for some countries like Japan and also some European countries the break of the Second World War had a considerable effect on sectoral growth rates. For the period 1913–39 more than half of the Western countries had higher productivity growth in industry than in agriculture. For the entire period for which data are available up to the Second World War all European countries experienced higher productivity growth in industry than in agriculture, as is shown in the table at the end of this note.

   In European countries comparative advantage in industry increased relatively to Australia, and to a lesser degree relatively to the USA, except for France which had the same gap as the USA. Although some European countries pursued autarchic policies, they actually exported relatively more industrial products and imported more agricultural products. For instance in Germany the share of manufactured products in exports increased from 63 per cent in 1880 to 89 per cent in 1939, whereas the share of agricultural products in imports increased from 33 per cent to 40 per cent (Sommariva and Tullio 1987: 49–50).

Growth rates of labour productivity in agriculture and industry in selected Western countries before the Second World War (%)

	Period covered	*Agriculture*	*Industry*	*Gap*
Japan	1885–1939	1.8	4.1	-2.3
Netherlands	1921–1939	2.0	3.2	-1.2
Sweden	1870–1939	1.4	1.9	-0.5
Denmark	1850–1939	0.9	1.8	-0.9
Germany	1850–1938	0.9	1.7	-0.8
France	1856–1936	0.6	0.8	-0.2
UK	1861–1938	0.2	1.9	-1.7
USA	1889–1939	1.0	1.2	-0.2
Australia	1861–1939	1.5	1.0	0.5

Source As for Table 2.1.

6. In a vent for surplus type of growth as described by Myint (1958 and 1980) and Lewis (1970) output per worker increased, but this was the result of increased labour input per worker (more working hours per year) and is therefore not the result of increased output per hour worked.
7. In general, however, technological developments have increased possibilities for transportation and trade of fresh and perishable products, such as vegetables and flowers. Especially in the EC and the USA such products are daily transported over large distances by road and air.
8. This was shown for the USA and Argentina by Stanneveld, Van Ooststroom and Van der Meer (1984). See also Van der Meer and Yamada (1986).
9. Similar mechanisms helped to generate considerable exports of rice in the second half of the nineteenth century from countries with favourable production conditions, such as Burma, Thailand, Cochin China, and Taiwan. This vent for surplus type of export oriented growth also played a role in the period after the Second World War when land-locked areas in Thailand were opened up for surplus production by road systems (Rijk and Van der Meer 1984).
10. The relatively advanced position of Dutch agriculture is shown in Van der Meer and Yamada (1986) and Van der Meer (1988).
11. Fiji is the only country in the Pacific included here. In the following we shall briefly speak of Asia. Japan is not included in this group, but in the group of industrial economies. See Appendix Table A.1, p. 169.
12. See notes in Appendix A about weighting for non-agriculture.

13. For consistency the same group of countries was used as in Table 2.9. Countries omitted from the original data set are given in note 14.
14. The countries that had to be dropped from our data set were Botswana, Central African Republic, Congo, Cyprus, Fiji, Gambia, Guyana, Hong Kong, Jamaica, Liberia, Mauritania, Niger, Panama, Sierra Leone, Singapore, Taiwan, Togo, Libya, and Saudi Arabia.

Chapter three: International comparison of agricultural productivity

1. The countries are selected on the following criteria: their importance in world agricultural development, their record of productivity performance, data availability, our familiarity with these countries, and comparability with other studies.
2. Statistics for agricultural production and labour input in the 1950s exist as well, but we did not use them because their reliability is lower.
3. The three- and five-year averages of farm production for the years 1961–5 and 1984–6 are used only to avoid strong effects on growth estimates from yearly fluctuations of farm production. The 1975 output data are single year data, directly taken from the FAO (1986), and are overestimates of Japan's output level because that year was a good crop year.
4. The study by the FAO (1986) which was prepared by D.S. Prasada Rao is the most important of the comparative studies. Our study uses it as a main data source.
5. Theoretically net factor productivity is the best indicator. However, in this study we mainly focus on labour productivity (gross value added per worker) and no effort was made to estimate net factor productivity. Although the net value added concept is more preferable because it also excludes double counting of fixed capital consumption, available data do not permit us to make a comparison for many countries on the basis of that concept.
6. The calculation method is as follows. First the prices are converted into comparable units using the calculated conversion rate of the jth country's currency, R_j, to the *numeraire* currency, US dollars. The P_i and R_j can be simultaneously calculated by use of the Geary–Khamis method which solves an interdependent system of linear equations as follows (FAO, 1986: 21):
   For each commodity i, the P_i is given by

   $$P_i = \sum_{j=1}^{M} R_j P_{ij} Q_{ij} / \sum_{j=1}^{M} Q_{ij}$$

   and for each currency R_j in terms of US dollars is given by

   $$R_j = \sum_{i=1}^{N} P_i Q_{ij} / \sum_{i=1}^{N} p_{ij} Q_{ij}$$

where p_{ij} is the price of the *i*th commodity in the *j*th country, *M* the number of commodities, and *N* the number of countries. These equations form an $M+N$ system with $M+N$ unknowns, which can be solved and result in unique positive solutions for the unknowns P_i and R_j. The P_i are expressed in units equivalent to dollars, but not the same as US dollars. These units are referred to as 'International dollars' in FAO (1986). The P_i and R_j estimated by the FAO (1986) according to the Geary–Khamis method are utilized for the present study.

7. In Appendix B, we discuss the likely extent of underestimation for some countries.
8. Hayami and Ruttan (1971) used US and Japanese data to estimate current inputs for all countries. Van Ooststroom and Maddison (1985) estimated the current input items seed, feed, fertilizer, and agricultural chemicals from the FAO sources and expressed them in USA prices. They made assumptions of the use of current input for all countries based on their use in the USA. FAO (1986) used differences in fertilizer prices between countries to estimate Purchasing Power Parities for agricultural inputs. This means that the relative differences in prices of all intermediate inputs are assumed to be similar to those of fertilizers, which is very unlikely. Besides, for most countries the gross value added ratios were estimated from bold regression results.
9. In developing countries modern current inputs are in general expensive relative to product prices while these are relatively cheap in developed countries, in particular where output prices are supported by the government. This implies that the estimated data in this study relatively tend to underestimate real gross value added in the former cases, and overestimate in the latter.
10. Use of a flow concept of labour input, such as working hours or working days, would be better, but this is impossible because of lack of data.
11. As referred to in note 3, the 1975 output level of Japanese agriculture may be overestimated because of the good crop year. If three-year averages were taken for comparison, the growth rate of gross value added became even slightly negative for 1960–75 in 1975 national prices.
12. As shown in Figure 3.6, the level of current input per worker is related to gross value added per worker. However, it should not be included conceptually as a determinant variable of productivity on a gross value added basis and, therefore, it is not included as a variable in equations.

Chapter four: Agricultural development in Japan and the Netherlands

1. For the nineteenth century estimates are available from Van Zanden (1985) for the benchmark years 1810, 1850 and 1880. Recently, Van der Meer and Van Ark (1987) provided tentative estimates of volume series for total production, and current inputs and gross value added for the period 1880–1950. Subsequent research by Knibbe and Van

der Meer aims at improved and expanded annual series of total production, current inputs and gross value added in current and constant prices for the period 1870–1950.

2. For Japanese agriculture the 1920–38 period was a distinct period of stagnation so that 1920 would be a good year for periodization for Japan (Hayami, *et.al.* 1975: 29). However, 1913 is taken for comparison here because 1913 is a common benchmark year for Western economic history.
3. Usually 1973 is taken as the turning point in post-war economic growth. However, the choice of 1975 is motivated by the fact that 1975 is a major benchmark year for international comparisons, and we also selected it for comparisons of real output and productivity in Chapters 3 and 5. In fact growth in agriculture is less effected by business cycles than in industry and the difference between 1973 and 1975 is minor.
4. This is true for the pre-war period since the time spans of the two pre-war periods were rather long. However, for the post-war period, each sub-period was rather short so that the use of a single year as a benchmark resulted in a certain bias. In Japan, 1975 was a good crop year. In 1975 prices total production in 1975 was 3.2 per cent higher than the average of 1974–6, final output 3.4 per cent, and gross value added 5.9 per cent. Value added in 1960 was also 1.7 per cent higher than the 1959–61 average. This means that for 1960–75 the growth rate of gross value added is 0.17 per cent per annum on the basis of a single year data while it is –0.10 per cent for three-year averages. (Data are based on Yamada 1987a).
5. For 1880–1920 the annual growth rates of final output and gross value added are 1.8 and 1.7 per cent, and only 0.6 and 0.2 per cent for 1920–38, respectively.
6. If three-year averages were used for comparison, even for 1960–75, gross value added declined slightly (Yamada 1987a).
7. Capital for Japan is gross value of capital stock at 1975 prices for new capital goods given by MAFF, *Cost of Production Report* (1975) without deducting its depreciation. For the Netherlands it is net value, i.e. depreciation deducted from gross value. Depreciation in Japan is a constant amount for respective capital goods based on the purchased value, while the constant rate method, based on the current value is used in the Netherlands.
8. Product groups are arable crops, horticulture, and livestock, and current input groups are feed, seed, fertilizer and chemicals, fuel, other materials, maintenance and services, and depreciation.
9. In Japan product groups are rice, other crops, and livestock and sericulture, and input groups are farm intermediate products, fertilizer, feed, agricultural chemicals, and others.
10. Because of an upward bias of the 1975 output figures from a smoothed trend which uses three- or five-year moving averages mentioned in note 4, the Japanese growth rates for 1960–75 would be a little over-estimated while those of 1975–85 are underestimated.

11. The upward bias of the 1975 output figures in Japan may affect the calculated changes in land productivity.
12. Because of the data availability, the 1984 weights are applied to the weights in the 1985 price indexes.
13. An alternative land share for the Netherlands was also calculated according to the same method as for Japan by use of some available land prices and the interest rate, although these are not necessarily appropriate. In that case the shares of land in final output are 20.3, 11.7 and 8.0 per cent and 30.7, 18.2 and 13.9 per cent in gross value added for respective benchmark years. The total factor productivity index by use of those shares was also calculated, but the trend and level was by and large the same as the case shown. The estimated share of land for Japan may be overestimated since the applied interest rate would be higher than the actual rate of return to real estate.

Chapter five: How productive is present Japanese agriculture?

1. The production and current input weights in the price statistics had to be adjusted to national accounts definitions because they include more intermediate agricultural products (farm to farm sales) than included in the sectoral accounts.
2. See Appendix D for motivation of the choice of years.
3. In principle if proper evaluation of feed prices is made, i.e. taking cost of transportation into account as a separate input, real productivity on farms operated on purchased fodder could be expected to be lower.
4. The basic price data in Van der Meer and Yamada (1988, annex Tables A.1–A.8) contain sufficient information for this purpose.
5. This is related to the fact that the share of by-products is higher on Dutch small farms while the prices for by-products are higher in Japan (see Van der Meer, Yamada, and Egaitsu, 1987).
6. Apparently the higher milk price of the other regions compensates the higher land price and has a positive effect on the productivity ratios (see Van der Meer, Yamada, and Egaitsu, 1987).
7. If depreciation of cows is included and historical value is used as the base for depreciation of machines and buildings, the difference between the Netherlands and Japan would be bigger (see Van der Meer, Yamada, and Egaitsu, 1987, annex Table A.5). This, however, would hardly affect the differences between Hokkaido and the other regions.
8. However, in 1985/6 labour productivity declined as a result of the introduction of the milk quota system (LEI, 1987).
9. Based on labour input in days data MAFF, 1985 *Agricultural Census*, vol. 4, p. 70.
10. See Van der Meer and Yamada (1988: chapter 5.2), for a discussion of several countries.
11. Already in the nineteenth century paddy prices in Japan were a few times higher than in exporting countries in Southeast Asia, such as Thailand, and also considerably higher than in Indonesia, and the

difference has grown over time. Data provided by Anderson, Hayami, and Honma (1986: Table 2.2) show a nominal rate of protection ranging between 9 per cent in 1903–7 to 45 per cent in 1933–7. Their calculation is based on border prices for Southeast Asian rice. Calculations by Manarungsan show a bigger gap. Japanese farmers received about two times higher prices than Thai farmers already in the nineteenth century and the gap has increased over time. Also on Java, prices were lower than in Japan. (Brown rice prices for Japan from Ohkawa, *LTES*, paddy prices for Thailand compiled by S. Manarungsan, and for Indonesia by P. van der Eng for current Ph.D. research.)

12. A discussion of the characteristics of the implicit deflators used is given in Van der Meer and Yamada (1988: 32–6).

Chapter six: The eclipse of Japanese agriculture

1. In a dynamic situation with changing technology and lagging factor allocation adjustment, it is of course more difficult to indicate what the optimum is. For this we refer to the discussion of the inverse U-shape hypothesis (in Chapters Two and Three).
2. See Binswanger (1978) for an explanatory overview.
3. See Van der Meer and Yamada (1988: 15–17, 58) for persons interviewed.
4. LEI/CBS (1988: 17, 21), based on NEG-classification, types 2 and 5.
5. Calculated from MAFF, *Agricultural Statistical Yearbook 1986/87*: 167 and from data provided by USDA.
6. Calculated from MAFF, *Agricultural Statistical Yearbook 1986/87:* 171 and data published in USDA, *Agricultural Statistics 1986*: 395.
7. Cost of production calculations show that in 1950 gross productivity per hour was about 2 kg for paddy and 1.7 kg for wheat.

Bibliography

Anderson, K., Hayami, Y., and Honma, M. (1986) 'The growth of agricultural protection', in K. Anderson and Yujiro Hayami (eds) *The Political Economy of Agricultural Protection*, Sydney/London/Boston: Allen and Unwin.

APO (1987) *Productivity Measurement and Analysis: Asian Agriculture*, Tokyo: Asian Productivity Organization.

——(1987 and previous issues) *Comparative Information on Productivity Levels and Changes in APO Member Countries*, Tokyo: Asian Productivity Organization.

Asian Development Bank (1987 and previous issues) *Key Indicators of Developing Member Countries*, Manila.

Bank of Korea, *Economic Statistics Yearbook*, various issues, Seoul.

Binswanger, H.P. (1978) 'Induced technical change: evolution of thought', in H.P. Binswanger, and W. Ruttan (eds) *Induced Innovation, Technology, Institutions and Development*, Baltimore and London: The Johns Hopkins University Press.

Boserup, E. (1965) *The Conditions of Agricultural Growth*, Chicago: Aldine.

——(1981) *Population and Technology*, London: Blackwell.

CBS (1969) *70 jaren statistiek in tijdreeksen* [70 years of statistical time-series], The Hague.

——(1982) *Statistische onderzoekingen, landbouwprijs-indexcijfers*, Heerlen.

——(1988 and previous issues) 'De toegevoegde waarde in de land- en tuinbouw en het agrarisch inkomen' in: *Maandstatistiek van de landbouw*, [Sector account for agriculture], The Hague.

Chayanov, A.V. (1966) *The Theory of the Peasant Economy*, edited and introduced by Daniel Thorner, Basile Kerblay and R.F. Smith, Illinois: Irwin.

Chen, Yueh-eh (1987) 'Taiwan study', in APO, *Productivity Measurement and Analysis*.

Clark, C. (1957) *The Conditions of Agricultural Progress* (3rd ed) London: Macmillan.

Cochrane, W.W. (1958) *Farm Prices, Myth and Reality*, Mineapolis: University of Minnesota Press.

Corsel, R.R. (1986) 'Labour input and patterns of growth in Thai agriculture, by region', unpublished M.Sc. thesis, Groningen: Faculty of Economics, University of Groningen.

Council for Economic Planning and Development (1987) *Taiwan Statistical Data Book*, Taipei.

Department of Agriculture and Forestry (1985, 1986 August) *Taiwan Agricultural Prices & Costs Monthly*. Taipei: Taiwan Provincial Government.

——(1986 and previous issues) *Taiwan Agricultural Yearbook*, Taipei: Taiwan Provincial Government.

Economic Planning Board, *Korea Statistical Yearbook*, Seoul, various issues.

Elfring, T. (1988) 'Service employment in advanced economies: A comparative analysis of its implications for economic growth', unpublished Ph.D. thesis, Groningen: University of Groningen.

Ellis, F. (1988) *Peasant Economics*, Cambridge: Cambridge University Press.

Eurostat (1987 and previous issues) *Economic Accounts for Agriculture*, Luxemburg.

——(1988 and previous issues) *Agricultural Statistical Yearbook*, Luxembourg.

FAO (1981 and 1988) 'Questionnaire on agricultural sector accounts' (unpublished) Rome.

——(1983) *Potential Population Supporting Capacities of Lands in the Developing World*, Rome.

——(1986) *Inter-country Comparison of Agricultural Production Aggregates*, FAO Economic and social development paper no. 61, Rome.

——(1988 and previous issues) *FAO Production Yearbook*, Rome.

Fei, J.C.H., and Ranis, G. (1964) *Development of the Labour Surplus Economy: Theory and Policy*, Homewood, Ill.: Irwin.

Goossens, F. (1986) 'Comparison in real values of final agricultural production for 1984, Seminar use of purchasing power parities' (unpublished), Luxemburg: Eurostat.

Hayami, Y. (1988) *Japanese Agriculture Under Siege*, London: Macmillan Press.

Hayami, Y., Akino, M., Shintani, M., and Yamada, S. (1975) *A Century of Agricultural Growth in Japan*, Tokyo: University of Tokyo Press.

Hayami, Y. and Ruttan, V.W. (1971 and 1985 revised) *Agricultural Development: an International Perspective*, Baltimore: The Johns Hopkins University Press.

Hillman, J.S. and Rothenberg, R.A. (1988) *Agricultural Trade and Protection in Japan*, Aldershot: Gower.

ILO (1987 and previous issues) *Yearbook of Labour Force Statistics*, Geneva.

Ishikawa, S. (1967) *Economic Development in Asian Perspective*, Tokyo: Kinokuniya.

Johnson, D.G., Hemmi, K., and Lardinois, P. (1985) *Agricultural Policy and Trade: Adjusting Domestic Programs in an International Frame-*

work, NewYork/London: New York University Press.
Johnson, G.L. and Quance, C.L. (1972) *The Overproduction Trap in US Agriculture*, Baltimore: The Johns Hopkins Press.
Johnston, B.F. (1951) 'Agricultural productivity and economic development in Japan', *Journal of Political Economy* 59: 498–513.
Kawagoe, T. and Hayami, Y. (1985) 'An intercountry comparison of agricultural production efficiency', *American Journal of Agricultural Economics*: 87–92.
Kayo, N. (ed.) (1977), *Nihon nogyo kiso tokei* [Japan agricultural basic statistics] Tokyo: Nosei Chosa Iinkai.
Knibbe, M. (forthcoming) *Dutch Agricultural Production 1870–1950*, Groningen: University of Groningen.
Kravis, I. Heston, H.H., and Summers, R. (1982) *World Product and Income: International Comparison of Real Gross Product*, Baltimore: The Johns Hopkins University Press.
LEI (1980 and 1987) *Melkkoeien 1980 and 1987* [Milk Cows 1980 and 1987], The Hague.
——(1982) *Resultaten van torensilobedrijven* [Results from farms with tower silos], The Hague.
——(1984) *Slachtkuikens 1984* [Broilers], The Hague.
——(1985) *Bedrijfsuitkomsten in de landbouw 1980/81–1983/84*. [Farm results 1980/81–1983/84], The Hague.
LEI/CBS (1988 and previous issues) *Landbouwcijfers 1988* [Agricultural Statistics 1988], The Hague.
Lewis, W.A. (1954) 'Economic development with unlimited supplies of labour', *Manchester School of Economic and Social Studies* 22 (May 1954): 139–91.
——(ed.) (1970) *Tropical Development 1880–1913*, London: George Allen & Unwin.
——(1978) *Growth and Fluctuations 1870–1913*, London: Allen & Unwin.
Maddison, A. (1970) *Economic Progress and Policy in Developing Countries*, New York: Norton.
——(1982), *Phases of Capitalist Development*, Oxford: Oxford University Press.
MAFF (1955, 1970 and 1984) *Chikusanbutsu seisanhi chosa* [Survey on Cost of Production of Livestock (CP)], Tokyo.
——(1974) *Time-series of Agricultural Economic Statistics, vol. 5: Cost of Production Surveys*, Tokyo.
——(1985) *Agricultural Census*, Tokyo.
——(1987 and previous issues) *Norinsuisansho tokeihyo* [Agricultural Statistical Yearbook], Tokyo.
——(1987 and previous issues) *Cost of Production Report*: Tokyo.
——(1987 and previous issues) *Noka keizai chosa* [Farm Household Economic Survey], Tokyo.
——(1987 and previous issues) *Nogyo oyobi noka no shakaikanjo* [Social Accounts of Agriculture and Farm Households]: Tokyo.
——(1988) *Pocket Statistics of Agriculture, Forestry and Fisheries*, Tokyo.
Mellor, J.W. (1966) *The Economics of Agricultural Development*, Ithaca

and New York: Cornell University Press.
Mensink, G.J.A. (1966) *Comparisons of Labour Productivity in the United Kingdom and the Netherlands*, The Hague: CBS Statistical Studies.
Minami, R. (1973) *The Turning Point in Economic Development, Japan's Experience*, Tokyo: Kinokuniya.
Ministry of Agriculture and Fisheries (1986) *Statistical Yearbook of Agriculture, Forestry and Fisheries*, Seoul.
Myint, H. (1958) 'The classical theory of international trade', in *The Economic Journal*: 317–37.
——(1980) *The Economics of the Developing Countries* (fifth edn), London: Hutchinson University Library.
OECD (1984) *Science and Technology Indicators: Resources Devoted to R&D*, Paris.
—— (1988a and previous issues) *National Accounts Statistics*, Paris.
——(1988b and previous issues) *Labour Force Statistics* 1965–1985, Paris.
Ohkawa, K. and Shinohara, M. (1979) *Patterns of Japanese Economic Development*, New Haven and London: Yale University Press.
Ohkawa, K., Shinohara, M., and Umemura, M. (eds) (1967) *Estimates of Long-term Economic Statistics of Japan since 1868*, vol. 8, Prices, Tokyo: Toyo Keizai Shinposha.
Paige, D. and Bombach, G. (1959) *A Comparison of National Output and Productivity*, Paris: OECD.
Pilat, D. (1988) *Dutch Agricultural Export Performance 1846–1926*, research memorandum of the Institute of Economic Research no. 296, Groningen: University of Groningen.
Rijk, A.G. and Van der Meer, C.L.J. (1984) *Thailand Agricultural Sector Assessment*, Manila: Staff Study Paper, ADB.
Ruttan, V.W. (1982) *Agricultural Research Policy*, Minneapolis: University of Minnesota Press.
Schultz, Th.W. (1953) *The Economic Organization of Agriculture*, New York: McGraw-Hill.
——(ed.) (1979) *Distortions of Agricultural Incentives*, Bloomington: Indiana University Press.
Shinohara, M. (1982) *Industrial Growth, Trade and Dynamic Patterns in the Japanese Economy*, Tokyo: University of Tokyo Press.
Sommariva, A. and Tulio, G. (1987) *German macro-economic history, 1880–1979: A Study of the Effects of Economic Policy on Inflation, Currency Depreciation and Growth*, New York: St Martins Press.
Stanneveld, A.M.H., van Ooststroom, H.P.C. and van der Meer, C.L.J. (1984) 'Comparison of levels of agricultural output and productivity: past and present', *Proceedings of the IVth European Congress of Agricultural Economists, vol. 5 Kiel*, Kiel: University of Kiel/European Association of Agricultural Economists.
Statistics Bureau (1986 and previous issues) *Japan Statistical Yearbook*, Tokyo.
——(1987) *Annual Report on the Labour Force Survey*, Tokyo.
Szirmai, A. and Pilat, D. (1989 forthcoming) *The International Comparison of Real Output and Labour Productivity in Manufacturing: a Study*

for Japan, South Korea and the USA for 1975, Research memorandum, Institute of Economic Research, Groningen: University of Groningen.

Tracy, M. (1982) *Agriculture in Western Europe, Challenge and Response 1880–1980*, (second ed), London: Granada.

Umemura, M., Yamada, S., Hayami, Y., Takamatsu, N., and Kumazaki, M. (1966) *Estimates of Long-term Economic Statistics of Japan Since 1868, vol. 9, Agriculture and Forestry*, Tokyo: Toyo Keizai Shinposha.

US Dept. of Commerce, Bureau of Economic Analysis (Sept. 1981 and July 1982) *Survey of Current Business*, Washington.

——(1975) *Historical Statistics of the United States, Colonial Times to 1970*, Washington.

——(1985) *Statistical Abstract*, Washington.

USDA (1987 and previous issues) *Agricultural Statistics* Washington: US Government printing office.

Van der Meer, C.L.J. (1983a) 'Growth and equity – experience in developed countries with market economic system', in A. Maunder and K. Ohkawa (eds) *Growth and Equity in Agricultural Development, Proceedings of the Eighteenth International Conference of Agricultural Economics*, Aldershot: Gower.

——(1983b) 'Lange-termijn trends in agrarische ontwikkeling in welvarende landen' [Long-term trends in agricultural development in developed countries], in C.L.J. Van der Meer, (ed.) *Landbouw en ontwikkeling* [Agriculture and development], The Hague: VUGA.

——(1986) 'Agrarisch grondgebruik in Nederland 1985–2025' [Agricultural land use in the Netherlands 1985–2025], in C.L.J. Van der Meer, and D. Strijker *De toekomstige ontwikkeling van het agrarisch grondgebruik in Nederland*, The Hague: Landbouw-Economisch Instituut.

——(1987a) *Employment and Labour Input in Dutch Agriculture 1849–1986*, Research memorandum no. 221, Institute of Economic Research, Groningen: Faculty of Economics, University of Groningen.

——(1987b) 'Analysis of productivity, trends and patterns', paper written for the APO seminar Agricultural productivity measurement and analysis (16–23 February 1987) (unpublished), Tokyo.

——(1988) 'Agricultural growth in the EC and the effect of CAP', in *Proceedings of the XX international conference of agricultural economists August 24–31, 1988, Buenos Aires, vol. I, invited papers,* Buenos Aires: International Association of Agricultural Economists.

Van der Meer, C.L.J. and van Ark, B. (1987) 'Growth and productivity in Dutch agriculture: a comparative perspective', in B. van Ark, H.J. Brinkman, J.W. Drukker, A. Maddison, C.L.J. van der Meer, H. van der Meulen, and B. Slot. (1987) *Economic Growth in Northwestern Europe: the Last 400 Years. Local Contributions to the Groningen Workshop on Quantitative Economic History, September 2–4, 1985.* Research memorandum of the Institute of Economic Research, no. 214, Groningen: University of Groningen.

Van der Meer, C.L.J. and Yamada, S. (1986) *Agricultural Development in the Netherlands and Japan*, Research Memorandum no. 182: 28–30, Institute of Economic Research, Groningen: University of Groningen.

——(1988) *Comparison of Real Output, Productivity and Effective Protection in Dutch and Japanese Agriculture for 1975, 1980 and 1984*, Research memorandum of the Institute of Economic Research, no. 267, Groningen: University of Groningen.

——(1989) *Productivity and Income in Intensive Livestock Farming in Japan and the Netherlands in 1983/84*, Research memorandum of the Institute of Economic Research, Groningen, University of Groningen.

Van der Meer, C.L.J., Yamada, S., and Egaitsu F., (1987) *Productivity and Income in Dairy Farming in Japan and the Netherlands in 1983/84*, Research memorandum of the Institute of Economic Research, no. 230, Groningen: University of Groningen.

Van Oostroom, H.P.C. and Maddison, A. (1984 and 1985 revised), 'An international comparison of levels of real output and productivity in agriculture in 1975' (preliminary paper), Groningen: Faculty of Economics, University of Groningen.

Van Zanden, J. L. (1985) *De Economische Ontwikkeling van de Nederlandse Landbouw in de Negentiende Eeuw 1800–1814* [Economic development of Dutch agriculture in the nineteenth century 1800–1914], Utrecht: HES uitgevers.

World Bank (1987 and previous issues), *World Tables*, Washington: World Bank.

——(1988 and previous issues) *World Development Report*, New York/Oxford: Oxford University Press.

Yamada, S. (1975) *A Comparative Analysis of Asian Agricultural Productivities and Growth Patterns*, Tokyo: Asian Productivity Organisation.

——(1982a) 'The secular trends in input-output relations of agricultural production in Japan, 1878–1978', in C.M. Hou and T.S. Yu, (eds) *Agricultural Development in China, Japan and Korea*, Taipei: Academia Sinica.

——(1982b) 'Problem of food security in Japan', in A.H. Chisholm and R. Tyers, (eds) *Food Security, Theory, Policy and Perspective from Asia and the Pacific Rim*, Lexington, Massachusetts, Toronto: Lexington Books.

——(1987a) 'Country study on agricultural productivity measurement and analysis: Japan', in APO (1987) *Productivity Measurement and Analysis*.

——(1987b) 'Agricultural growth and productivity in selected Asian countries', in APO (1987) *Productivity Measurement and Analysis*.

Yamada, S. and Hayami, Y. (1979) 'Agricultural growth in Japan, 1880–1970', in Y. Hayami, V.W. Ruttan, and H.M. Southworth (eds) *Agricultural Growth in Japan, Taiwan, Korea, and the Philippines*, Honolulu: APO, Tokyo and East West Center.

Yamada, S. and Ruttan, V.W. (1980) 'International comparisons of productivity in agriculture', in J.W. Kendrick and B.K. Vaccara (eds) *New Development in Productivity Measurement and Analysis*, Chicago and London: University of Chicago Press.

Index